OKINAWA 1945

OKINAWA 1945

Final Assault on the Empire

SIMON FOSTER

ARMS AND
ARMOUR

Arms & Armour Press
A Cassell imprint
Villiers House, 41–47 Strand, London WC2N 5JE

Distributed in the USA by Sterling Publishing Co Inc, 387 Park
Avenue South, New York, NY 10016-8810

Distributed in Australia by Capricorn Link (Australia) Pty Ltd,
2/13 Carrington Road, Castle Hill, New South Wales 2154

British Library Cataloguing-in-Publication data: A catalogue
record for this book is available from the British Library

ISBN 1 85409 195 6

Cartography by Peter Burton

Edited and designed by Roger Chesneau/DAG Publications Ltd
Printed and bound in Great Britain

Printed and bound by
Hartnolls Ltd, Bodmin, Cornwall

Contents

Preface

The invasion of the island of Okinawa in April 1945 was the largest and most complex amphibious operation undertaken by the Americans in the Second World War. The operation hinged on the Americans' retaining command of the seas around Okinawa in order to maintain their logistic chain and keep their mobile airfields, the fast carriers of Task Force 58, near enough to ensure that air support was available to the ground forces until airfields could be established ashore. In pursuit of this objective, the Americans exposed themselves to the full fury of Japanese suicide attacks and suffered heavy losses.

This account is related primarily from the naval point of view since, to a certain extent, the ground war—bitter though it was—was a foregone conclusion. It was at sea that the outcome of the invasion would be decided. The Japanese 32nd Army on Okinawa was cut off and beyond reinforcement. It was only a matter of time before American quantitative and qualitative superiority prevailed. I therefore apologize in advance to the officers and enlisted men of the Tenth Army if they feel that their efforts have not received sufficient recognition.

I am grateful to many people for their help with this book, but in particular I thank the staffs of the US Naval Historical Center, the Library of Congress and the Imperial War Museum in London for permission to use some of the photographs of the British Pacific Fleet.

Any errors in the pages that follow are exclusively my own responsibility.

S.F.

1

The Plan

The Joint Chiefs of Staff have directed the Commander in Chief Pacific Ocean Areas to occupy one or more positions in the Nansei Shoto, target date 1st March 1945.—Directive issued to Admiral Nimitz by the Joint Chiefs of Staff

BY April 1945, the two-pronged Allied assault on Japan had resulted in the establishment of a string of bases stretching westwards from Hawaii and northwards from Australia from which the final assault on Japan could be launched. Throughout 1944 operations in the Pacific had been directed to this aim. From Hawaii the chain stretched through the Marshalls and West Carolines, while from Australia it ran north through the Solomons and Manus in the Admiralty Islands. Both chains converged at Leyte and Mindoro in the Philippine Islands, the geographical focus of lines of communication not only from the United States in the east and Australia in the south but also with India and the United Kingdom to the west via the Moluccas. The capture of the Philippines in 1944 led to the establishment of bases on a strategic line some 1,300 miles from Japan and lying directly across her lines of communication with the oil fields to the south, vital to her prosecution of the war effort. The occupation of Iwo Jima, where organized resistance ceased on 16 March 1945, provided an air base at the eastern end of the line. Now all that was required was the advance of the western end of the line to provide a jumping-off point near the Japanese Home Islands from where the invasion could be launched.

The Japanese could offer little resistance to this inexorable advance. The annihilation of the Imperial Japanese Navy at the Battle of Leyte Gulf in October 1944 was a crucial point from which the Japanese could not recover. Six months after the battle, the Japanese Navy was merely of nuisance value. The Achilles' heel of the Americans, the long seaborne lines of communication along which all their supplies had to travel, was never exploited by the Japanese, who were thrown back on to the defensive and could only respond to Allied initiatives by static operations, by air attack and by the increasing use of suicide weapons.

However, every Japanese island or possession which was captured presented the Americans with a dilemma at the heart of their policy. For obvious reasons, the prospect of a fully fledged invasion of Japan was viewed with a considerable degree of foreboding. Both the Americans and the British had always hoped that Japan could be starved into surrender by an air and sea blockade implemented by securing bases on the Chinese mainland such as Amoy and Hong Kong, but from July 1943 onwards the prospect of an invasion of Japan loomed ever larger and the Americans reluctantly began to consider such an eventuality.

They now had to decide how best to implement the policy. The US campaign in the Pacific was organized into two fronts, the South-West Pacific commanded by General of the Army Douglas MacArthur and the Central Pacific under Fleet Admiral Chester Nimitz. Though nominally complementary, the two were really in competition and reflected divisions within the US military. South-West Pacific was seen as an 'Army' command and was thus bitterly resented by the Navy, while Central Pacific reflected the US Navy's view of the war and was considered more important in that its axis lay directly across the Japanese lines of communications.

The discussions on how to proceed with an invasion of Japan reflected these divisions. MacArthur wished to advance up through the Philippines and then bypass the island of Formosa, just as he had bypassed Truk and Rabaul, before invading Japan. MacArthur reckoned without the opposition of Fleet Admiral Ernest King, Chief of Naval Operations, who believed that the capture of Formosa was a prerequisite of a successful invasion of the Philippines. However, King's preference for Formosa was damaged when in May 1944 Japanese forces in China began a drive south of the Yangtse river to eliminate US B-29 bomber bases established there in preparation for the final offensive against Japan. The offensive was successful on the ground but also in its effect on planning in Washington. The option of acquiring bases in China now seemed distinctly unattractive, especially in the light of the establishment of bases in the Marianas. Additionally, the failure of Chiang Kai Shek's Nationalist forces to put up any resistance worthy of the name in the face of the Japanese offensive served to discredit the idea of establishing bases on the Chinese coast. At the same time the American planners were discovering that an invasion of Formosa was presenting more problems than could be solved, particularly in view of the great distances involved and the fact that the Marianas could provide adequate base and harbour facilities for such an attack. This consideration clearly favoured MacArthur's choice of the Philippines, where Manila Bay was large enough to provide just such an anchorage.

It was at this juncture, when US planning was somewhat confused over which direction to take regarding the invasion of Japan, that a third option presented itself. King had asked Admiral Raymond Spruance, the commander of the Fifth Fleet, what should follow the invasion of Guam. Spruance suggested an attack on Okinawa in the Ryukus chain. Okinawa, in the Nansei Shoto (the South-Western Islands) was an island possessing potential airfields from where almost any type of aircraft could reach the Japanese industrial heartland of Kyushu, 350 miles away, and where space in terms of both land and suitable harbours was sufficient for the mounting of the final assault on Japan

However, Spruance qualified his recommendation with a rider to the effect that such an operation was only possible if satisfactory means of transferring ammunition at sea were found. Previously US ships had always ammunitioned while at anchor in harbour. The immense distances involved in an invasion of the Ryukus meant that ships would have to carry out this replenishment at sea, particularly as the scale of air attack experienced in the Philippines meant that ammunition expenditure would be considerable. Additionally, Spruance recommended the capture of Iwo Jima in the Bonins as a forward air base from which to support the attack on Okinawa and the eventual attack on Japan.

King had a high regard for Spruance but took some time to digest his proposal. His eventual decision was hastened by the fact that the war against Germany was not going to end as soon as hoped and that therefore there would be insufficient troops released from Europe for an invasion of Formosa. This view was also held by Nimitz, who, together with Spruance, met King at San Francisco in September 1944 to discuss the matter. However, Nimitz did have sufficient soldiers and Marines within his command to execute the operations against Okinawa and Iwo Jima. In pressing this view on King, both Nimitz and Spruance stressed that the occupation of Okinawa would give the Americans a base that would be important not only for the invasion of Japan but also because it lay astride Japanese communications to the south and across the China Sea. Thus King's preference for Formosa was scuppered by his own subordinates. The recommendation was formally adopted in a JCS (Joint Chiefs of Staff) Directive of 3 October 1944. The operation was code-named 'Iceberg'. The Directive was issued to Nimitz, who was to

> . . . establish bases from which to:—
>   (i) attack the main island of Japan and their sea approaches with naval and air forces;
>   (ii) support further operations in the regions bordering the East China Sea;
>   (iii) sever Japanese air and sea communications between the empire and mainland of Asia, Formosa, Malaya and the Netherlands East Indies.
>   To establish secure sea and air communications through the East China Sea to the coast of China and the Yangtze Valley.
>   To maintain unremitting military pressure against Japan.[1]

Detailed planning for the operation had begun before the JCS had issued their directive. Okinawa presented the Americans with some formidable problems. Its distance from bases in the Marianas and the Carolines meant that a huge logistic train would have to be gathered together to keep the ships supplied at sea. The corollary of this problem was that Okinawa was perilously near to the Japanese mainland, where there were thought to be between 3,000 and 4,000 aircraft. In the early stages of the operation air support for the troops ashore would have to be furnished by the carriers, which would thus be exposed to the full weight of Japanese air attack—which would, given the experience of the Americans in the Philippines, include suicide attacks.

Nimitz proposed that the thrust against Okinawa be in two parts. The first would involve the capture of Iwo Jima in the Bonins, and this would be followed by the assault on Okinawa itself. The date for the attack on Iwo Jima was set for 20 February in order to allow for the construction of airfields on the island from which B-29 bombers could fly against targets on Okinawa. In the event, bad weather and delays in the conquest of the Philippines meant that the capture of Iwo Jima was put back to 20 March and that of Okinawa to 1 April. Concern was felt that the timing of both operations was becoming very tight: if the invasion of Okinawa were put back any further it would run into the summer typhoon season, with potentially disastrous consequences.

On 3 January 1945 Spruance completed the broad operational plan for the invasion of Okinawa. Less than five weeks later Admiral Kelly Turner produced the detailed operational orders and on 1 February both plans received the formal assent of the JCS. The operational concept was in three stages. The southern portion of Okinawa was to be captured first, including small adjacent islands where advance base facilities were to be established. This was to be followed by the seizure of the remainder of Okinawa and Ie Shima, and the development of base facilities in appropriate areas. Finally, mopping-up operations were to be conducted throughout the Nansei Shoto with such forces as were locally available.

'L-Day', the day of the assault, was set, rather inauspiciously, for 1 April. Although the Joint Chiefs had specified 1 March in their Directive, the shortage of transport shipping (a perennial problem in the Pacific), the delay in completing the occupation of Luzon and the possibility of typhoons meant that the date had to be put back.

The launch of 'Iceberg' coincided with a reorganization in the command structure of American forces in the Pacific. Hitherto the two theatre commanders, General of the Army Douglas MacArthur in the South-West Pacific Area and Fleet Admiral Chester Nimitz in the Pacific Ocean Areas (or Central Pacific), were autonomous in their own areas and reported directly to the Joint Chiefs of Staff in Washington. On 5 April 1945, four days after the landings at Okinawa, the joint Chiefs promulgated a series of amendments on the grounds that the rapid advance on Japan had reduced the operational requirements considerably and that there was thus no longer the need for two autonomous theatre commanders. MacArthur was appointed Commander-in-Chief US Army Forces Pacific (CINCAFPAC) and made responsible for all US Army personnel and resources in the Pacific theatre less those in the Alaskan Department and those assigned to South-East Asia, in

13

which latter theatre the British Admiral Lord Louis Mountbatten's status as 'supremo' was unchanged. Nimitz was given command of all US Navy and Marine forces in the Pacific, less those in South-East Asia, although Admiral Ernest King, jealously guarding his prerogatives, reserved the right to allocate US Navy forces as he saw fit. Henceforth the Joint Chiefs of Staff would allocate forthcoming operations to either MacArthur or Nimitz as appropriate, leaving it to each commander to assist the other in the supply of forces.

The details seem to have been left deliberately vague and the new arrangement never really worked as intended, but it was probably the best way of combining the fiefdoms of two powerful personalities, neither of whom would relish being subordinated to the other. Organization and habits developed over nearly four years of warfare could be dismantled at a stroke by administrative fiat. In fact, the decision led to lot of confusion in the US higher command in the Pacific as to who was responsible for what. Thus, although most of the forces allocated for 'Iceberg' came from Nimitz's old Pacific Ocean Areas command, his supply bases in the Philippines came under the authority of General MacArthur's South-West Pacific command. In the end common sense won, and during 'Iceberg' both commanders continued to maintain their areas and rely on separate logistic chains as before.

The situation was further complicated in that, although Nimitz and MacArthur possessed their 'own' air forces—Nimitz had the Strategic Air Force, Pacific Ocean Areas, and Forward Area, Central Pacific, while MacArthur controlled the Far Eastern Air Force—the Twentieth Air Force (consisting of XX Bomber Command operating in India and China and XXI Bomber Command working from the Marianas) under General of the Army Henry 'Hap' Arnold and the China-based air force under Lieutenant-General A. C. Wedermeyer were controlled directly from Washington. In the original brief Nimitz was allowed to call on aircraft of XXI Bomber Command in a tactical or strategic emergency. However, XXI's commander, Major-General Curtis Le May, was so desperate to lay his hands on the Okinawa airfields in order that his B-29s could begin the demolition of Japan's industry that he indicated to Nimitz that his forces were available to him whether an emergency existed or not. Thus for five weeks before the invasion Nimitz had the unrestricted use of this powerful and well-equipped force to destroy the Japanese aerial offensive capability and to compel the enemy to retain for home defence aircraft which otherwise could have been used against the assault forces.

The forces involved in the capture of Okinawa broke down into four components, each responsible to the Joint Chiefs of Staff:

1. Twentieth Air Force (General of the Army H. A. Arnold), consisting of XX Bomber Command, charged with neutralizing enemy installations in northern Formosa, and XXI Bomber Command, released in support of CINCPAC;

2. China-based forces (Lieutenant-General A. C. Wedermeyer), for aerial reconnaissance and strikes over the Chinese coast;

3. Pacific Fleet and Pacific Ocean Areas (Fleet Admiral C. W. Nimitz), to establish and maintain control of the approaches to the East China Sea by capturing positions in the Nansei Shoto in order to provide facilities for further advances on Japan;

4. South-West Pacific Forces (General of the Army D. MacArthur), responsible for air attacks from Luzon in the Philippines on enemy bases in Formosa and the neutralization of airfields in Formosa and for reconnaissance and rescue over the China Sea, the Strait of Formosa and sea areas east of Formosa.

General of the Army Douglas MacArthur was, at 65, almost at the peak of his professional career. After his ignominious expulsion from the Philippines in March 1941 he had conceived and implemented the brilliant strategy of 'island-hopping'. The heart of this strategy was to bypass the large, heavily defended islands and instead to seize smaller, less well defended islands, develop them as bases and move on. In this way his forces had retaken northern New Guinea and the Solomons, while in October 1944 he had made good his promise to return to the Philippines with his landing on Leyte.

General MacArthur was a commander about which it is very difficult to be neutral. He was undoubtedly ambitious, vain and flamboyant to a degree. He was disparagingly known as 'Dug-Out Doug'. However, even his detractors had to admit that the man was a military genius. In the view of the eminent military historian Basil Liddell-Hart, MacArthur was

> . . . supreme . . . His combination of strong personality, strategic grasp, tactical skill, operative mobility and vision put him in a class above Allied commanders in any theatre.[2]

MacArthur's counterpart in the Central Pacific, Fleet Admiral Chester Nimitz, was as different from him as chalk from cheese. Nimitz had had a varied career, including service in submarines, battleships and aircraft carriers together with staff appointments and a period at the Naval College. He was appointed to command the Pacific Fleet in place of Admiral Husband Kummel after the Pearl Harbor débâcle and did much to restore confidence and morale. His bold and skilful exploitation of intelligence gained from decoded Japanese signals enabled him to deploy his numerically inferior forces to compensate for the odds stacked against him. His perceptive and positive decisions led, time and again, to the ideal disposition of his forces, enabling his commanders at sea to meet the enemy under conditions of the greatest advantage. His accessibility, his regard for his subordinates and his quiet strength of character inspired the deepest devotion.

It was Nimitz who was selected to conduct the Okinawa landings. The forces at his disposal were large and widely flung. His main 'executive' force was the Fifth Fleet under the command of Admiral Raymond Spruance with its fast aircraft carrier task forces, each of which was a self-contained 'fleet' in its own right. Admiral Raymond Spruance was a quiet and unassuming figure with a background of engineering and technical appointments. At the outbreak of the Second World War he was in command of the cruisers in Admiral William Halsey's carrier task force and it was only the latter's illness on the eve of the Battle of Midway that sent him on the path to high command. His appointment to command the American carriers at Midway was a surprising decision but one which was justified by Spruance's handling of these irreplaceable ships during the battle. Spruance was criticized for being too cautious, particularly during the Battle of the Philippine Sea in that his tactics permitted the bulk of the Japanese ships to escape. However, the decimation of the Japanese Navy's air arm brought about by his defensive tactics served to eliminate Japanese sea power as effectively as sinking their ships. Spruance was an intellectual, retiring man not given to seeking publicity and thus he has often been denied the recognition as a great commander which is rightly his.

Behind the striking power of the Fifth Fleet lay a hinterland of support and logistic forces essential for the prosecution of operations at such great distances from the Americans' main bases. Some, such as the Marshalls-Gilberts Force under Rear-Admiral W. K. Harrill, guarded lines of communication by holding positions necessary for security. A force under Vice-Admiral F. J. Fletcher contained the Japanese in the North Pacific. The South Pacific Force under Vice-Admiral W. L. Calhoun provided logistic support as directed, as did Rear-Admiral R. E. Ingersoll, Commander Western Sea Frontier (United States) and Lieutenant-General R. C. Richardson Jr, commanding the Army Forces of the Pacific Ocean Areas. The Service Force Pacific Fleet under Vice-Admiral W. W. Smith and the Air Force Pacific Fleet under Vice-Admiral G. E. Murray provided logistic support for Commander Logistic Support Group (TG.50.8) who furnished direct logistic support to the forces in and around the combat zone. Vice-Admiral Murray was also responsible for the supply of replacement aircraft, air crews and aviation spares to forward area bases. The Submarine Force under Vice-Admiral C. A. Lockwood was widely dispersed across the Pacific to conduct reconnaissance, undertake lifeguard duties and engage in the continual attrition of Japanese shipping. The Forward Area Central Pacific to which ships returned for rest and replenishment was under the control of Vice-Admiral J. H. Horner, who also controlled naval and air forces for anti-submarine cover, the neutralization of enemy airfields, lifeguard duties and so on. The Strategic Air Forces Pacific Ocean Areas under Major-General W. H. Hale were required to neutralize enemy bases in the Carolines, the Nanpo Shoto, the Nansei Shoto and Japan and provide fighter cover for XXI Bomber Command's B-29s during their raids over Japan.

The forces required for 'Iceberg' were organized into two groups: the Covering Force and the Joint Expeditionary Force. The Covering Force (see Appendix 1) consisted of two fast carrier task groups, one American and one British. The American force, TF.58,[3] was under the command of Vice-Admiral M. A. Mitscher, who was succeeded on 28 May by Vice-Admiral J. S. McCain.[4] Mitscher was one of the pioneers of aviation in the US Navy and, in the words of the Official Historian, 'had grown up with the flat-top'.[5] He was a lean, wiry figure with a leathery face invariably topped by a long-visored baseball cap. Naval aviation was his abiding passion and he had little time for the traditions and customs of the 'Blackshoe Navy'. Since March 1944 Mitscher had commanded Nimitz's fast carrier forces and justified his appointment by his superb performance during the Battle of the Philippine Sea. He had also won the loyalty of those in his command by his concern for their welfare, in particular his concern to rescue downed aviators. Mitscher's somewhat unorthodox manner was more than balanced by that of his flag-captain, Captain Arleigh Burke, a famous destroyer commander who had earned the nickname 'Thirty One Knot Burke'. The two men, very different in character, worked well together. Whenever a destroyer came alongside Mitscher's flagship to fuel, he would jokingly order Burke to be lashed to a stanchion lest he be tempted to 'jump ship'!

TF.58 consisted of four groups of carriers protected by a screen of capital ships, cruisers and destroyers, each group making up a balanced force. In the event that the surviving capital ships of the Japanese Navy made a sortie, a Striking Force code-named TF.59 could be formed under Vice-Admiral W. F. Lee. The fast carriers had the onerous responsibility of destroying Japanese air power prior to the landings and thereafter preventing enemy interference with operations ashore. The battleships had to provide heavy AA fire for the carriers but also had a bombardment role. TF.58 carried 919 aircraft, of which 70 per cent were fighters and the remainder bombers.

The British Carrier Force (TF.57) under Vice-Admiral Bernard Rawlings, although dignified with the status of a Task Force, was little bigger than a single group from the American fast carrier force, having 218 aircraft (see Appendix 2). It was given the exclusive task of protecting the left flank of the operation by attacking the airfields in the Sakishima Gunto group of islands. It was formed from the British Pacific Fleet (Commander-in-Chief Admiral Sir Bruce Fraser) and was, in theory, self-sufficient, having its own fleet train (TF.112) under Rear-Admiral D. B. Fisher. However, in reality the fleet train proved totally incapable of supplying TF.57's requirements and the shortfall had to be made up from American supplies. Although operating in Admiral Nimitz's area, the British fleet's bases were in MacArthur's area at Leyte and Manus, while its only shore base was in Australia.

The Joint Expeditionary Force included all the elements directly concerned with the landings. Vice-Admiral Richmond Kelly Turner, Commander Amphibious Forces, US Pacific Fleet (TF.51), was charged with the capture, occupation and defence of islands in Okinawa Gunto and the construction of advanced base facilities. 'Iceberg' would be Turner's fifth major amphibious operation in the Pacific: his experience went back to Guadalcanal, Tarawa and the Marshalls, and he was more familiar with such operations than probably any other officer in the United States. Turner was a quick, nervous man who was often appallingly rude to his subordinates, but for all his roughness he was ready to respond to the ideas of others. A total of 1,213 ships were employed by TF.51 during the operation together with 451,866 officers and men. The Expeditionary Force Troops (TF.56) consisted of the US Tenth Army under Lieutenant-General Simon Bolivar Buckner Jr (the son of a Confederate general of the Civil War), who would die watching the US Marines advance on Okinawa. The Tenth Army was a new formation and Buckner himself was very much an unknown quantity: his previous appointment had been Commander of US Army formations in Alaska.

The Tenth Army may have been a new formation, but its two constituent corps were veterans of the Pacific War. The XXIV Corps US Army, commanded by Major-General John R. Hodge and made up of the 7th and 96th Infantry Divisions, had captured Leyte, while the Marines of III Amphibious Corps, under the command of Major-General Roy Geiger USMC and consisting of the 1st and 6th Marine Divisions, had taken Guam. These men were not new to the Pacific War. Buckner also had the 2nd Marine and 77th Infantry Divisions (with the 27th Infantry Division in reserve) as Army troops, together with such HQ and support echelons as was appropriate.

The two Corps were split into two assault forces, the Northern Landing Force (TG.56.2), made up of III Amphibious Corps, and the Southern Landing Force (TG.56.3), made of XXIV Army Corps. The assault forces were to be landed by, respectively, the Northern Attack Force (TF.53) under Rear-Admiral L. F. Reifsnider USN and the Southern Attack Force (TF.54) commanded by Rear-Admiral J. L. Hall Jr USN. Other assault forces included the Western Islands Attack Group (TG.51.1) under the command of Rear-Admiral J. L. Kiland USN, which was to land the 77th Infantry Division (TF.56.4: Major-General A. D. Bruce US Army) and capture the archipelago of Kerama Retto to the west of Okinawa before the main landings for use as an advanced base; and the Demonstration Group (TF.51.2), which was to engage in diversionary operations to deceive the Japanese in advance of the landings and which consisted of the 2nd US Marine Division under Major-General T. E. Watson USMC together with an RCT[6] from each of III Amphibious Corps and XXIV Corps.

In reserve was the Expeditionary Force Floating Reserve (TG.51.3) under Commodore J. B. McGovern USN which consisted of the 27th Infantry Division (Major-General G. W. Griner US Army). This force remained at Ulithi until committed on orders from TF.51, Vice-Admiral Turner. Finally, the Area Reserve consisted of the 81st Infantry Division (TF.51.4) under the command of Major-General Meuller US Army, which, in the event, was not required. All Army and Marine formations engaged in the operation were under the immediate command of Vice-Admiral Turner until such time that he was sure that the assault had been successful and the lodgement secure. At that moment he was to turn over command to General Buckner, who would henceforth report direct to Nimitz.

A new feature in the composition of the assault forces was the Gunfire and Covering Force (TF.54), commanded by Rear-Admiral Morton L. Deyo USN. TF.54 consisted of ten old battleships (*Texas, Maryland, Arkansas, Colorado, Tennessee, Nevada, West Virginia, Idaho, New Mexico* and *New York*) divided into five Fire Support Units each with screening cruisers and destroyers. A sixth Fire Support Unit consisted of two seaplane tenders for spotting purposes. TF.54 provided continuous naval gunfire support for the ground forces throughout the operation.

Backing these up was the Amphibious Support Force (TG.52) under Rear-Admiral W. H. P. Blandy, who was also charged with the capture of Kerama Retto and support for the subsequent main landings. TG.52 was by far the most flexible element of the assault forces. From his headquarters ship the USS *Estes*, Rear-Admiral Blandy commanded a force composed of all the elements required to support the landings. The components of TF.52 were as follows:

TG.52.10	Air Support Control Unit
TG.54.1	Fire Support Group consisting of the heavy fire support ships assigned from the Gunfire and Covering Force.
TG.52.1	Support Carrier Group consisting of fourteen escort carriers and screen.

TG.52.2	Mine Flotilla comprising 75 minesweepers organized into fifteen sweep units and an Investigation Unit.
TG.52.8	Net and Buoy Group.
TG.52.11	Underwater Demolition Flotilla consisting of ten UWD teams organized in two groups.
TG.52.25	Advanced Support Craft: four gunboat support divisions, three mortar support divisions and a Rocket Landing Ship Group.
TG.51.1	Western Islands Attack Group, including the Western Islands Landing Force (TG.56.4) transports, landing ships and a screen of destroyers.
TG.51.15	SOPA (Senior Officer Presently Afloat) Kerama Retto, who commanded the Kerama Retto screen, ammunition ships, oilers and all vessels whilst engaged in replenishment, maintenance and repairs.
TG.51.20	Seaplane Base Group.

For every unit involved, the invasion of Okinawa was the culmination of four years of amphibious warfare in the Pacific. The commanders and their forces were well seasoned in combat. Their naval, ground and air doctrines had been thoroughly tested throughout the Pacific.

NOTES TO CHAPTER 1

1. Admiralty, Naval Staff History, Battle Summary No. 47: 'Okinawa: Operation Iceberg, March–June 1945' (London, 1950), p.2.
2. Keegan, John, and Wheatcroft, Andrew, *Who's Who in Military History: From 1453 to the Present Day*, Routledge (London, 1987), p.201.
3. On 27 May control of all Fifth Fleet units passed to the Third Fleet under Admiral W. F. Halsey. Unit designations were changed so that TF.50 became TF.30.
4. On 17 April TF.58.2 was dissolved after heavy losses and action damage. Its ships were used to reinforce the remaining three groups.
5. Morison, Samuel E., *The Two Ocean War: A Short History of the United States Navy in the Second World War*, Little, Brown (1963), p.334.
6. RCT = Regimental Combat Team.

2

The Objective

One plane for one warship. One boat for one ship. One man for ten enemy. One man for one tank.—Battle slogan of Japanese XXXII Army defending Okinawa.

THE Ryuku Islands are composed of three main archipelagos, or *gunto*, marking the eastern boundary of the East China Sea as they extend along an arc running from the southern tip of Kyushu to the north-eastern end of Formosa. In north to south order these archipelagos are Amami Gunto, Okinawa Gunto and Sakishima Gunto. The island of Okinawa, the largest of the Okinawa Gunto, was a logical choice for the advanced base for the invasion of Japan proper. It lies only 325 miles from Japan and has plenty of room for airfields, and it has two protected anchorages on the east coast.

Okinawa was not unknown to the Americans. In 1853 Commodore Matthew Perry had raised the Stars and Stripes on a hill near Shuri, the scene of much bloody fighting in 1945, and compelled the King of the Ryukus to sign a treaty allowing the Americans to set up a coaling station at the port of Naha and guaranteeing good treatment to visiting US ships and personnel. Japan only took over the islands in 1879, but the native Okinawans were never totally assimilated into Japanese society or culture.

The Okinawa Gunto, the northernmost of two groups of islands which make up the Ryukus, is a densely populated group of rugged islands situated in the approximate centre of the Nansei Shoto. It consists of Okinawa Shima, the largest and most populated island of the chain, and numerous smaller islands including Kerama Retto, Keise Shima, Ie Shima and the South-East Islands, the whole covering an area of 90 miles east to west by 65 miles north to south. The strategic position of Okinawa Shima may be judged from the distances from the island to the Japanese bases at Kiirun (Formosa; 330 nautical miles), Shanghai (450) and Kyushu (Kagoshima; 360). It lay, as it were, at the gates to Japan.

The island of Okinawa lies north-east and south-west, is about 60 miles long and varies from three to ten miles in width. The south-western and north-eastern parts of the island are very different in character. The north-eastern section is mountainous, wooded, rugged and sparsely populated, with hardly any cultivated land. The few roads which exist run along the coast, which is rocky and precipitous, broken by only a few beaches and alluvial flats at the mouths of rivers and streams. By way of contrast, the south-western portion of the island is well populated, with a community numbering nearly 500,000.[1] The landscape consists of hills and plateaux which are intensively cultivated. However, the countryside is broken up by numerous ravines, scarps and ridges and nearly all the low-lying land is overlooked by high ground. The largest areas of flat terrain are around the edges of Nagagusuku Bay (renamed Buckner Bay by the Americans after the death of General Buckner) on the east and from about ten miles north of Cape Yakimu, the south-western point of the island, to Machinato. Elsewhere the shores are formed by cliffs or steep slopes, with few significant beaches. The town of Naha in the south-west of the island had a harbour which could accommodate destroyers but which was very exposed to westerly gales.

Okinawa afforded two fleet anchorages, in Nagagusuku Bay and Chim Bay, both on the east coast of the island and the only substantial such facilities available south of Kyushu. The anchorages were protected by a fringe of reefs and islands, known as the Eastern Islands, one of which, Tsuken Shima, dominated the entrance to Nagagusuku Wan and was strongly garrisoned by the Japanese.

There are also a number of 'satellite' islands around Okinawa which were to feature in the landings. The largest of these is Kerama Retto, a group of small islands lying between 10 and 20 nautical miles west of Okinawa proper, of which the largest is Tokashiki Shima. The islands are very rough and hilly, and densely forested, and have very steep and irregular coasts with the occasional coral sand beach. However, they do offer excellent anchorages—of which the Americans were to make maximum use in the operation. Keise Shima is a group of three islands with sand

and pebble beaches and lies between Okinawa and Kerama Retto. These islands, the largest of which is Nagandu Shima, were uninhabited except during the fishing season, when temporary reed huts were built by the fishermen. They lay only 20,000 yards from the beaches selected for the assault on Okinawa and so would be quickly occupied and used as gun positions.

Ie Shima, four miles off the tip of the Motobu Peninsula on the west coast of Okinawa, comprises a slightly elevated plateau with good, firm beaches at its south-eastern end but with rocky coasts elsewhere. The Japanese had three airfields on the island, each approximately 5,000 feet long. The remaining islands, Tori Shima, Iheya Shima, Aguni Shima and Kume Shima, lie to the west of Okinawa and would be used by the Americans as warning and fighter-direction stations.

The areas selected for the assault of Okinawa extended over 10,000 yards on the south-west side of the island between Zampa Misaki and Chatan. The beaches on this stretch of coastline are not continuous but are interrupted by bluffs which drop vertically into the sea. Other factors which would impede the landings were a shortage of exits from the beach and the presence of sea walls and off-shore reefs. Despite these disadvantages, the site was chosen because it was sheltered from the easterly winds which prevailed during the spring, the conditions of gradient, surf and reef were good and the area behind the beach offered ample opportunity for manœuvring a large assault force and quick access to the airfields at Yontan and Kadena.

A shallow fringing reef with scattered coral heads borders the entire coast. The average depth of water over the reef at low tide is three feet. Throughout much of its length the reef is more like a barrier reef, with deeper water between its lip and the shore. The distance between the shore and the outer edge of the reef at the northern end of the assault area was about 1,300 yards, narrowing to some 200 yards in the centre of the assault area and widening to about 900 yards at the southern end. The beaches are composed largely of coral sand and vary in width from three to thirty yards. The beach gradients vary from gentle to moderate in the southern sector and from moderate to steep in the northern. The spring tides average about 5½ feet. For more than half their length the beaches are backed by a very narrow fringe of trees and bushes. Immediately behind the beaches is an uplifted terrace which rises from 20 to 70 feet, abruptly in places and particularly so in the northern sector. Most of the beaches have at least one good road exit; these varied in width from six to twelve feet and some of them had coral surfacing. The southern beaches have fewer roads, but there were larger cleared areas adjacent to the shore, permitting adequate dispersal.

During the period from October to March the Nansei Shoto is under the influence of the winter monsoon which blows from the north and north-east. Over the open sea its strength is between Force 4 and Force 5 but has been known to approach gale force, causing very rough seas in exposed areas. From June to the end of August the summer monsoon prevails, with light winds from the south-west and south-east. All through the year the islands lie in path of typhoons, twelve of which pass by Japan in an average year.

As the Second World War progressed and as, in tandem, Japan's military position became bleaker, the Ryukus assumed a more significant position in Japanese defence plans. This first became evident in September 1943 when an 'Absolute National Defence Zone' was established; at the end of 1943 joint Army/Navy talks were held at IGHQ on the subject. The talks produced a concrete result in March 1944 when the 32nd Army was formed. The primary objectives of this force were the defence of the Ryukus against an invasion and the defence of the airfields and anti-submarine bases on islands in the chain. The new commanding officer of the Army, Lieutenant-General Masao Watanabe, left Japan to take up his command on 29 March 1944 and from that time the build up of forces on the islands accelerated. On 3 May that year three mixed brigades, an anti-aircraft battalion and three medical units, together with ordnance, communications and airfield construction troops, were transferred to the 32nd Army. However, only one of the mixed brigades, the AA battalion, the communications unit and two of the field hospitals arrived: the remainder were lost when their transports were sunk on passage.

The American landings in the Marianas, especially the capture of Saipan in June 1944, served to accelerate planning for the defence of the Ryukus. Since the Japanese were unsure of where the Americans would strike next, they evolved an intricate defence plan called *Sho-Go* which envisaged four scenarios:

Sho-1: The Philippines

Sho-2: The Ryukus, Formosa and the east and south coasts of China.

Sho-3: The Home Islands (excluding Hokkaido)

Sho-4: Hokkaido

The Ryukus occupied a central position in all these plans except for *Sho-1*, since in order to capture any of the objectives listed in *Sho-2, 3* and *4* they would have to be taken, or at least neutralized, first. As a result, reinforcements now poured into the islands, and four infantry divisions, the 9th, 24th, 28th and 62nd, arrived in June 1944 together with the 59th Independent Mixed Brigade and a host of supporting units. Simultaneously the Japanese evacuated tens of thousands of native Okinawans to Kyushu and Formosa, thus turning the islands into a fortress.

It all looked very good on paper to see these units arriving in the Ryukus. Watanabe, however, was constantly having to adjust his plans to take account of the latest directive from IGHQ. For example, no sooner had the 28th Division landed in Okinawa than they were ordered to the islands of the Sakishima Gunto although remaining under Watanabe's command. This switching of resources was characteristic of Japanese defence plans for Okinawa. The threat to the islands was real, and perceived as such in Tokyo, yet, almost as it supplied reinforcements for the islands with one hand, IGHQ would take away what it had recently given with the other. Watanabe therefore had a thankless task, and he must have been relieved when he was replaced by Lieutenant-General Mitsuru Ushijima in early August 1944. Ushijima was an officer of considerable experience and one who had a deceptively soft manner. In contrast, his Chief of Staff, Major-General Isamu Cho, was a fire-eater in the best traditions of the Japanese Army.

The American invasion of the Philippine Islands in October 1944 caused another rethink in Tokyo. The Japanese, rightly, believed that the Americans would have to take the Ryukus as a prerequisite to an invasion of Japan. But which way would they come? Would the thrust come through China and Formosa or would it be through the Bonins, including Iwo Jima? In November 1944 IGHQ believed that Formosa was where the Americans would attack next; at this stage in the war Japanese and

American plans were remarkably similar. In the light of this thinking, IGHQ felt that the garrison on Formosa was under strength and needed reinforcements. But instead of finding these reinforcements from forces in Japan or the massive Kwantung Army in China, it decided to strip Ushijima's command of one division, the 9th, which represented 33 per cent of his infantry strength. To make matters worse, the 9th was the best of Ushijima's three divisions and the promise of the 84th Division in replacement sounded rather hollow. Ushijima's scepticism was well-founded. In January 1945 he was told that the orders for the 84th Division to embark for Okinawa had been cancelled since it was considered too risky to send such a large number of troops by sea in the face of the American submarine offensive and because many officers at IGHQ were convinced that the final apocalyptic battle for Japan's survival would take place in the Home Islands. In these circumstances, reinforcing the islands on Japan's periphery was a waste of resources.

With the capture of the Philippines, it became very clear that *Sho-Go* had been made redundant by events. In January 1945 the Japanese unveiled another plan for the defence of their homeland, this time entitled *Ten-Go*. The new doctrine emerged in the shape of an 'Outline of Army and Navy Operations' which became the basis for all future defence planning. The Japanese realized that the final decisive battle of the war would be waged in Japan proper and that the best means of defence lay in holding the Americans off and using air power, particularly suicide attacks, to sink or cripple sufficient US shipping to prevent an invasion of the Home Islands. A series of Army/Navy conferences culminated in a meeting on 6 February 1945 and a joint agreement:

> All Army and Navy forces in the homeland will be concentrated in the East China Sea area during the months of February and March 1945. This concentrated air strength, together with air units in Formosa plus reinforcements from other areas, will crush any enemy attempt to invade points within this area.
>
> Primary emphasis will be laid on the speedy activation, training and mass employment of air special attack units.
>
> The main target of Army aircraft will be enemy transports and of Navy aircraft carrier task forces.[2]

For the first time in a Japanese operational plan, a formal role was given to the Special Attack Units, better known in the west as *Kamikaze* units. Suicide has always been a part of the Japanese military code, but usually only in desperate circumstances. Now the idea of giving one's life for the Emperor was placed on an organized footing. The Special Attack Units were composed of volunteers prepared to crash their aircraft on to American ships, losing their life in the process. It is important to stress that, contrary to contemporary American propaganda, the *Kamikaze*s were not unwilling conscripts, nor were they 'hyped' on drugs or alcohol before their operation. They were for the most part young men who believed passionately that they were doing what was right and carrying out what was expected of them by their culture and their military code. The concept of ritual suicide is abhorrent to those brought up in the liberal Christian tradition, but there were no such feelings in Japan. The Japanese forces were imbued with the idea that 'duty is more weighty than a mountain, death is no heavier than a feather'. One Japanese officer about to embark on a suicide mission wished that he had 'but seven lives to give for his Emperor'.

The Special Attack Units came under the command of Vice-Admiral Matome Ugaki, Commander of the Fifth Air Fleet. Ugaki was one of the pioneers of Japanese naval aviation and had been Vice-Admiral Chiuchi Nagumo's Chief of Staff for the attack on Pearl Harbor. Ugaki had developed the *Kamikaze* concept from an idea put forward by Vice-Admiral Takajiro Onishi, who had commanded the First Air Fleet during the Philippines Campaign. Both men combined a powerful belief in mythology and mysticism—*Kamikaze* was the name given to the 'Divine Wind' which had saved Japan from the Mongol invasion in the Middle Ages—with a belief in the benefits to be derived from suicide attacks. Their proposals did not meet with universal approval. Admiral Soemu Toyodo, Commander-in-Chief of the Grand Fleet, considered the idea valuable but wasteful in terms of air crews and aircraft. Toyodo believed strongly that better results could be achieved by the new generation of aircraft coming into service. However, during the Philippines Campaign the first suicide attacks were made and the die was cast.

For the defence of Okinawa, Ugaki was given command of the Japanese Sixth Air Army in addition to his own Fifth Air Fleet. *Ten-Go* did not meet with Ugaki's approval, for it called for his aircraft to concentrate on the supply ships and landing craft.

Ugaki was sufficiently familiar with American practice to realize that any landing would be preceded by a wave of strikes by carrier-borne aircraft, and if he followed *Ten-Go* to the letter his aircraft would be wiped out on the ground. He managed to persuade Toyodo to allow him some flexibility in choosing his targets.

In the first months of 1945 Ushijima consolidated his plans for the defence of the islands (the Japanese order of battle is summarized in the accompanying table). Though his infantry strength had been weakened by the dispatch of the 28th and then the 9th Divisions to Sakishima and Formosa respectively, he possessed considerable reserves of artillery, well dug-in, but little armour (only the 27th Tank Regiment, consisting of fourteen medium and thirteen light tanks, was assigned to his command) since his defence was to be a static one. However, Ushijima was blessed in his artillery commander, the formidable Lieutenant-General Kosuke Wada, and in having a considerable reserve of artillery, largely because of the fact that many weapons destined for the Philippines had been retained on Okinawa for want of shipping. Wada had more artillery at his disposal than the Americans had yet encountered in the Pacific, and this German-trained artillery officer prepared a fire plan which made the most of his assets. Wada possessed more than 250 guns of 70mm calibre or larger, including 150mm howitzers. The Japanese were also well equipped with mortars, including the fearsome 320mm spigot mortar, labelled the 'Flying Boxcar' by the Americans. There was also an ample supply of automatic weapons, especially heavy machine guns.

In January 1945 Ushijima's forces began to take up their positions, the 24th Division and the 44th Independent Mixed Brigade in the centre of the island with the 62nd Division in reserve in the south. However, the strategy adopted by Ushijima was new and owed much to Japan's experience during the American amphibious campaign across the Pacific. The classic Japanese Army doctrine of 'attack on any and every occasion, irrespective of conditions, and with no calculation as to the real chances of success' had been proved wrong in New Guinea and the Solomons, when waves of charging Japanese infantry had been scythed down by American firepower; so, too, did the theory of 'impregnable defences' collapse in the face of American firepower

JAPANESE ORDER OF BATTLE
FOR THE DEFENCE OF OKINAWA

HQ Staff   **1,070**
32nd Army Headquarters Staff

Infantry   **38,310**
24th Division
62nd Division
44th Independent Mixed Brigade
1st–3rd, 26th–29th Independent Battalions (Naval Infantry)
223rd, 224th, 225th Garrison Companies
3rd, 4th Commando Units

Armour and Artillery   **11,476**
27th Tank Regt
5th Artillery Command (3 regiments)
100 Heavy Artillery Battalion
1st Artillery Mortar Regiment
1st, 2nd Light Mortar Battalions
3rd, 7th, 22nd Independent Anti Tank Companies
27th, 79th, 80th, 81st Independent AA Artillery Battalions
21st AA HQ
103rd, 104th, 105th MG Cannon Battalions
3rd, 4th, 14th, 17th, 23rd Independent MG Battalions

Shipping and Engineers   **4,465**
23rd, 26th Shipping Engineer Regiments
66th Independent Engineer Battalion
Shipping HQ and two Sea Duty Companies

Line of Communications Troops   **7,333**
36th Signal Regiment
32nd Army Field Freight Depot
32nd Army Field Ordnance Depot
72nd Land Duty Company
Field hospital plus ancillary medical units

Army Air Force (Ground)   **6,936**
Miscellaneous Air Force command and control units,
maintenance units and airfield construction units

Naval units   **3,500**

Other miscellaneous troops   **3,359**

TOTAL   **77,199**

in the Gilberts, Marshalls and Marianas. Accordingly, Ushijima adopted a defensive system aimed at prolonging each action to the utmost and inflicting the maximum number of casualties on the Americans. The Japanese garrison in Okinawa dug-in into the cliffs and hills and prepared to fight the Americans in a campaign of attrition in which the latter would be allowed to land but would then be forced to fight for every mile of ground. Lieutenant Tomiichi Hidara was an officer in the 89th Infantry Regiment, part of the 24th Division:

> When I reached my unit, I was surprised to find little preparation being made to repulse the Americans on the beaches. Instead, everyone was digging, laying barbed wire and mines and working out zones of fire for more heavy machine guns and mortars than I had ever seen. I felt totally useless, for nothing in Officer School had prepared me for planning a defence. All we had been told was how to attack. Nevertheless, despite the strange orders coming down from Army Command, all the officers and men seemed imbued with the feeling that this time the Americans were going to be beaten.[3]

It was to be at Shuri, the ancient capital of the islands, that Ushijima's forces would make a stand. The area was particularly suitable, being honeycombed with old caves, tombs and workings which made ideal defensible positions. There the troops of the 32nd Army dug in and waited.

NOTES TO CHAPTER 2

1. The last recorded survey, in 1935, established the population as being 451,620.
2. Pineau R., *History of the Second World War: Okinawa*, Purnell & Sons (London), Vol 6, p.3549.
3. Tomiichi Hidara to author, 29 September 1993. This is not his real name: he changed his identity after the war to escape the ignominy of having surrendered.

3

Preparatory Operations

*It cannot be too often repeated that in modern war, and
especially in modern naval war, the chief factor in achieving
triumph is what has been done in the way of thorough
preparation.*—President Theodore Roosevelt.

ONE of the cardinal principles of the American campaign in
the Pacific was never to give the Japanese pause to recover
and regroup. On 24 March 1945, the same day that
resistance ended on Iwo Jima, the fast carrier groups of the Pacific
Fleet sailed from Ulithi for preparatory strikes off Okinawa.
Minesweeping operations, carried out under the protection of the
big guns of the battleships of the fast carrier force and protected
by an awesome air umbrella, began ten days later.

In fact, the effort against Okinawa had started as early as
September 1944 when the first aerial reconnaissance missions
were flown. Since Okinawa was a prefecture of Japan, information of military value was difficult to come by. Although captured
Japanese charts furnished a certain amount of hydrographic
data, and while other captured documents and the interrogation
of prisoners and former inhabitants yielded some basic intelligence, it was clear that detailed information about the islands
would have to come from photographic reconnaissance.

The nearest Allied airfield was 1,200 miles away, which meant
that the initial surveys would have to be performed by B-29
bombers or carrier-based aircraft. Small-scale coverage of the
island for mapping purposes was completed by 29 September
1944 by B-29s of XXI Bomber Command. With the exception of
the northern part of the island, which was obscured by cloud,
good coverage was obtained of Okinawa itself and the outlying
islands. From then until the assault date, coverage was continually updated by Army or carrier-based aircraft, although the
weather, the distance from suitable airfields and restrictions on

Above: Admiral Chester W. Nimitz, Commander-in-Chief Pacific Fleet and in overall command of Operation 'Iceberg'. (US Navy)
Below: General Douglas C. MacArthur, whose initial preference was for an attack up through Formosa. (US National Archives)

Above: Vice-Admiral Raymond Spruance, Commander Fifth Fleet, who produced the initial operational plan for 'Iceberg'. (US National Archives)
Right: Vice-Admiral Marc Mitscher, Commander of TF.58, the fast aircraft carriers and battleships, which composed the main striking force of the Fifth Fleet. (US National Archives)

Left: Vice-Admiral Richmond Kelly Turner, amphibious warfare specialist and responsible for the detailed planning of the landings. (US National Archives)

Right: Turner (left) with Major-General Alexander A. Vandegrift, Commandant of the US Marine Corps. Vandegrift was to be a persistent critic of the conduct of operations on Okinawa. (US National Archives)

Below: Lieutenant-General Simon B. Buckner Jr (left), Commander of the Tenth Army, with Major-General Roy S. Geiger USMC, Commander of III Amphibious Corps. (US National Archives)

Above: Task Force 58 at anchor at Ulithi—one of the greatest concentrations of sea power ever assembled. In the centre of the photograph are five *Essex* class carriers. (US National Archives)

Below: B-29 bombers on Saipan being readied for an operation against targets in southern Japan. B-29s of XXI Bomber Command played an important role in the preliminary operations against Okinawa in terms of both bombing operations and photo-reconnaissance. (US National Archives)

Above: B-29 bombers of XXI Bomber Command flying over Mount Fuji in January 1945. Operations such as this heralded the attack on Okinawa and the eventual assault on Japan. (US National Archives)

Below: A Japanese air base at Kure under attack from carrier-based aircraft of TF.58 on 20 March 1945. Note that the aircraft are arranged with little or no camouflage. (US National Archives)

Above: The immense American armada required for the support of the Okinawa landings lying in the Transport Area—an irresistible target for any Japanese pilot. (US National Archives)

Right, upper: Rear-Admiral William H. Blandy, Commander of the Amphibious Support Force, TF.20, (far left), with (left to right) Rear-Admiral Harry W. Hill, Lieutenant-General Holland M. Smith and Vice-Admiral Richmond Turner. (US National Archives)

Right, lower: A Japanese midget submarine base in northern Okinawa under attack by aircraft from TF.58 in March 1945. The submarines are shown secured close into the shore, while in the upper part of the photograph a coaster is down by stern after a near miss. (US National Archives)

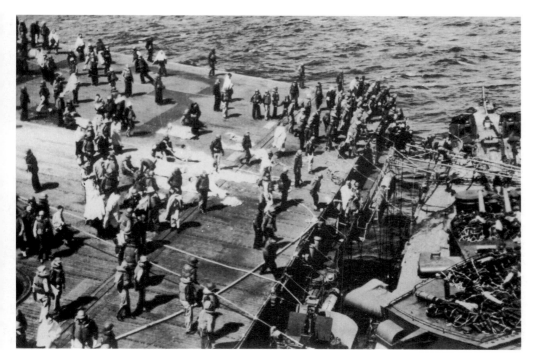

Left, upper: The USS *Franklin* listing and on fire after being struck by a *Kamikaze* on 19 March 1945. Only damage control of a very high order saved the ship. (US National Archives)

Left, lower: The conning tower of the USS *Franklin* after the ship had been struck. Debris is seen flying through the air and damage control parties on the flight deck are rushing to take cover. (US National Archives)

Above: Wounded are transferred from *Franklin* to the cruiser USS *Santa Fe* secured alongside the carrier. (US National Archives)

Below: *Franklin*'s ship's company gather for a service in the burnt-out hangar. Altogether 832 of her crew died in or after the attack. (US National Archives)

Above: Infantry moving ashore on Kerama Shima (Keram) on 26 March. There was slight resistance but the island was secured the next day. (US National Archives)
Below: LVTs and infantrymen of the 77th (Statue of Liberty) Division come ashore on Tokashiki Shima on 27 March 1945. Tokashiki Shima was part of the Kerama Retto group of islands, ten miles from the island of Okinawa. (US National Archives)

Above: The Stars and Stripes are raised on Kerama Shima by infantrymen of the 77th Division. (US National Archives)
Below: A captured *Shinyo* suicide boat is put through its paces by an American officer. The boat was found concealed on Kerama Shima. (US National Archives)

Above: Not all Japanese in the Kerama Retto group of islands gave themselves up immediately. This group surrendered to an American 'Flycatcher' patrol on 3 July 1945 and are seen wading out to the boat, carrying their clothes above their heads. (US National Archives)
Below: The Stars and Stripes are raised on Aka Shima on 27 March 1945. (US National Archives)

Above: The battleship USS *Tennessee* bombarding Okinawa before the landings on 1 April 1945. (US National Archives)
Below: An LSM(R) firing a salvo of rockets in the final bombardment before the troops went ashore on Okinawa. (US National Archives)

Above: A view of the invasion beaches from an LST anchored offshore. (US National Archives)
Below: LCAs manœuvre around assault transports during the morning of 1 April 1945. (US National Archives)

photo-reconnaissance missions on account of air strikes made it difficult for the Americans to obtain the large-scale photographs necessary for the detailed study of installations. However, on 10 October 1944 aircraft from the Fast Carrier Force flew sufficient missions over the island to provide the large-scale vertical and oblique coverage required.

Further B-29 missions were flown on 29 November 1944, 3 January and 28 February 1945, while the carrier-based aircraft covered the island on 22 January, 1 March and 22 March. In this last operation aircraft from two carriers, the USS *Bunker Hill* and the USS *Hornet*, supplied over 28,000 photographs between them. The coverage on most of these operations was good and permitted a close watch to be maintained on changes to Japanese defence installations. The small-scale coverage by the long-range B-29s, though not particularly suitable for detailed study, nevertheless effectively closed the gaps in that obtained by aircraft from the fast carriers.

From 25 March (L–7), when the Amphibious Support Force (TF.52) arrived at the objective, photographic reconnaissance came under the control of Rear-Admiral W. H. P. Blandy. The effort and resources required for photographic-reconnaissance operations on such a scale often pass unnoticed amid the more combat-orientated preparations, but the technical and logistical effort in obtaining such a comprehensive picture of the islands was immense.

The fact that the Okinawa operation involved the drawing together of cargo and troops from many widely dispersed locations—the United States, Hawaii, the South-West Pacific, the Marshalls and Carolines and Leyte—precluded a joint rehearsal of all the units taking part. Instead, the various elements assembled and conducted their rehearsals individually. This was perhaps not the best way to approach a large-scale amphibious operation, but after nearly four years of amphibious warfare in the Pacific the Americans were seasoned campaigners and knew their drill.

The Gunfire and Covering Force (TF.54) worked up from 5 to 21 March at Ulithi, joined by the Amphibious Support Force (TF.52) from 11 to 21 March. The Northern Attack Force (TF.53) trained at Guadalcanal from 1 to 8 March, while the Southern Attack Force (TF.55) exercised at Leyte from 14 to 21 March. The Western

Islands Attack Group (TG.51.1) assembled at Leyte from 9 to 16 March, while TG.51.2, the Demonstration Group, practised their techniques at Saipan from the 16th to the 21st of that month. The reserve forces, the Floating Reserve (TG.51.3) and the Area Reserve (TG.51.4), formed at Espiritu Santo and Noumea respectively.

It was envisaged that the ships of the Gunfire and Covering Force and those of the Amphibious Support Force would assemble at Ulithi on 5 March and until 21 March would be available for training, rehearsal repair and replenishment. In the event, ships arrived at Ulithi right up to the day of departure. Many late arrivals came directly from operations off Iwo Jima and were badly in need of repair and rest for their crews; moreover, they had not received any plans concerning the Okinawa operation before their arrival at Ulithi. Training at Ulithi was further downgraded by the constant need to provide radar picket ships around the island, which was subjected to frequent Japanese air attacks. In one such attack the carrier USS *Randolph*, part of the fast carrier force, was damaged on 11 March and did not rejoin her group until 8 April.

When the various groups of the Joint Expeditionary Force sailed for the combat area after final rehearsals and replenishment, most had one or more escort carriers from the Amphibious Support Force assigned to provide cover while on passage. The various forces then proceeded directly to their objective areas—the Western Islands Attack Group to Kerama Retto, the Northern and Southern Attack forces to a point off the main landing beaches on the west coast of Okinawa and the Demonstration Group to the eastern side of the island. These movements were carried out without opposition from the Japanese, although as a bonus two Japanese submarines were sunk. At 2333 on 22 March the destroyer USS *Haggard*, which was steaming twelve miles ahead of a task group nearing Okinawa, attacked a radar contact with depth charges. *Haggard* continued the attack and at 0028 the next day a submarine, the Japanese *I-371*, was blown to the surface. *Haggard* turned to ram and her bow sliced into the submarine just aft of her conning tower. The submarine rolled over to port, exploded and sank, leaving no survivors. However, *Haggard* had been so badly shaken by the explosions of her own depth charges and by the shock of the ramming that she was considered unfit to proceed with the operation so was sent back to Ulithi escorted by the destroyer USS *Uhlmann.*

At 2039 on 30 March the destoyer USS *Stockton* in the Logistic Support Group attacked a submarine about 65 miles south-east of Okinawa. The submarine, *I-8*, was detected on the surface and sunk by gunfire after she had been illuminated by flares dropped by an anti-submarine patrol aircraft. One survivor was picked up, together with some mangled human remains.

It was the fast aircraft carriers of TF.58 which began the offensive against Okinawa. After supporting the landings at Iwo Jima, Mitscher had led his carriers back to Ulithi for ten days of repair and replenishment. On 14 March his ships left Ulithi to attack airfields on the mainland of Japan in order to eliminate airborne resistance to the forthcoming landings. Mitscher believed that his primary task was to conduct air strikes over Japan in order to eliminate as many aircraft as possible, either in the air or on the ground, while destroying the facilities at the principal airfields. He hoped that, in this way, he would prevent the Japanese mounting an air attack of any size on the landings. The targets were selected on the basis of the number of primary airfields in Kyushu, Shikoku and southern Honshu, and each of Mitscher's four Task Group Commanders was assigned a target area. Airfields were designated as the primary targets of all fighter sweeps; bomber strikes from all Task Groups could be concentrated on a single target or targets in the same general area, in order to provide a maximum concentration of bombs and mutual protection.

The strikes were to be carried out over a two-day period, 18 and 19 March. Mitscher's carriers fuelled on 16 March and by dawn on the 18th were in position 100 miles east of Kyushu and ready to commence flying-off operations. The strikes went ahead unabated and succeeded in their primary object of disabling the Japanese Army and Naval Air Forces to such a degree that they were incapable of mounting any strong attacks against the invasion force until a week after the landings.

The pilots reported that air opposition over Kyushu had been light and that their attacks had been concentrated against airfields and associated installations. The absence of Japanese aircraft was deliberate: Ugaki had held back fifty of his precious aircraft and now sent them out looking for the carriers. It was

Rear-Admiral Radford's TG.58.4, in position about 75 miles south of Shikoku, which received the concentrated Japanese attack. *Enterprise* was hit by a bomb which failed to explode at 0725. However, her luck did not hold, for she was subsequently disabled by 'friendly' gunfire. A 'Betty'[1] which attempted to crash on *Intrepid* was shot down so close to the ship that the explosion of the aircraft killed two of the carrier's crew and started a serious fire in the hangar. Shortly after 1300 *Yorktown* was attacked by three 'Judys'[2]: two missed, but the third hit the signal bridge and passed through one deck before exploding near the ship's side, making two big holes and killing seven and wounding twenty-six of her crew.

On the 19th Mitscher's ships moved north to undertake a series of strikes against Japanese warships, including the mammoth battleship *Yamato*, located at Kure and Kobe the previous day. Other ships attacked included the carriers *Amagi*, *Katsugari* and *Ryuho*, the battleships *Haruna* and *Hyuga* and the cruisers *Tone* and *Oyodo*. A good deal of damage was inflicted on installations ashore and the carrier *Ryuho* was badly damaged, but otherwise the strikes were only moderately successful on account of heavy AA fire over the ports.

The Japanese continued their attacks on the fast carriers throughout the 19th, this time choosing TG.58.2 commanded by Admiral Davidson as their target. USS *Wasp* (Captain O. A. Weller USN) had just secured from General Quarters after launching two-thirds of her air group. A Japanese aircraft somehow got through the screen undetected and dropped a single bomb on *Wasp* at 0710. The bomb hit the flight deck and penetrated to the hangar, where it caused an aircraft to explode before passing through mess decks on No 2 deck and detonating in a galley on No 3 deck, where most of the ship's cooks and mess attendants were about to serve breakfast. Fires broke out simultaneously on five decks, fuelled by avgas which poured down from the hangar. Six fire mains were ruptured, but *Wasp*'s ship's company were so well drilled in damage control that the flames were out in fifteen minutes and at 0800 the carrier was able to recover her aircraft. Nevertheless, 101 officers and men had been killed or subsequently died of their wounds and 269 had been wounded. *Wasp* continued to operate for several more days before returning to Ulithi for repairs.

Admiral Davison's flagship USS *Franklin* (Captain Leslie H. Gehres USN), affectionately known to her crew as 'Big Ben', was launching her second wave of aircraft just after 0708 when she was hit by two bombs from another Japanese aircraft which, again, penetrated the screen without being detected. The first bomb exploded on the hangar deck, wrecked the forward elevator and started huge fires thoroughout the hangar—where many aircraft were parked, fuelled and armed ready for operations—and No 3 deck. Everyone in that part of the hangar was killed. The second bomb struck the flight deck and exploded above the hangar, spreading fires among planes which were running up their engines ready to launch. The explosion blew the after elevator up and over to one side. Almost immediately *Franklin* was enveloped in a pall of black smoke and it seemed to those in other ships nearby that the carrier was as good as lost.

Captain Gehres, on the bridge, was knocked down by the first explosion and after picking himself up saw the fires in the forward part of the ship and ordered full right rudder in order to bring the wind on to the port side, in the hope of keeping the flames away from the massed ranks of aircraft parked at the after end of the flight deck. However, he soon noticed that the after end of the flight deck was also in flames, and so he swung *Franklin* to port in order to bring the wind on to the ship's starboard beam.

Franklin was now shaken by explosions as the ordnance on the aircraft ranged on the flight deck began to detonate. Some of the explosions were very violent: Admiral Mitscher, aboard his flagship *Bunker Hill*, heard six coming from *Franklin* when she was still below the horizon. The 11.75-inch 'Tiny Tim' rockets fitted to some of the aircraft went up spectacularly. *Franklin*'s Executive Officer, Commander Joe Taylor USN, recalled:

> . . . some screamed to starboard, some to port and some straight up in the air. The weird aspect of this weapon whooshing by so close is one of the most awful spectacles a human has ever been privileged to see. Some went straight up and some tumbled over end over end. Each time one went off the fire-fighting crews would instinctively hit the deck.[3]

Before the fires were brought under control, all the ready-use ammunition in lockers and around the gun positions aft of the island had exploded.

Admiral Davison transferred his flag to the USS *Hancock* and advised Captain Gehres that he was considering abandoning the damaged carrier. Gehres was having none of this and told Davison that he thought he could save his ship. However, Gehres was no fool and he ordered all but key officers and men to abandon ship. The cruiser *Santa Fe* (Captain Hal C. Fitz) was ordered by Davison to stand by *Franklin* (and, indeed, had been rescuing those members of the carrier's crew who had been forced overboard by the heat and flames), and shortly after 0930 Fitz brought his ship alongside *Franklin* and began taking off her crew. A total of 826 men crossed over to *Santa Fe* in just under half an hour.

By 1000 *Franklin* lay dead in the water, her fire and engine rooms having been evacuated on account of the intense smoke and heat. But by noon Gehres was able to report that the fires were practically under control, that the ship's list had stabilized at 13 degrees and that all the wounded had been evacuated. The cruiser *Pittsburgh* (Captain John E. Gingrich) secured a towline and, after *Santa Fe* had cast off, brought the carrier round to a southerly course, gradually working up to a speed of 6 knots. By 0300 the next day power had been restored and by 1100 *Franklin* was steaming at 15 knots, although without a compass—'Down by the tail but reins up,' in the words of Captain Gehres. Making only one stop, at Pearl Harbor, *Franklin* made the 12,000-mile voyage to New York under her own power.

Franklin sustained heavier damage than any other American carrier during the Second World War. Altogether 724 officers and men of her crew were killed or listed as missing and there were 265 wounded. Cruisers and destroyers rescued 1,700 of *Franklin*'s crew from the water. Among the casualties was Captain Arnold J. Isbell USN, the Commander of the highly successful 'hunter-killer' groups in the Atlantic, who was aboard *Franklin* as an observer. The casualty figures were in fact a record for a US ship surviving an enemy attack and were exceeded only by those of the sunken USS *Indianapolis*.[4] The heroism displayed by her crew was outstanding. Lieutenant-Commander Joseph T. O'Callaghan, the ship's RC chaplain, organized fire-fighting parties in addition to his pastoral duties and led two sailors trailing fire hoses to cool down a 5-inch shell magazine in which the temperature was hovering at the danger limit. Lieutenant (JG) Donald A. Gary discovered 300 men trapped in a compartment, managed to identify an escape route and made three trips into the compartment to bring them out.

However, it was more than just gallantry which saved *Franklin*. She would have surely been lost, as would all the other ships struck by Japanese suicide planes during the Okinawa campaign, had it not been for the careful attention paid to fire-fighting by the US Navy. 'Get the fear of fire out of the sailor' was the maxim of the damage-control schools established throughout the length and breadth of the United States. New fire-fighting techniques such as the use of atomized water sprays instead of solid streams were developed and taught to every ship's damage-control party. Equipment for fire-fighting and damage control was provided on a lavish scale. The *Essex* class carriers, which were already equipped with fourteen fire mains run on ship's power, were fitted with another two independently powered mains driven by gasoline engines. One of these ran continuously for eight hours on board *Franklin* when all the other mains were knocked out. Damage-control equipment was standardized throughout the Navy and equipment was designed with the emphasis on portability and manœuvrability in confined spaces. If the conduct of the war so far in the Pacific had failed to show the benefits of such training, events off Okinawa over the next three months would certainly do so.

The fast carriers retired slowly after their strikes on the Inland Sea on 18 and 19 March but kept air patrols over southern Kyushu throughout 20 March to discourage any Japanese aircraft from flying. In the afternoon of the 20th TG.58.2, still screening the damaged *Franklin*, was attacked by a 'Zeke'[5] which went for the carrier *Hancock*. The plane missed the carrier but was hit by the barrage of defensive anti-aircraft fire and ploughed into the destoyer *Halsey Powell* which, having refuelled, had just sheered away from *Hancock*. The aircraft crashed on to the destroyer's main deck near the after 5-inch mounting, wrecked the steering gear and caused a good deal of other damage. Fortunately the bomb which the 'Zeke' was carrying went straight through the destroyer's thin hull without exploding. Nevertheless, casualties amounted to twelve killed and 29 wounded.

Later that evening a series of raids on carriers was mounted between 1600 and 2000. The attacks were not well pressed home, other than that by one aircraft which bombed and strafed *Enterprise*. The bomb missed, but in the confusion the carrier was struck by 'friendly fire' from the other ships in the Group and was unable to operate aircraft.

The next day saw further attacks upon the carriers by 'Betty' bombers carrying, for the first time, the one-man piloted bomb known to the Japanese as *Ohka* ('Cherry Blossom').[6] This was a fearsome weapon, although its effectiveness was lessened by the fact that the weight of the *Ohka* so slowed the aircraft down that the latter were easy prey for the CAP fighters—which was fortunate since, once in flight, the *Ohka*s were so fast as to be impossible to shoot down. The attack was met by a force of 24 Hellcat fighters from TG.58.1 which shot down every one of the attackers for the loss of only two aircraft. By 22 March the carriers were outside the radius of Japanese land-based aircraft and were able to take on fuel from the tankers of the Logistic Support Group.

The results of the carrier strikes were mixed. The Americans claimed to have destroyed 528 Japanese aircraft in the air and on the ground during the two days. The Japanese admitted to the loss of 161 aircraft out of 193 committed, together with an indeterminate number on the ground. These losses prevented Japanese aircraft from participating in the defence of Okinawa in the immediate aftermath of the assault, and it was not until 6 April, when sufficient replacements had been amassed, that Japanese air assets became a serious factor in the campaign. In the words of the American Official Historian, 'Ten-Go was no-go'.

The Japanese claimed to have sunk five aircraft carriers, two battleships and three cruisers. Admiral Ugaki confidently proclaimed that the American assault on Okinawa would have to be postponed at the least. Not for the first time in the war, hopelessly over-exaggerated claims by Japanese field commanders influenced the planners at Imperial General Headquarters; if any of the staff at IGHQ had any doubts they kept them to themselves. Consequently the Japanese were lulled into a sense of false security. On the other hand, three valuable US aircraft carriers had been damaged and forced to retire without one American having set foot on Okinawa, while 168 American aircraft had been lost, mainly aboard the damaged carriers: 52 aircraft were destroyed in *Franklin* alone.

On 23 March the carriers began direct attacks on Okinawa and the adjacent islands. All known enemy installations were extensively bombed in order to prepare for the minesweeping operations which would precede the actual landings and for the planned assault on Kerama Retto. There was virtually no air opposition and it became clear that the carrier strikes of 18–19 March had been more successful than first thought.

In the morning of 28 March there were indications that the remains of the Japanese surface fleet might be planning a sortie through Bungo Suido. Admiral Spruance told Admiral J. J. Clark, commanding TG.58.1 (consisting of the carriers *Hornet*, *Bennington*, *Belleau Wood* and *San Jacinto*, screened by the battleships *Massachusetts* and *Indiana* with four cruisers and thirteen destroyers), that he was free to reduce his operations over Okinawa if he could get his carriers to within striking distance of the projected position of the Japanese ships south and west of Kyushu. Accordingly Clark's ships sped north at high speed and at 1430 launched a strike against the Japanese vessels, reported to be 225 miles away. The strike was backed up by fighter sweeps over Kanoya and airfields in southern Kyushu to keep Japanese air cover occupied, but the presence of the Japanese ships proved illusory.

In the morning of the 29th TG.58.1 joined up with TG.58.3 and TG.58.4, which had moved north in support after fuelling. Search aircraft were launched at dawn but there was no sign of the Japanese ships. Instead the carriers launched aircraft in a wave of strikes against shipping and airfields in southern Kyushu. The aircraft from TG.58.3 in particular had a string of successes against shipping and the Task Group Commander, Rear-Admiral F. C. Sherman, wrote:

> . . . on no other single day were so many shipping targets presented, or was so much shipping damage inflicted by this Task Group.[7]

The strikes by the fast carriers preceded the less glamorous but equally important task of preparing the invasion beaches by minesweeping, underwater clearance and bombardment. At daylight on 24 March the fast battleships of TF.59—*New Jersey*, *Wisconsin*, *Missouri*, *Washington*, *North Carolina*, *South Dakota*, *Indiana* and *Massachusetts*—were temporarily detached and, together with three divisions of destroyers, formed TG.59.7 under

41

the command of Vice-Admiral W. A. Lee Jr. The ships proceeded towards the south-east coast of Okinawa to bombard coastal defences as a diversion (the landings were scheduled to take place on the other side of the island) and to protect the minesweepers which were to begin operations in that area.

The battleships opened fire at 0922 at extreme range, but the absence of any opposition allowed them to close the range to 14,000 yards while the destroyers screened the big ships to seaward. Watched by Admiral Spruance from his flagship, the cruiser USS *Indianapolis*, the battleships fired 1,375 16-inch shells before ceasing fire at 1400 and withdrawing to rendezvous with the carriers.

Minesweeping operations were planned to provide for the approach of the fast battleships of TF.59 to within bombardment range of the coast of south-eastern Okinawa outside the 100-fathom line; to clear the approaches to Kerama Retto and the passage between Kerama Retto and Tomachi Shima; to find the northern limits of the minefield between Okinawa Shima and Sakishima Gunto; to clear the water to the shore line for the attack force landings and close fire-support craft; and to clear the approaches to Okinawa for the attack force. Additionally, daily sweeps were to be maintained of the swept channels.

Mine Group 1 (TG.52.3) of the Amphibious Support Force arrived off Okinawa on 24 March and commenced operations under the protecting fire of the fast battleships. When the remaining echelons of TF.52 arrived the following day, the protection of the minesweepers was the responsibility of Gunfire Support Group (TG.54.2) and the Advance Support Craft Group (TG.52.25). Admiral Mitscher's carriers provided CAP on the first day but thereafter the escort carriers of the Support Carrier Group (TG.52.1) assumed this duty.

During L–8 and L–7 minesweeping and UDT operations went ahead without interference and no mines or obstacles were found, but on L–5 delays were encountered when the minefield off the Hagushi beaches on the west coast of Okinawa was found to be more extensive than anticipated. This delayed UDT operations of these beaches until L–3 and was further complicated by the fact that the Japanese had laid additional drifting or moored mines during the night in areas which were hitherto considered 'safe'. The practice of withdrawing the support craft at night without leaving covering patrols undoubtedly helped the Japanese in this regard, although in retrospect they did not take advantage of this opportunity.

The dangerous nature of this work was shown on 26 March when the destroyer USS *Halligan* lost her bows after being torpedoed by the submarine *Ro-49*.[8] The explosion caused *Halligan*'s two forward magazines to detonate and the entire forward part of the ship as far back as No 1 stack was blown off. On 28 March the minesweeper USS *Skylark* was sunk after hitting two mines. Nevertheless, the clearance of the areas off the beaches was complete by L–3 and the way was clear for a close-range bombardment of the beach defences.

The minesweeping operations which preceded the Okinawa landings were certainly the largest such sorties ever undertaken. Seventy-six minesweepers were engaged in clearing over 3,000 square miles of ocean, some areas of which had to be swept several times. A total of 177 mines were swept and 80 floating mines were destroyed—not a great number by any account, but it takes only one mine to sink a transport packed with troops. As the official British account of the operation records,

> The immunity with which great numbers of bombardment and assault ships closed the assault beaches without significant loss was evidence of the thoroughness with which the mine-sweepers carried out their task.[9]

Hand in hand with the minesweeping operations went the work of the Underwater Demolition Teams (UDT) to prepare the beaches for the assault. Their work was complex and included beach reconnaissance on Okinawa, Kerama Retto and Keise Shima, the preparation of charts for the assault forces, diversionary reconnaissance operations in southern Okinawa and the supply of guides for all the assault battalions in the initial landings. The responsibility of the UDT teams stopped at the high-water mark and ceased completely once harbour engineers were available to take over beach and port development.

TG.52.11, the Underwater Demolition Flotilla, was divided into two groups, Group A, of four teams, and Group B, of six. Group A concentrated on Kerama Retto and Keise Shima, beginning work on L–7 and completing their task by L–6. No opposition other than small-arms fire was encountered. The six teams of Group B concentrated exclusively on the Hagushi beaches and began their surveys on L–3. Light resistance was encountered in the form of small-arms and mortar fire but was quickly dealt with by the covering forces. Obstacles were encountered in the shape of 2,900 wooden posts inserted in six of the beaches in as many as four rows. Demolitions were carried out on the morning of L–2. Watchers on the support craft could see the frogmen placing their charges on the posts before being collected by LCVPs, but some 200 posts were still in position on L-Day. It was decided to leave these in place and have guides ready to advise the assault troops to keep clear. The UDT teams carried on their work up to L+4, blasting channels and trimming the edge of the reef.

Preparatory work for the diversionary operation on southern Okinawa was carried out by Group A and was apparently successful since Tokyo Radio announced that landings were imminent on south-eastern Okinawa as well as the western beaches. Total casualties in the UDT operations were astonishingly light—no more than one killed and two wounded.

Once the approaches to Okinawa were clear then the work of the bombardment group could begin in earnest. The fire-support ships were under the control of the Amphibious Support Force TF.52 and were provided by the Gunfire and Covering Force TF.54 and the Advance Support Craft Group TG.52.25 (landing craft support only). The heavy ships from TF.54 were under dual control: for their bombardment missions they came under TF.52, but they had an independent role in the event of a sortie by the Japanese fleet and while on passage to the assault area or while covering other shipping. Under these circumstances they had their own commander, Rear-Admiral Morton L. Deyo.

For the bombardment of Okinawa the ships were organized into five Fire Support Units under Rear-Admiral B. J. Rodgers. Unit 1 was assigned to the south-eastern coast of Okinawa and Unit 2 was to bombard the Naha area and support the landings on Kerama Retto. Units 3, 4 and 5 were all allocated to the Hagushi beaches in support of the main landings and early ground operations.

The fire-support plan followed that which had successfully been developed in the American advance across the Pacific. Three lanes of ships were provided, each increasing in firepower seaward from the beach. Gun landing craft formed the first line, covered by destroyers in the second line. Beyond the destroyers were the cruisers and battleships using their secondary and AA batteries to neutralize all ground from 300 to 1,000 yards inland and their main armament on specific targets as indicated to them.

The battleships of the bombardment group—*Tennessee, Texas, Maryland, Arkansas, New Mexico, New York, Colorado, Nevada, West Virginia* and *Idaho*—began operations on 26 March and continued up to L-Day. However, it was not until L-3, when minesweeping and UDT operations were complete, that the ships could close the shore and engage targets with direct fire. The bombardment encountered little or no opposition but targets were difficult to locate since the Japanese had taken considerable care over camouflage. However, all known coastal guns were destroyed and positions believed likely to harbour Japanese defenders were also subjected to shelling. By L–1 Deyo estimated that preparations were complete for a successful landing. During the bombardment 5,162 tons of ammunition were fired—27,226 shells of various calibres from 5-inch to 16-inch, with 5-inch AA ammunition accounting for a further 4,098 rounds. The amount of ammunition used of calibres below 5-inch is impossible to quantify.

In addition to suffering gunfire support, Okinawa was vigorously worked over by aircraft from the Support Carrier Group (TG.52.1) as well as the fast carriers. From L–7 to L-Day targets were continually strafed. Japanese aircraft and airfields were the main priority, followed by what the Americans had identified as 'amphibious tanks' (but were in fact suicide boats) and island installations. In addition to strike missions the support carriers and the fast carriers also furnished CAP over the islands. CAP would arrive on station 45 minutes after first light and leave 45 minutes before sunset. The Japanese were evidently aware of this pattern, for all their suicide attacks took place before the morning CAP was on station.

The Japanese ground forces made little or no attempt to interfere with any of the preparatory operations. Even the minesweepers were left unmolested, despite being within range of known Japanese gun positions. If the Japanese hoped that inactivity on their part would preserve their positions from attack they were mistaken, for most of the coast defences which could oppose the landings were destroyed by the coastal bombardment.

There were, however, a number of attacks by midget submarines and suicide boats. On 27 March the destroyers USS *Callaghan* and *Porterfield* attacked a midget submarine in 26°26'N 127°39'E and brought up debris marked with Japanese characters. On the same day the cruiser USS *Portland* had an inconclusive action with a similar vessel off Zampa Misaki in 26°29'N 127°45'E. The following day the light minelayer USS *Tolman* was unsuccessfully attacked in the early hours off Nago Wan by eight MTBs. She destroyed two and damaged several of the others before the attack was broken off. Suicide boats made further attacks in the morning of 29 March and eight were destroyed in return for damage to *LCI(G)558*.[10] On 31 March the destroyer USS *Barton*, part of the screen for Fire Support Unit 3, made sonar contact with a submarine to the west of Okinawa and claimed to have sunk the boat with her second depth charge attack—a claim which was not confirmed by post-war analysis.

Japanese air attacks proved more damaging. Within forty-eight hours of the commencement of preliminary operations, the Japanese gave notice that they were aware that an assault was imminent. On 26 March eight enemy aircraft attacked shipping near Kerama Retto, where landings were due to take place that day. Several of the enemy were destroyed by CAP or gunfire, but the high-speed transports *Gilmer* and *Knudson* of Demolition Group A, the minelayer *R. H. Smith* and the minesweeper *Skirmish* received minor damage, while the destroyer *Kimberly*, part of the Western Islands Attack Group screen, was so badly damaged that she required dockyard facilities for repair. In the Fast Carrier Group the destroyer *Hickox* was also slightly damaged.

During the night of the 26th/27th a force of fifteen Japanese aircraft attacked the ships off Okinawa. TF.54 received the heaviest attack early in the morning, the Japanese deceiving the Americans as to the number of aircraft involved by use of 'Window'. Suicide hits damaged the destroyer USS *Porterfield* and the cruiser USS *Biloxi*, both in Fire Support Unit 4, while in Fire Support Unit 6 the destroyer-escort *Foreman* was badly damaged. The battleship USS *Nevada* took a direct hit but her stout construction meant that damage was confined to a blackened area on the upper deck. The suicide attacks arrived before CAP was on station; however, a conventional attack using torpedo bombers on the Fast Carrier Force was decimated by CAP, although not before the high-speed minesweeper USS *Dorsey* and the destroyer USS *Murray* had been damaged.

There were no further air attacks until the morning of 29 March. AA fire from the ships accounted for thirteen of the attackers and CAP another three. The level of the attacks was quite high. The destroyer USS *Preston* suffered four attacks, *Wiley* five, *M. F. Bauer* six and *Twiggs* seven. None of these ships was damaged, but *LCI550* was dismasted and *LSM(R)188* was badly damaged together with the attack cargo ship *Wyandot*.

The most serious casualty was the cruiser USS *Indianapolis*, Admiral Spruance's flagship, which was hit during the morning of 31 March. The pilot of the aircraft was deterred by the huge volume of the AA fire put up by the cruiser and swerved at the last moment, crashing into the sea. However, the bomb which he released struck the port side of the main deck and went through the ship before exploding under the hull. Two holes were blown in the ship's bottom and the cruiser settled by the stern, though she was able to proceed under her own power. *Indianapolis* had to return to the United States for repairs and Admiral Spruance shifted his flag to the battleship *New Mexico*.

The last element of the preparatory operations was the seizure of Kerama Retto. The capture of these islands was dictated by the necessity of establishing a replenishment and naval repair base, the need for which arose from the fact that the Okinawa operation was being conducted at a vast distance from the nearest Allied advanced or permanent base. A subsidiary role was that of a repair base, for shipping casualties anticipated in the assault on Okinawa and the subsequent invasion of Japan. That the islands be seized was the proposal of Admiral Turner, and almost every element of the command which studied the proposal rejected it for a variety of reasons, the proximity of land-based Japanese air power being the main factor. But the heavy losses encountered during the seizure of Iwo Jima emphasized the requirement for a forward repair base, so Turner got his way. Events fully justified this decision. The large number of ships damaged off Okinawa made for a very heavy load on the repair facilities, and eventually four floating docks were needed at Kerama Retto to cope with the work. As the operation on Okinawa developed, so the role of Kerama Retto increased, not just as a repair base but also as a general replenishment and rearmament facility.

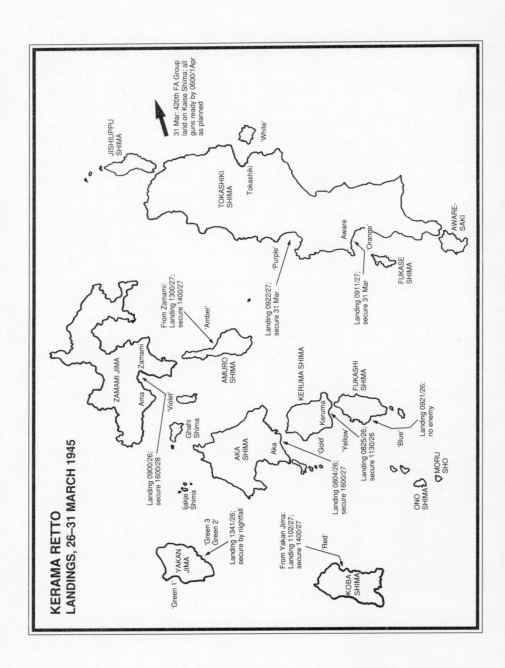

KERAMA RETTO
LANDINGS, 26–31 MARCH 1945

31 Mar: 420th FA Group
land on Kaise Shima; all
guns ready by 0600/1 Apr
as planned

JISHUPPU
SHIMA

'White'

TOKASHIKI
SHIMA

Tokashiki

AWARE-
SAKI

Aware

'Orange'

'Purple'

FUKASE
SHIMA

From Zamami:
Landing 1300/27;
secure 1400/27

'Amber'

Landing 0922/27;
secure 31 Mar

Landing 0911/27;
secure 31 Mar

ZAMAMI JIMA

Ama   Zamami

'Violet'

Ghahi
Shima

AMURO
SHIMA

KERUMA SHIMA

FUKASHI
SHIMA

Keruma

Landing 0921/26;
no enemy

Landing 0900/26;
secure 1600/28

AKA
SHIMA

Aka

'Gold'

'Yellow'

'Blue'

Ijakje
Shima

Landing 0804/26;
secure 1600/27

Landing 0825/26;
secure 1130/26

MORU
SHO

ONO
SHIMA

'Green 1'   YAKAN
            JIMA

'Green 3'
Green 2'

Landing 1341/26;
secure by nightfall

From Yakan Jima:
Landing 1102/27;
secure 1400/27

'Red'

KOBA
SHIMA

48

Admiral Turner believed that Kerama Retto could be seized by a reconnaissance battalion, since air reconnaissance indicated that the garrison of all islands did not exceed 400 men and only two of them possessed fixed defensive positions in the form of machine guns or light artillery. However, Rear-Admiral Ingolf N. Kiland USN, Commander of the Western Islands Attack Group (TG.51.1) and responsible for the operation, demurred. He had no intention of using small forces to fight desperate actions with isolated Japanese parties on individual islands: instead he would land simultaneously on five of the six larger islands using men of the 77th (Statue of Liberty) Infantry Division commanded by Major-General A. D. Bruce US Army.

Kiland's Western Islands Attack Group consisted of one transport squadron with sufficient lift to take a reinforced infantry division. The Amphibious Support Force provided two cruisers, four destroyers, twelve LCI(M)s (RCM), 24 LCI(G)s and twelve LSM(R)s to permit independent movement. The group sailed from Leyte on 19 March in three sub-divisions, and by the night of 25/26 March all elements were in position.

The enemy air action that night, referred to earlier, did not disrupt the plan and at 0804 on 26 March the battleship USS *Arkansas* began the bombardment which preceded the landings proper. The first landfall was made by a battalion landing team on Aka Shima against light rifle and mortar fire. By 1600 on 27 March the garrison of 200, together with an equal number of Korean labourers, had been overcome. Among the enemy equipment captured were 38 suicide boats located in caves along the north-west coast.

Throughout the 26th four more landings were made: on Keruma Shima (sometimes spelt Geruma Shima), which fell in three hours; on Zamami Jima, where the garrison took to the hills and were finally mopped up the next day; and on Fukashi Shima and Yakan Jima, which were undefended. On 27 March, at 0911, a regimental combat team landed on 'Orange' Beach on Tokashiki Shima and a few minutes later a battalion landing team took 'Purple' Beach on the same island. There was no resistance and, as on Aka Shima, numerous suicide boats were located in caves and coves on the eastern beaches. The Japanese commander on Tokashiki Shima was invited to surrender by American-born Japanese negotiators. He refused, but he indicated that he would not fire on American troops on the beaches so long as his camp in the hills was left alone. This uneasy co-existence persisted until the Japanese surrender when, after being shown a copy of the Imperial Rescript, he finally capitulated. Also on 27 March detachments from Zamami Shima and Yakan Jima took the islands of Amuro Shima and Koba Shima with only token resistance.

The islands had been taken remarkably easily. US casualties amounted to 31 killed and 88 wounded; Japanese losses were 516 killed and 166 taken prisoner. Once the islands were secure, then the establishment of the base began. By 28 March 22,000ft of anti-submarine nets had been installed, yet even before the nets were in position Admiral Kiland's vessels were 'serving' ships of the fire-support groups with fuel and ammunition. Despite the proximity of the islands to Okinawa and the densely packed shipping in the roadstead, other than the occasional air raid and sporadic sniper fire from the shore the islands were virtually ignored by the Japanese. The sole attack came when two enterprising swimmers swam out and clambered aboard *LST884* and killed the sentry while another entered a destroyer through a hole in her bow.

The last stage of the operation was the seizure of Keise Shima. This went ahead on 31 March without opposition and the same day two battalions of the 420th Artillery Group equipped with 155mm guns were landed. By 0600 on L-Day, 1 April, all guns were emplaced and zeroed-in.

The preparatory operations were now complete and Okinawa had been effectively isolated. The entire series of operations had been a model of inter-service co-operation, yet it was the general opinion of many American officers that, despite the lack of evidence that the Japanese would resist the landings, the actual operation could be as bloody as Tarawa.

NOTES TO CHAPTER 3

1. 'Betty' was the Allied code-name for the Mitsubishi G4M twin-engine bomber.
2. 'Judy' was the Allied code-name for the Yokosuka D4Y single-engine bomber and reconnaissance aircraft.

3. Morison, Samuel E., *History of United States Naval Operations in World War II. Vol. XIV: Victory in the Pacific 1945*, Little, Brown (1968), p.96.

4. The USS *Indianapolis* was torpedoed on 30 July 1945 by the Japanese submarine *I-58*.

5. 'Zeke' was the Allied code-name for the Mitsubishi A6M single-engine fighter.

6. The *Ohka* was 19ft long, with a 16ft 5in wing span, and carried a 2,640lb warhead fitted with a nose fuze and four base fuzes. The craft was powered by three rockets ignited electrically by the pilot. After release from the carrier aircraft it glided, the rockets being ignited only for the final dive, during which speeds of 620mph were attained. The pilot had no means of exit from the projectile.

7. Admiralty, Naval Staff History, Battle Summary No. 47: 'Okinawa: Operation Iceberg, March–June 1945' (London, 1950), p.26.

8. Some sources, however, including Morison and the Naval Staff History, indicate that *Halligan* was mined.

9. Admiralty, Battle Summary No. 47, p.29.

10. CTF.52's action report confirms the craft damaged as *LCI(G)558* but 'Operations in Pacific Ocean Areas, April 1945' names the craft as *LCI(G)588*.

4

The Landings

How wrong everybody was. What we thought to be difficult proved to be easy and after the easy part was over the tough fighting began.—Samuel Eliot Morison

BY 31 March Rear-Admiral Blandy, CTF.52, considered that all the preparatory operations were complete and that weather conditions would permit the landings to go ahead on 1 April in accordance with the plan. The southern half of the island, the part lying south of a line from Shirachi to Chimu, including the small islands off the eastern coast, was selected as the first objective for the assault. It was intended to isolate the southern half of the island by capturing the Ishikawi isthmus in order to prevent Japanese reinforcements coming from the north. At the same time the assault forces were to occupy a general east–west line from Kuba Saki at the head of Nagagusuku Wan in order to prevent enemy reinforcements coming from the south. The northern half of the island would then be secured, followed by the remainder. It was very important that the airfields at Yontan and Kadena be captured quickly in order to provide operating facilities for shore-based aircraft. Other important objectives included the Katchin Peninsula on the northern side of Nagagusuku Wan, to assist in securing the latter as a naval anchorage and unloading port, the port of Naha and the airfields at Machinato and Yonabaru. The capture of the four airfields was critical to the success of the plan since the landings would be the first to take place within staging distance of fighter aircraft from Japan.

The plan called for simultaneous landings on beaches north and south of Hagushi by the Tenth Army, with two corps abreast, each corps landing on a two-division front. XXIV Corps, consisting of the 7th and 96th Infantry Divisions, would take the right flank covered by the Southern Attack Force (TF.55) while III Amphibious Corps, consisting of the 1st and 6th Marine Divisions, would land on the left flank covered by the Northern Attack Force (TF.53). If, for one reason or another, it proved impossible to implement this operation, an alternative plan provided for landings on the eastern and south-eastern beaches of Okinawa, also with four divisions landing abreast one another.

At 0600 on 1 April, two and a half hours before the scheduled landing, Vice-Admiral Turner took command of TF.52 and gave the traditional order 'Land the landing force'. Rear-Admiral Blandy assumed command of TG.51.19, the Eastern Fire Support Group charged with covering the diversionary landings to be made on the south-eastern side of Okinawa near Sikabaru Saki. These diversionary landings were under the command of Rear-Admiral J. Wright, CTG.51.2, who had one transport squadron at his disposal with the 2nd Marine Division under the command of Major-General Watson USMC embarked, together with one tractor flotilla and the necessary screening and support vessels. The operation was to simulate a landing in every way possible. The waters adjacent to the beaches had been swept and the UDT teams had exploded real, but unnecessary, demolition charges to simulate preparations for the landings. The troops of the 2nd Marine Division were embarked and combat loaded—a necessary precaution in case they were required to support the landings if the alternative plan were implemented.

The main body of TG.51.2 arrived off the beaches early in the morning of 1 April, L-Day. As the ships entered the Transport Area[1] they were attacked by enemy aircraft which, for some reason, were not detected either by radar or by the look-outs until they were too close for avoiding action to be taken. A suicide aircraft smashed into the port quarter of *LST884* at 0549. The LST, with 300 Marines on board, burst into flames and, as her cargo of ammunition began to explode, had to be abandoned. Twenty sailors and Marines were killed and a further 21 wounded. A fire party from the destroyer USS *Van Valkenburgh* boarded the LST and succeeded in bringing the fire under control by 1100. Another suicide plane hit the transport *Hinsdale*, flooding the machinery spaces and causing a complete loss of power. Sixteen of the ship's crew were killed and 39 wounded. Both vessels were subsequently towed to Kerama Retto.

The battleships *Texas*, *Arkansas* and *Maryland*, screened by the cruiser *Tuscaloosa* and eight destroyers, made up Admiral

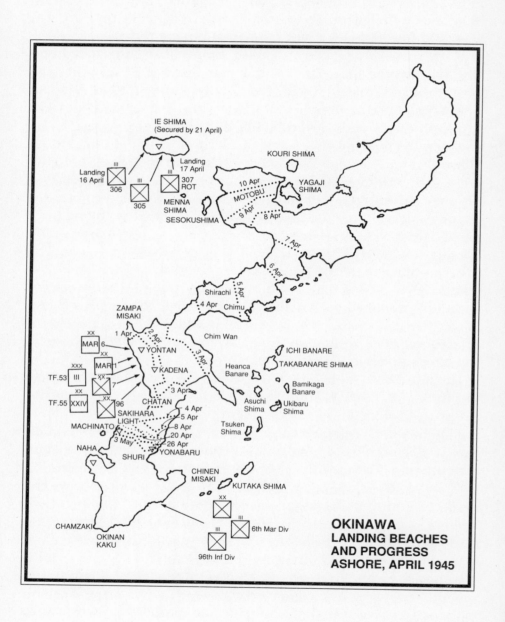

IE SHIMA
(Secured by 21 April)

KOURI SHIMA

Landing
16 April

306

305

Landing
17 April
307
ROT

MENNA
SHIMA

SESOKUSHIMA

MOTOBU

10 Apr

9 Apr

8 Apr

YAGAJI
SHIMA

7 Apr

6 Apr

5 Apr

Shirachi

4 Apr   Chimu

ZAMPA
MISAKI

1 Apr

2 Apr

Chim Wan

ICHI BANARE

TAKABANARE SHIMA

MAR 6

MAR 1

YONTAN

KADENA

3 Apr

Heanca
Banare

Bamikaga
Banare

TF.53   III

7

3 Apr

Asuchi
Shima

Ukibaru
Shima

TF.55   XXIV   96

CHATAN

SAKIHARA
LIGHT

Tsuken
Shima

MACHINATO

NAHA

3 May

4 Apr

5 Apr

8 Apr

20 Apr

26 Apr

SHURI   YONABARU

CHINEN
MISAKI

KUTAKA SHIMA

CHAMZAKI

OKINAN
KAKU

6th Mar Div

96th Inf Div

OKINAWA
LANDING BEACHES
AND PROGRESS
ASHORE, APRIL 1945

Blandy's Eastern Fire Support Group and commenced their pre-landing bombardment. This was followed at 0800 by a bombing and rocket attack on the beaches by support aircraft. The actual demonstration consisted of a feint towards the beach by seven waves of landing craft, each composed of 24 LCVPs from the line of departure, at seven-minute intervals. The LCVPs would be preceded by two divisions of LCI(G)s and flanked by two divisions of LCI(M)s on the left and two of LCI(L)s on the right. The operation went ahead with only slight opposition from the beaches, and when the fourth wave crossed the line of departure at 0830, the time of the main landing on the other side of the island, all the boats reversed course and returned to their ships, covered by smoke laid by aircraft and the LCIs. All the while the Eastern Fire Support Group maintained heavy neutralizing fire on both sides of the demonstration beaches. By 1500 all the boats had been recovered and the force retired at 1530, although Admiral Blandy's command ship, the USS *Estes*, and her screen remained off the beaches overnight.

The only reaction to the landings was a desultory salvo of four rounds which landed close to the USS *Gregory*, one of the screening destroyers, while the battleship *Arkansas* reported being fired on by a coast defence gun just south of Naha airfield. *Arkansas'* 14-inch guns lacked the range to engage the gun, so the USS *Maryland*, veteran of Pearl Harbor and a number of landings in the Pacific, was brought in to silence the weapon with her longer-range armament.

The demonstration was repeated on L+1, 2 April, with similar timing and with an equal lack of interest from the shore, and on 14 April the 2nd Marine Division was released from the operation and returned to Saipan. It is difficult to assess how effective the deception was. It certainly drew the only air activity on L-Day, since the huge array of ships off the western coast was left unmolested until that evening. Whether the Japanese were taken in or not is unclear, but their radio triumphantly claimed to have repulsed a landing 'with heavy losses'. While Radio Tokyo was claiming a victory, US troops were pouring ashore unopposed on the other side of the island.

After leaving Ulithi, the transports containing the troops of the Joint Expeditionary Force ran into heavy seas, gale force winds and even typhoon warnings. Such adverse weather conditions did little for the morale of the troops embarked. Training and preparation for the operation continued en route and particular emphasis was placed on civil affairs since, for the first time in the Pacific War, a considerable number of civilians would be encountered and would have to be looked after. In their intelligence briefings the Americans stressed that there were many cultural differences between the Japanese and native Okinawans, and the sensitive handling of civil issues would go some way to exposing these differences and exploiting them for the Americans' cause. To this end, propaganda leaflets had been showered over the island stressing that the Americans came more as liberators than as conquerors. However, most of the troops approached the islands with a sense of grim foreboding, particularly after reports of the heavy casualties sustained during the capture of Iwo Jima. This was a Japanese 'home island', and the troops noted that, although the Japanese had ceased to defend the beaches, the nearer the Americans came to Japan, the greater the ferocity with which the defence was conducted. Okinawa was undoubtedly 'The Big One', and many troops felt that they would be lucky to get off the beach, let alone contemplate the prospects of well dug-in Japanese troops in the interior, of snakes, of disease and of a hostile civilian population.

The weather on the day would be crucial, so considerable effort was put into weather reporting, with submarines positioned in the Yellow Sea, off Kyushu, in the Tokyo area, in the Shikoku area, off Amami Oshima and off Okinawa specifically for this purpose. As it happened, the weather which had been almost perfect for the preparatory operations remained splendid on the day of the assault itself. At H-Hour (0830) the skies were almost clear, with only three-tenths cloud cover at 3,000 feet. The wind was easterly, at 13 knots, and visibility was reduced to six to eight miles by early morning haze and smoke from the pre-invasion barrage. The sea was slight, with a chop, but there were no waves or swell over two feet. The remainder of the day was substantially the same. Cloud increased throughout the morning and by 1600 was seven-tenths cover, although after 1800 the skies cleared. The wind being offshore, there was little or no surf or swell on the reef.

The main landing over the Hagushi beaches was preceded by an immense bombardment. This had two objectives, firstly to blast holes in the sea walls on the beaches to provide exits for

56

amphibians and armoured vehicles and secondly to pour continuous interdiction fire on to the roads leading to the beaches, to prevent Japanese reinforcements from reaching them before the Americans had time to deploy and concentrate. However, the length of the landing area, almost 10,000 yards, and the navigational hazards off the beaches meant that the density of fire that could be provided at any one time was very limited. The large number of troops being deployed also meant that the bombardment had to be rigidly controlled by aerial spotting.

The direct fire support of troops was under the control of the respective attack force commanders. TF.55, commanded by Rear-Admiral J. L. Hall Jr, supported XXIV Army Corps with the battleships *Nevada*, *Tennessee* and *Colorado*, the cruisers *Wichita*, *Minneapolis*, *Birmingham* and *St Louis* and seven destroyers. Rear-Admiral L. F. Reinfsnider's TF.53 provided gunfire support for III Amphibious Corps with the battleships *West Virginia*, *Idaho*, *New Mexico* and *New York*, screened by the cruisers *Salt Lake City* *Biloxi*, *Portland* and *Pensacola* and eight destroyers. Also involved were nearly 200 support landing craft of various types. The new rocket ships firing the 5-inch projectile were used successfully for the first time although their design and construction had been carried out extremely quickly. The support landing craft were on station at sunrise on L-Day and provided continuous cover until H+60 (2030 on 3 April), after which call fire became available.

Air cover was provided by TG.58.1, 58.3 and 58.4 of the Fast Carrier Force and the escort carriers of TG.52.1, which flew a total of 1,027 sorties. Air support was controlled by the Air Support Unit in the USS *El Dorado* with subsidiary Air Support Control Units for the northern beaches and southern beaches embarked in the USS *Panamint* and USS *Teton* respectively. Up to H-Hour, and shortly thereafter, air strikes concentrated on supposed blockhouses and bunkers on the beaches, together with such targets of opportunity as presented themselves.

To those watching, the bombardment was awesome. It was, in fact, the greatest concentration of naval gunfire ever unleashed on a shore target. Yet the absence of any return fire led one seasoned Marine veteran of Saipan and Iwo Jima to comment (with a side-swipe at the South-West Pacific Front), 'Hell, this is just like one of General MacArthur's landings!' That the bombardment worked so well was the result of years of practice. In particular, the covering fire provided at Okinawa was organized on a flexible basis rather than by adhering to a rigid timetable. Thus it did not especially matter that the first waves of amphibians landed ten minutes late—the fire controllers could easily adapt their programmes. The only real problems were those brought about by the rapid advance of the troops inland, out of the range of the air spotters. On these occasions Direct Support Groups and Roving Patrols were used, operating some distance ahead of the troops.

Under cover of this massive bombardment, the troops of the Tenth Army went ashore shortly after 0830. Opposition to the landings was light—surprisingly so in view of what the troops had experienced at Iwo Jima. Most of the defences on or near the beach had either been destroyed by the bombardment or abandoned. There was intermittent artillery and mortar fire which was distracting but which caused no casualties and did little damage. The armoured amphibians which led the assault went inland immediately out to a distance of 4,000 yards, where they halted to wait for the infantry to come up in support. For the first time in the Pacific War the armoured amphibians were being used as artillery under the command of the Divisional Artillery Regiment.

On the beach men and *matériel* poured ashore. Amphibians disgorged infantry before returning across the reef to bring in supplies. Tanks of both Corps began to land by noon. The tanks were fitted with detachable pontoon floats: on XXIV Corps' front they were carried to the reef in landing ships and craft before launching, but on III Amphibious Corps' front they were launched from 5,000 to 8,000 yards out to sea and left to make their own way to the beach.

Across the whole front the advance continued eastwards all day, with III Amphibious Corps facing negligible opposition from the north and XXIV Corps facing slight resistance to the south. By noon both Yontan and Kadena airfields had been captured and before dark on L-Day the Tenth Army had some 50,000 troops ashore in a beach-head between 4,000 and 5,000 yards in depth and secure from small-arms fire. This represented the line General Buckner had hoped to reach by L+3.

With such a large assault involving so many men over so large a front, it is difficult to get a picture of what actually happened. However, this description by the American historian Samuel

Morison is a classic example of its *genre*. Morison was describing the landing of the 7th Infantry Division on XIV Corps' front by Transportation Group 'Dog':

Very early the big attack transports (*Harris*, flag) heave-to about seven and a half miles off shore. Beaching craft proceed to area four miles nearer, control craft mark the line of departure 4,000 yards off shore and 17 'specialist' beaching craft (supply, water, hospital and so on) together with LSD *Epping Forest* carrying boated tanks in her womb, heave-to seaward of the LSTs. Each control craft displays a banner of the same color as the beach with vertical stripes to distinguish between Nos 1 and 2 of the same color. This is carried out consistently. Every boat's wave guide flies a pennant of similar color and design, and each landing craft of the initial wave has it painted topside. First wave ashore sets up beach markers about ten feet high, brightly painted on canvas.

Battleship *Tennessee* (Captain John B. Hefferman) with Rear Admiral Deyo embarked and cruiser *Birmingham* (Captain H. D. Power) with Rear Admiral Bertram J. Rodgers embarked, close to 1,000 yards from the beach. En route a Japanese dive-bomber makes for them but is splashed just astern of *Birmingham*, whose crew, in view of their earlier experiences, are pleasantly surprised at their escape. At 0640 the naval bombardment opens and continues intermittently until 0735, when it is raised to allow carrier based planes to play their part. The sound of the naval cannon is stilled, but the air is filled with the drone of airplane motors, the rolling rumble of exploding bombs and the sharp, unmistakable crack of rocket fire.

At 0800 the cry goes up, 'Here they come!' In the van are 12 LCI gunboats, moving in perfect alignment at a deliberate three knots in order not to outdistance the LVTs. They pass around the battleships and open fire, their 3-inch guns rattling like old time musketry. In ten minutes' time, three boat waves, each flanked by flag-flying guide boats, have swept round the battleship *Tennessee*'s bow and stern, reforming on her landward side directly under her guns, which are shooting 14-inch, 5-inch and 40mm projectiles over the men's heads. The troops in green coveralls and camouflaged helmets gaze curiously at the battleship's flashing guns. The LCI(G)s are now close to the shore, their gunfire sounding like a roll of drums. Just as the fourth wave passes *Tennessee*, planes come in for their last pre-landing strafing and rocket fire, making a noise like a giant cotton sheet being ripped apart. The fifth boat passes, troops standing on the afterdeck to see 'what goes on.' And a marvellous sight it is, these waves of landing craft extending parallel to the coast as far as the eye can see, all moving with a precise deliberation that well represents the stout though anxious hearts they are carrying.[2]

The very successful landing and advance inland caused its own problems. The landing schedule for supplies could not be adjusted to take advantage of the rapid advance and thus, although artillery-spotting aircraft were operating from Yontan and Kadena from 2 April, it was not until 7 April that the first garrison aircraft were flown to Okinawa from the ferry CVEs. Admiral Turner made strenuous efforts to expedite the operation of the airfields. The task of unloading supplies was subordinated to that of getting the aviators and their equipment ashore.

Aerial opposition to the landings was slight, the Japanese seemingly distracted by the diversion off the island's south-eastern coast. There was an air raid at twilight in which the transport Alpine was hit at 1910 by a suicide plane which tore a hole 30 feet square from main deck to waterline. Five minutes later the veteran battleship West Virginia was also hit, but she remained operational. At 2200 the destroyer Vammen in the Transport Screen struck a seemingly innocuous group of planks. The 'collision' was swiftly followed by an explosion similar to that of a 300lb depth charge, which caused slight damage to one of the destroyer's propeller shafts: the 'planks' had been booby-trapped and Vammen was lucky to escape with such slight damage.

With the initial assault evidently successful, priority was now given to consolidation and bringing sufficient supplies ashore to allow the troops to move inland. In the Northern Sector the Marines had landed over nine beaches: 'Green 1' and '2'; 'Red 1', '2' and '3'; 'Blue 1' and '2' and 'Yellow 1' and '2'. A further pair of beaches, code-named 'Black', were not used, while 'Yellow 3' was not used until the afternoon of L-Day on account of doubts as to its suitability. The reef which fronted the beaches had proved immune to the attentions of the UDT teams and thus the only craft which could cross it were LCVPs and LCMs—and then only for a four-hour period at high water. Transfer points using cranes were established on the reef to move supplies at low water. Further factors which delayed the landing programme were a shortage of exits from the beaches, and of engineering equipment to make them, and the Marines' unfortunate (but understand-able) habit of commandeering LVTs and DUKWs required for unloading duties and using them to support their move inland before their own vehicles were sent ashore.

By 2 April, however, Major-General Geiger was confident enough to order general unloading to commence, noting that the work was proceeding with 'minimum satisfactory progress'.[3] So as to make the most of the high-water period, unloading went on all night using searchlights, despite the risk of air attack, while those transports as yet unloaded by nightfall remained in the anchorage instead of joining in the general night retirement. The situation in the Northern Sector improved day by day, showing that the logistics plan was just flexible enough to cope with the unexpectedly easy landing.

In the Southern Sector the assault was made over eleven beaches stretching from 'Purple 1' to 'Brown 4'. The 'Brown' beaches were abandoned after the assault waves had landed since the reef proved to be an impenetrable obstacle. The reef which fronted all the beaches in the southern sector dried out at low water so that vehicles could then be disembarked from all types of landing ships and craft. However, the depth of water over the reef was insufficient to allow landing craft to pass over it even at high water, and accordingly the continuous operation of a transfer line was necessary.

Engineers built causeways by bulldozing from the edge of the reef to the beach, which increased the flow of supplies considerably since less reliance was thereby placed on cranes than in the Northern Sector. However, delays were caused by a shortage of wheeled transport. Soft-skinned vehicles had been combat-loaded in the expectation that it would take the soldiers some time to establish a beach-head of any size, and the rapid advance of the troops resulted in a need for this transport while it was still aboard ship. As a result, the turn-around time of lorries en route from the beach to the front was greater than anticipated. Moreover, stores were piling up on the beach and not being cleared speedily enough. This led to amphibians being used to move them inland, with the result that there were insufficient amphibians available to bring supplies from the reef to the beach.

Despite these problems, by L+3 the organization was working like clockwork. On L+3 garrison beach parties replaced the naval beach parties, which were withdrawn at 1600. Meanwhile the troops were racing eastwards with little or no opposition. By L+2 the two corps had severed Japanese north–south communications, effectively cutting the island in half. In XXIV Corps' sector, troops could now receive direct fire support from ships on the eastern side of the island, which was reached on 3 April. XXIV Corps now halted to replenish and regroup before wheeling south.

The Japanese persisted with their air raids off the beaches. On 2 April the transports *Achernar* and *Tyrell* were damaged by suicide planes during night retirement and the same evening the ships and screen of Transport Squadron 17 sustained a heavy air attack while retiring south of Kerama Retto, the assault transport *Henrico* and the high-speed destroyer-transport *Dickerson* being damaged. These attacks continued on 3 April. The destroyers *Prichett* and *Foreman* were damaged, as was *LST599*. *LCI82* was hit by a suicide MTB and sank the next day as a result of the damage sustained. Despite these attacks, Turner felt confident enough about the position to order that night retirement be discontinued except for hospital ships.

What were the Japanese doing? Lieutenant Hidara remembers:

> We saw hordes of the Americans pour ashore from their landing craft together with a wealth of supplies the like of which we had not seen for years. The temptation to strike swiftly was immense: this, after all, was in accordance with our national tradition. However, our orders were unambiguous: we had to resist the desire to attack. We were to lie low, to wait. We were to use skill and cunning to kill as many Americans as possible. And this is what we did. We stayed in our bunker and watched this huge Army come ashore. In the short term I felt confident that we could certainly stall the Americans . . .[4]

NOTES TO CHAPTER 4

1. 'Transport Area' was a term used by the US Navy to indicate the point where landing craft would be released or lowered from their mother ships. It corresponds to the term 'Lowering Position' used by the Royal Navy.
2. Morison, Samuel E., *The Two Ocean War: A Short History of the United States Navy in the Second World War*, Little, Brown (1963), pp.534–5.
3. Admiralty, Naval Staff History, Battle Summary No. 47: 'Okinawa: Operation Iceberg, March–June 1945' (London, 1950), p.43.
4. Tomiichi Hidara to author, 29 September 1993.

5

A Multitude of Threats

ONCE the beach-head had been established, a mass of shipping such had seldom been assembled in history lay off the coast of Okinawa carrying supplies and reinforcements. It was expected that the Japanese would stop at nothing to attack and destroy the ships and would use every weapon at their disposal. The defence of the shipping therefore had to take into account every conceivable threat.

The defence plan was known as the Screening Plan and provided for attack by aircraft, surface ships, submarines, midget submarines and fast coastal craft. The Screening Plan also had to take into account the need to prevent the Japanese from moving troops and supplies up and down the coast of Okinawa by barge and between the various islands in the Gunto. Lastly, there was the ever-present threat of suicide weapons other than aircraft, such as explosive motor boats, human torpedoes and swimmers carrying limpet mines.

The Screening Plan eventually adopted was very complicated and involved a Surface Covering Group, radar pickets, a Radar Counter-Measures Screen, an Outer and Inner Anti-Submarine Screen, mobile 'hunter-killer' groups, special patrols against explosive motor boats (known as 'Flycatcher' patrols), boat patrols in the Transport Area and off the beaches, smoke and night retirement.

It was considered that, after the losses the Japanese had suffered at Leyte Gulf in the autumn of 1944, they would not commit their remaining capital ships in defence of the Ryukus, although a 'hit and run' raid was always a distinct possibility. Vice-Admiral Mitscher's fast carriers of TF.58, which were operating to the north and east of Okinawa, were handily positioned to intercept any Japanese ships coming south by a route east of the Nansei Shoto, while the British Pacific Fleet (TF.57) guarded the western flank. There seems to have been some confusion over the role of the British Pacific Fleet in this respect. Although Admiral Turner regarded TF.57 as the 'fence' on his western front, this role was never mentioned by Admiral Spruance, Commander Fifth Fleet, by Admiral Sir Bruce Fraser, CinC BPF or by TF.57's commander, Vice-Admiral Sir Bernard Rawlings. The responsibility for detecting the approach of surface forces to the west of the chain and preventing any attempt at either reinforcing or evacuating Okinawa was assigned to the Support Carrier Group (TF.52.1). Early-morning and late-afternoon searches were carried out by aircraft of the Support Carrier Group in the sectors to the north and north-west of Okinawa until this work was taken over by the Search and Reconnaissance Group (TG.50.5).

If a report of enemy surface forces were to be received during the daytime, it was felt that the bombardment vessels around Okinawa cound concentrate fairly quickly to provide a force capable of driving off the attack. In these circumstances a formation called the Surface Covering Group was to be formed from battleships and cruisers of Admiral Deyo's Gunfire and Covering Force (TF.54), screened by destroyers taken from the Transport Screen. Supporting and covering aircraft were to be funished by the Support Carrier Group. At night, however, it was a different matter. The fire support ships stationed off south-eastern and eastern Okinawa were few in number, and many valuable hours of bombardment time and fire cover for the minesweepers would have been lost in moving the ships to join those operating off the west coast of Okinawa at night. This particularly applied during the first few nights of the operation, when unswept waters to the west of Naha would have required the Eastern Fire Support Group to pass west of Kerama Retto while going to and from the concentration area.

Accordingly, the night plan was for the fire support ships on the west coast of Okinawa—some 80 per cent of the total—to gather in what was known as the Retirement Area off the north-west coast of the island, within three hours' steaming of the transport area and the beaches. The fire support ships on the east and south-east coasts, the remaining 20 per cent, deployed to a similar position off the north-east coast of the island. The eastern group, though numerically inferior to the western group, could count on the additional support of Admiral Mitscher's carriers. If

Right: An LSM(R) firing rockets against the Hagushi beaches during the intial phase of the assault. (US National Archives)
Below: LVTs heading for the beaches on 1 April. (US National Archives)

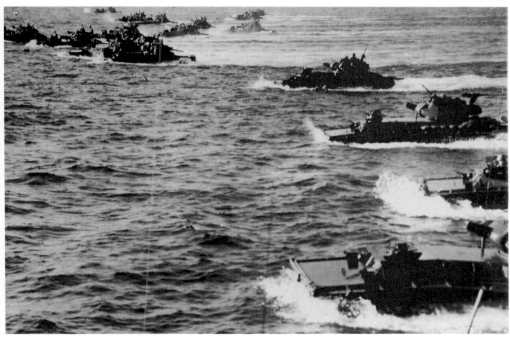

Left: An aerial view of the beaches, showing LVTs on their final run-in. (US National Archives)

Above: Camouflaged Marines of III Amphibious Corps leave their landing craft at the northern end of the beaches. Opposition to the landings was virtually non-existent. (US National Archives)

Below: A general view of the southern sector of the Hagushi beaches, showing the causeways built to facilitate the transfer of supplies from the reef to the shore. (US National Archives)

Above: Marines of III Amphibious Corps move inland. In the background an LST(III) is moored, while a stream of landing craft brings more men and supplies to the beach. (US National Archives)

Below: A Japanese aircraft explodes during a raid on the transport area. (US National Archives)

Above: LVTs of III Amphibious Corps on the perimeter of Yontan airfield, which was captured on 1 April—considerably earlier than the Command had envisaged. (US National Archives)
Below: A *Baka* piloted suicide weapon captured on Yontan airfield by III Amphibious Corps Marines, 1 April 1945. Note the *Kikusui* emblem on the nose. (US National Archives)

Above: Marines take cover while a flame-throwing Sherman tank destroys a Japanese strongpoint. (US National Archives)
Below: The transport *Achernar* burning after being damaged by a suicide attack during night retirement on 2 April 1945. (US National Archives)
Right: The forward section of the minelayer USS *Lindsey*, which was struck by two suicide planes south-west of Okinawa on 12 April. After temporary repairs at Guam, the ship proceeded to Norfolk Navy Yard, Virginia, for the fitting of a new bow. *Lindsey* remained in US Navy service until 1970. (US National Archives)

Left, upper: Marines head inland after the landings. The man on the left is carrying a BAR (Browning Automatic Rifle) while the one on the right is armed with a Garrand rifle. The two Marines in the background are carrying flame-throwers, weapons that were to become increasingly important in the fighting on Okinawa. (US National Archives)

Left, lower: The war correspondent Ernie Pyle, sharing his cigarettes with Marines on Okinawa on 7 April. Pyle was subsequently killed in the fighting on the island of Ie Shima. (US National Archives)

Below: Troops of the 77th Division relax on the upper deck of an LST(III) before the invasion of Ie Shima on 16 April. The island was not secured until 21 April, following some bitter fighting. (US National Archives)

Left, upper: Marines enter the town of Sobo, the first settlement of any size on Okinawa to be captured. (US National Archives)

Left, lower: Infantrymen provide cover for one of their number who tosses hand grenades through the aperture of a Okinawan tomb converted for use as a pill box. (US National Archives)

Above: Medical Corpsmen adminster fluids to a Marine wounded in the fighting in northern Okinawa. (US National Archives)

Above: Soldiers of the 27th Division cross a river using a pontoon bridge during the American offensive against the southern part of the island which began on 19 April. (US National Archives)

Below: US troops, covered by warships offshore, rest before the assault on Yonabaru, in the southern part of the island. (US National Archives)

Above: Two American flame-throwing Sherman tanks in action. The flame-throwers were very effective when used against Japanese strongpoints. (US National Archives)
Below: US forces advance down the southern half of the island. The photograph shows the topography to good effect and illustrates how the terrain favoured the Japanese defenders. (US National Archives)

Above: US artillery in action in the first of General Buckner's offensives against Japanese forces in the southern part of the island on 19 April. Indirect artillery fire proved to be ineffective against the carefully prepared Japanese positions. (US National Archives)

Below: US Marines in close-quarter fighting north of Naha, the main town on the island, after III Corps had been moved to join the battles in the southern half of the island. (US National Archives)

Above: Infantry advance behind a Sherman tank. In the thickly wooded and mountainous terrain, tanks proved highly vulnerable to mines, suicide attacks by Japanese armed with satchel charges and artillery fire. On the rear of the tank is a telephone enabling the infantry to keep the tank commander constantly informed of the situation. (US National Archives)

Below: American infantry use a white phosphorous grenade to clear a Japanese stongpoint. The Americans soon learned that blanket barrages were ineffective against the Japanese positions and that virtually every one would have to be cleared individually. (US National Archives)

Above: Infantrymen use a ladder to cross a narrow ravine during the advance on Shuri. The terrain in southern Okinawa did not favour infantry operations. (US National Archives)
Below: 6th Division Marines, led very carefully by a man armed with a flame-thrower, enter a cave which has been cleared of Japanese. (US National Archives)

the eastern force were to be threatened by an overwhelmingly superior Japanese group, Admiral Turner was prepared to take the risk of ordering the ships of the western group to support the eastern ships by passing through the unswept waters to the north of Okinawa which, Intelligence indicated, were not mined.

In connection with the possibility of a 'hit and run' raid, all transports not actually beached on the reef were supposed to retire from the beach-head at night and return the following morning. This practice does not seem to have been followed by the transports and landing ships after L+4, although the ships of the Gunfire and Covering Force continued to withdraw to their night stations. However, after the destruction of the battleship *Yamato* on 7 April, the risk of a raid by Japanese surface forces was considered to be very small. Thus the bombardment ships would remain in the Assault Area overnight, using smoke screens for cover, if required, all night. Later in the camapign, night retirement ceased altogether and all ships not actually engaged in night bombardment would remain in the Transport Area.

Shipping remaining in the Assault Area at night could be protected by smoke during enemy air attacks. Smoke screens were only ever used at night since CAP and AA fire were considered competent enough to deal with air attacks during the daylight hours. The plan consisted of stationing all ships equipped with smoke generators in a line across the windward side of the anchorage. In addition, two LCVPs equipped with smoke generators were assigned to each transport and stationed to windward of her. Smoke boats were provided for large warships and for transports carrying troops. Finally, 45 smoke generators were set up ashore. Smoke was made on the orders of SOPA, usually as a result of a radar warning, to give good coverage of the anchorage by the time enemy aircraft arrived. From 1 April to 16 May smoke was made on 36 of the 48 nights for an aggregate of 98 hours, or roughly 2hr 45min a night. From 17 May to 21 June it was used on 72 occasions for a total of 52 hours, an average of 1hr 27min a night.

The smoke screens were successful in preventing damage to transport ships even though the Japanese began dropping bombs at random through the screens as the operation progressed. However, the oil-laden smoke produced by the generators posed considerable problems in that the oil adversely affected the

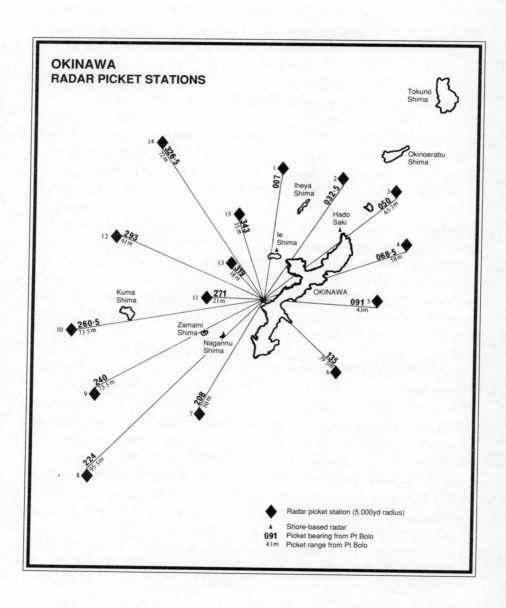

OKINAWA
RADAR PICKET STATIONS

Tokuno
Shima

Okinoerabu
Shima

14 **326·5**
72m

1 **007**

Iheya
Shima

2 **032·5**

3 **050**
65·3m

Hado
Saki

15 **343**
35m

12 **293**
61m

Ie
Shima

13 **319**
18m

4 **068·5**
58m

Kuma
Shima

11 **271**
21m

OKINAWA

5 **091**
43m

10 **260·5**
73·5m

Zamami
Shima

Nagannu
Shima

135
39·5m 6

9 **240**
73·5m

7 **208**
50m

8 **224**
95·5m

Radar picket station (5,000yd radius)

Shore-based radar

091 Picket bearing from Pt Bolo

43m Picket range from Pt Bolo

insulation on upper-deck electrical fittings such as cables, generators, motors and so forth, to the point where complete rewiring was often required.

The most important element of the defence of the shipping off Okinawa was the reporting carried out by the radar pickets and the fighter-direction ships occupying exposed positions to the north of the island. There were six Headquarters Ships, each carrying a Group Fighter Director, and nineteen Fighter Director Ships (sixteen destroyers and three minelayers). After the preliminary operations the Fighter Director Ships were assigned to fifteen radar picket stations (a sixteenth was added later) established at distances varying from 50 to 70 miles from the Transport Area covering all points of the compass but concentrated in the north and north-west—the directions from which attacks would most likely come. In the early stages of the operation, Stations 1, 2, 3, 4, 7, 10, 12 and 14 were filled, Station 9 being occupied later as nine stations were required for full cover. Once shore radar stations were established at the northern end of Okinawa on Hedo Saki on 21 April and on the island of Ie Shima two days later, however, the number of picket stations required was reduced to five. A new plan was drawn up under which only Stations 5, 7, 9 15 and 16 were filled.

The fighter-direction ships on picket duty manœuvred at a speed of 15 knots within a 5,000-yard circle, maintaining continuous radar air and surface searches. They also carried out their own anti-submarine defence by conducting periodic sonar searches on either beam. The whole line of picket ships controlled two to four divisions of fighter aircraft, each division containing four aircraft.

There seems to have been some difference of opinion in the American command governing the employment of the radar pickets. Vice-Admiral Turner, CTF.51 until 17 May 1945, considered that their primary duty lay in raid reporting and that the actual destruction of enemy aircraft could be left to CAP and AA gunfire. However, Vice-Admiral Hill, who relieved Turner on 17 May, considered that the pickets' primary duties were the destruction of enemy aircraft and the breaking up of attacking formations and that reporting was a secondary consideration.

The radar pickets played a vital role in disrupting Japanese attempts to attack the transports lying off Okinawa. They suffered heavy losses since their stations were often too far away for the CAP to intervene effectively and each ship lacked the firepower to deal with multiple attacks. Their ordeal will be dealt with in greater detail in the next chapter but, in brief, one was mined, four were sunk by suicide aircraft and eight were seriously damaged and three lightly damaged by suicide aircraft. Of the fourteen replacement ships, one was sunk and seven were damaged by suicide aircraft. Nevertheless, Admiral Spruance considered that the Japanese decision to expend so much effort on the radar pickets rather than the transports was a serious error. In an effort to give the pickets greater protection, groups of LCS(L)s, termed Radar Supports, were assigned to each station, and after the very heavy air raids of 12 April a special Picket CAP was supplied for each station. These measures eventually succeeded in reducing attacks on the pickets.

In addition to the pickets, the Americans also provided for a Radar Counter-Measures (RCM) Screen to prevent the Japanese locating targets off Okinawa using radar. Twenty LCI(R)s were spread out over the transport area, each maintaining a continuous watch for Japanese radar transmissions and ready to put up a comprehensive 'blizzard' of electronic interference to render any Japanese radar ineffective. RCM was only ever used once during the campaign—with evident success, for the Japanese made no further use of their radar.

Aircraft were one threat; submarines were another. The Americans maintained two Anti-Submarine (A/S) Screens off Okinawa. The outer consisted of a continuous line of A/S vessels—destroyers, destroyer-escorts etc—from a point south-east of Nagagusuku Wan, on the east coast of the island, south to Ie Shima, including Kerama Retto. This line was divided into seven sectors each occupied by five ships which patrolled screening stations 7,000 yards in length at a speed of 15 knots. The average distance of this screen to the shore or the Transport Area was ten miles. The function of the screen was the detection and prosecution of submarine contacts until relieved by a hunter-killer group. Four such groups were formed, each composed of two ships of the anti-submarine screen and one or two aircraft detailed by the Air Support Control Unit. Four hunter-killer stations were established, three just inside the outer A/S screen, to the north, west and south of the Transport Area and the fourth at Kerama Retto.

Their purpose was to take over A/S operations from ships on the screen once a contact had been made. In addition to the outer screen, a close semi-circular screen of A/S vessels was maintained around the Transport Area from shore to shore. It was divided into two sectors each patrolled by five ships.

Twenty-four-hour coverage was also maintained by six patrol aircraft from the Seaplane Base Group (TG.51.20) at Kerama Retto. One torpedo bomber was tasked for special searches over the transport area. The escort carriers *Anzio* and *Tulagi* of the Anti-Submarine Warfare Group (TF.50.7) searched the transport lanes to the south-east of Okinawa out to a distance of 200–300 miles since this area was one of two where the greatest concentration of Japanese submarines was to be found. The other area, applicable only to midget submarines, lay in the waters around the Okinawa Gunto.

On 29 April an aircraft from *Tulagi* attacked a submarine, *R-109*, in 24°15'N 131°16'E, thirteen miles south-south-east of Okino Ogari Shima, and sank it by depth charges. Two days later aircraft from *Anzio* surprised *I-12* on the surface in position 22°22'N 131°16'E while on a sweep between Okinawa and the Marianas and sank her. Although several attacks were made on Japanese submarines on the transport route to the south-east of Okinawa, no kills were made after the sinking of *I-8* by the destroyers *Stockton* and *Morrison* during the night of 30/31 March until 10 April, when the destroyer-escort *Fieberling*, in the screen of Task Unit 51.29.11 en route from Okinawa to Saipan, made a contact at 1651 south-east of Okino Ogari Shima. Together with the destroyer *Howorth* and the high-speed destroyer-transport *Barr*, *Fieberling* made eight attacks between 1651 and 1912. After the seventh attack contact was lost and several heavy underwater explosions were heard, with large bubbles and craters of air rising to the surface. Though no debris was recovered, it is now known that the submarine *I-44* was sunk in this attack.

On 27 April the high-speed destroyer-transport *Ringness*, escorting a convoy from Saipan to Okinawa, was credited with the possible destruction of a midget submarine, while the destroyer-escort *Hemminger* probably damaged a submarine during the night of 24/25 May, 60 miles south-east of Okinawa. At 1400 on 14 May an abandoned one-man midget submarine, probably a

Kaiten torpedo, was sighted in the fuelling and replenishing area south-east of Minami Ogari Shima in the Borodino Islands by Service Squadron Six (TG.50.8) and sunk by gunfire.

Admiral Mitscher's fast carriers of TF.58 were totally unmolested by Japanese submarine activity. TG.58.1 felt so secure that they abandoned anti-submarine patrols early in the operation in order to simplify the work of the fighter controllers. On 9 April the destroyers *Mertz* and *Monssen*, screening TG.58.4, each made five attacks on a submarine contact in 26°06'N 130°21'E, south-east of Okinawa, which resulted in the sinking of *Ro-46*. *Mertz* was also involved in the sinking of *I-56* on 18 April after a fourteen-hour hunt which also involved the destroyers *Heerman*, *Uhlmann*, *McCord* and *Collett*, assisted by aircraft from the CVE *Bataan*.

A total of eight Japanese submarines, excluding midget submarines and the suicide *Kaiten* weapons, were sunk during the Okinawa campaign in return for no sinkings of warships or transports. Given that the success of a submarine campaign is measured by what is known as the Exchange Rate—the ratio of merchant ships sunk to submarines lost—the Japanese figure of 0:8 is almost a disaster. The failure of the Japanese to interdict the extended American supply lines with their submarines must rank as one of their greatest lost opportunities of the war.

The Japanese made equally ineffectual use of their submarines off Okinawa. The midget submarine pens at Unten Ko in the north-west of the island were found to be empty when they were captured on 10 April. There were numerous reports of torpedoes being fired and very many counter-attacks were mounted, resulting in a prodigious expenditure of depth charges. There were, however, only two certain sinkings. At 0230 on 5 April *LCS115* detected a large submarine near Kume Shima. The destroyer *Hudson* was called to the scene and sank *Ro-41*. On the same day a midget submarine was caught against the reef around Zampa Misaki and sunk by the destroyers *Hyman*, *Starling*, *Impeccable* and *Fieberling* together with *PC855*.

In the evening of 20 May the Japanese made what appeared to be a co-ordinated attack using aircraft and midget submarines—the only occasion during the campaign when such an operation was carried out. The raid began with suicide aircraft making attacks on shipping around Ie Shima and to the north-west of the

Transport Area. At 1844 the minesweeper *Butler* was hit twice by suicide aircraft and damaged. At 1920 the high-speed destroyer-escort *Chase*, in screening station B.11, 25 miles north-west of Zampa Misaki, was disabled by a suicide aircraft. Simultaneously the high-speed destroyer-transport *Register*, in a station adjacent to *Chase*, was also hit by a suicide aircraft. At 1923 the destroyer *Thatcher* was hit and disabled by a suicide aircraft, also off Zampa Misaki. These attacks had the effect of tearing a gap in the anti-submarine screen to the west and north-west of the Transport Area and to the north of Ie Shima.

About an hour later a number of submarine contacts were established. The destroyer *Badger* sighted a midget submarine near Nago Wan but lost the contact. However, the destroyer-escort *Finnegan*, working with *Badger*, obtained a good contact and made two attacks, the second of which resulted in a series of underwater explosions believed to indicate a kill. At 2030 the destroyer-escort *Fieberling* made a contact in 350°, fourteen miles from Zampa Misaki, and made three depth-charge and two 'Hedgehog' attacks over a period of two hours. The contact disappeared in water of 100 fathoms and a submarine was thus believed to have been sunk. A number of other contacts were established and both *LCS58* and *LCS68* reported torpedo tracks, but there were no more sinkings; more importantly, there were no losses among the warships or transports. The only Japanese attempt at inter-arm co-operation had been a failure.

The operations of the Japanese explosive motor boats were equally unsuccessful. The Japanese had positioned a large number of *Shinyo* type suicide craft[1] on Okinawa and the outlying islands but most were accounted for by air strikes or in the preparatory bombardment. They were considered to be a substantial threat and thus special photographic sorties were mounted to identify the places where they might by hiding. Naval gunfire and air strikes were then ordered to destroy them.

The *modus operandi* of the suicide boats was to approach the target in groups of three from astern. For the boats fitted with depth charges, the tactics called for their dropping the charges three feet from the ship's side at a vital point and then—in theory anyway—make their withdrawal. The boats fitted with bow charges would likewise approach from astern but would then make a high-speed run-in and impact against the ship's side.

These craft had the facility to lock their wheels during the final approach to the target so that, should the operator's courage fail him at the critical moment, there was nothing he could do. Documents captured at Okinawa indicated that a number of these craft were intended to carry swimmers armed with limpet mines or primitive 'spar' type explosive charges.

To counter the threat from these boats an Anti-Small-Craft Screen was formed which stretched from Ie Shima south around the island to Chim Wan. The line was divided up into stations, each covering an area three miles long by two miles wide, the line of stations being about one mile off shore. Each was occupied by an LCI(S) fitted with radar and each group of five or six of such vessels was supported to seaward by a cruiser and destroyer, the whole being known as a 'Flycatcher' team. The functions of the 'Flycatcher' teams were to prevent operations by the *Shinyos* by means of illuminating and bombarding their likely hiding places and by destroying those which ventured forth. They performed the additional task of laying down dusk-to-dawn interdiction fire on Naha, Itoman and Yonabaru airfield to prevent their use by the Japanese.

Other measures to guard against the *Shinyos* consisted of providing each large ship in the Transport Area with either an LCVP or an LCPL which would patrol around the parent ship at a distance of between 300 and 500 yards. The landing craft were fitted with heavy machine guns and equipped with 5lb explosive charges and hand grenades to use against the *Shinyos* and assault swimmers alike. Further landing craft and amphibian patrols were established off the beaches. After the MTB attacks of 29 and 30 March (referred to in Chapter 3) there was no further activity by these craft until 3 April, when *LCI82*, operating on a 'Flycatcher' patrol in Nagagusuku Wan, was so badly damaged by a *Shinyo* that she had to be sunk the next day.

During the night of 8/9 April there was considerable enemy suicide-craft and other small-boat activity. A force of twelve to fifteen boats was sighted in the Kerama Retto area, five of which were destroyed by gunfire. At least fifteen assault swimmers were discovered and killed. Between 0330 and 0430 suicide boats operating out of the port of Naha attacked shipping in the southern transport area. One boat hit the destroyer *Charles J. Badger*: both her turbines were rendered inoperable for a short period, but there no casualities. A second boat was detected by the destroyer *Purdy* and, when fired on, dropped its depth charge and made off at high speed. The transport *Starr* was also damaged but was saved by the LSM secured alongside which took the full impact of the boat.

During the night of 26/27 April the destroyer *Hutchings* was damaged by a *Shinyo* while delivering fire support to the 7th Division from Nagagusuku Wan. The boat came in from the destroyer's port quarter and the explosion occurred about half a minute after it had turned away. A further twelve such boats were destroyed that night, while the following night the cruiser *St Louis* accounted for nine of the nineteen boats sunk. During the night of the 28th/29th *LCS37* destroyed one such craft, only to be damaged in turn by the explosion from the boat's depth charges. Several *Shinyo*s penetrated the screen that night but nearly all were destroyed. The only damage was that to the transport *Bozeman Victory*. Apart from an attack on the transport *Carina* on 4 May, this was the sum total of the *Shinyo*s' successes. Another nasty facet of Japanese defence planning was the presence of numerous booby traps, such as bundles of logs concealing one or more depth charges. These were used in considerable numbers and, in addition to damaging the destroyer *Vammen* as described earlier, were responsible for sinking *YMS92* and *YMS103* as well as an MTB.

It was in the course of these 'Flycatcher' operations that the destroyer *Longshaw* was sunk. She was one of the few US ships not sunk by air attack and the only one to be accounted for by shore artillery. *Longshaw* had been heavily engaged in providing fire support and during the previous week had expended over 1,500 rounds of 5-inch ammunition. On 17 May she arrived at Kerama Retto for some well-earned rest and replenishment but instead was required for night firing on Okinawa. The following day she was ordered round to the east coast of the island on another fire support mission and, probably because her officers and men were exhausted, ran aground on a reef off Naha airstrip. A survey of her hull found that the ship was intact, so the destroyer *Picking* tried to tow her off, but without success. A fleet tug, *Arikara*, then arrived and had just managed to secure her tow when heavy and accurate gunfire from the shore began to fall around *Longshaw*; evidently the Japanese commander could not restrain himself and chose to ignore his standing instructions not to fire on ships for fear of giving his position away. *Longshaw* sustained four hits in quick succession, one of which blew off her bow as far back as the bridge. Her commanding officer, Lieutenant-Commander Becker USN, severely wounded, gave the order to abandon ship. Her casualties were heavy: thirteen officers and 76 men had been killed or were missing and 61 had been wounded, and among the dead were her Commanding Officer and Executive Officer. *Longshaw*'s wreck was subsequently destroyed by gunfire and torpedoes, while the Japanese battery was silenced by counter-fire from the cruiser *Salt Lake City* and the destroyers *Picking* and *H. L. Edwards*.

One other aspect of Japanese small-craft operations was their use to land forces behind the American lines on infiltration missions. The most important of these occurred on 4 May and was co-ordinated with sea and air attacks. The operation began with considerable small-boat activity in Nagagusuku Wan during the night of 3/4 May. This was dealt with by the 'Flycatchers', although the transport *Carina* was damaged. After 0130 on 4 May the air attacks began, and these lasted until 0445 without any success. These attacks were followed by the landing of a force of between 500 and 600 Japanese soldiers from a number of barges west of Machinato airfield. Some 250 of these men were killed on the beach but the remainder escaped into the town carrying light weapons. On the east coast another attempt to land troops was completely foiled when three of the nine boats involved were destroyed by American troops and the remainder by naval gunfire. After 0745 there was a second series of fourteen air raids which resulted in the sinking of the destroyers *Luce* and *Morrison* and two LSMs; all these ships were on radar picket station. In the same raid the light cruiser *Birmingham*, the destroyer *Ingraham* and the light minelayer *Shea* were damaged, the last by a *Baka* bomb. In the evening a third attack resulted in damage to the escort carrier *Sangamon* and light minelayer *Gwin*. However, the infiltration tactics were successfully repulsed and the Japanese lost 137 aircraft in return for five US machines shot down.

All the preprations made by the Americans to defend their shipping against air, submarine and small-boat attack worked well, but in order to do so they had depended on efficient communications to draw all the threads together. Alas, as Admiral Spruance noted ruefully in his report, communications were the weak link in the chain. There were not enough personnel, so that the radio operators on Turner's staff were working 'watch and watch'[2] for 46 days, with consequent effects on efficiency. Moreover, a large amount of radio equipment had been destroyed on Iwo Jima and had not been replaced. Ships not actually in the assault area were ruthlessly stripped of radio equipment in order to make sure that those in the assault area could utilize the three TBS VHF radio channels available. The Screening Plan worked, however: supplies and men poured ashore on Okinawa.

NOTES TO CHAPTER 5

1. The *Shinyo* explosive motor boat had a displacement of 1.35 to 2.15 tons, with dimensions of 21ft 4in oa × 6ft 1in × 1ft 2in. The machinery comprised one 134bhp engine, giving a speed of 28 knots. The armament was an explosive charge consisting either of a quantity of TNT or of two depth charges stowed in the bow, plus two 4.7in rockets to distract the enemy gunners' aim during the run in.
2. Four hours on, four hours off.

6

The Battle for Air Supremacy

*I desire to record that the history of our Navy was enhanced
on 11 May 1945. I am proud to record that I know of no
record of a destroyer's crew fighting for one hour and thirty-
five minutes and against overwhelming aircraft attacks and
destroying twenty-three planes.*—Commanding Officer of
USS *Hugh W. Hadley*

THE suicide attacks on the shipping of the Expeditionary Force constituted the outstanding feature of the Japanese attempt to repulse the landings. The enemy's tactics came as no surprise to the Americans, who had first endured this type of assault on 24 October 1944 during the battle for Leyte Gulf. At Okinawa, however, the Japanese attacks reached a climax, resulting in the loss of many ships and severe damage to many more, which in turn placed a considerable strain on the repair organization.

The attacks were launched from the flanks of the Expeditionary Force—from Formosa and the islands of the Sakishima Gunto to the west and from Kyushu and Amami Gunto to the north and east. The forces operating from Formosa were augmented by aircraft drawn from formations in China and South-East Asia, while the whole of Japan, the protectorate of Manchukuo and Korea were ransacked for aircraft to operate from Kyushu. Japanese air opposition had been expected, and it was as part of the preliminary operations that the fast carriers of Mitscher's TF.58 had engaged in the strikes on Kyushu before the landings, together with the bombers of XXI Bomber Command. The success of these strikes was shown in the lack of Japanese air opposition to the landings.

From L-Day onwards the left flank of the Expeditionary Force was guarded by the British Pacific Fleet (TF.57) and the US Navy's Escort Carrier Group, while Mitscher's veteran carriers guarded the right flank. Both forces engaged in a constant, wearing series of strikes on Japanese airfields in which they were joined by XXI Bomber Command from 16 April at the request of Admiral Spruance. In fact, by the end of the operation 40 per cent of XXI Bomber Command's sorties were being directed against airfields on Kyushu. Spruance rightly recognized that airfields were the least vulnerable of targets to bombing, but he felt that he had no option but to sanction the continuance of the strikes on account of the known inflexibility of the Japanese' planning, their tendency to be thrown off balance easily and their difficulties with aircraft maintenance.

The air war over Okinawa soon developed into a grim battle of attrition. In the early stages of the operation the Japanese appeared to be capable of mounting a major attack every few days in addition to the daily nuisance raids. A total of 1,465 Japanese aircraft from Kyushu participated in ten massed suicide raids between 6 April and 22 June 1945. Eight hundred and sixty were from the Navy's 5th Air Fleet while the remainder came from the Army's 6th Air Army. From Formosa a total of 250 suicide attacks were made, 50 by Army aircraft and 200 by the Navy. As well as the massed suicide (*Kikusui*) attack, there were the conventional raids by bombers and torpedo bombers. The Japanese Navy mounted 3,700 sorties over Okinawa and the Army mounted 1,100.

The *Kikusui* attacks were very difficult to counter. Any pilot who had decided to kill himself could hit a ship unless shot down; even an aircraft disabled by AA fire could still crash on to a ship with devastating effect. Although such attacks were ineffectual in sinking capital ships, cruisers and carriers because of these vessels' excellent and sophisticated protection and damage control, they were very effective against smaller ships. Moreover, the damage they could inflict on a ship might be such that the vessel concerned was rendered a 'mission kill', i.e. the target was so badly damaged that she was unable to carry out her assigned duties. Fifty-seven destroyers, destroyer-escorts, high-speed minesweepers and other light craft were thus immobilized during the Okinawa Campaign.

The Japanese were well aware of the performance and limitations of the American search radar and IFF equipment and had successfully developed a receiver which enabled them to identify 'fade' areas, that is, areas where the radar coverage was poor or the signal distorted, which they would then use when making their approach. Attacks that took place at dawn were the most successful, although the Japanese made less use of these than had been expected. The American carriers would launch CAP, strikes and other sweeps at morning twilight and thus within a few moments the area around the Task Group would be flooded with friendly aircraft. The Japanese would have infested the area around the Task Group from about 30 minutes before first light with aircraft at all altitudes and protected by cloud cover. It was therefore a comparatively simple matter for them to approach the Task Group by imitating American IFF transmissions. Dawn attacks made it difficult for the Expeditionary Force Commander to judge whether or not to deploy his forces into their daylight positions or keep the ships in the Night Retiring Disposition while hostile aircraft were in the neighbourhood. Dusk attacks were also employed, designed to catch the carriers while they were recovering their CAP. Again, less use was made of dusk attacks than the Americans thought would be the case and Admiral Morton Deyo considered this to be a major Japanese failing.

Air support for the Expeditionary Force was initially furnished by TF.58 and the Support Carrier Group, TF.52.1. However, as a result of the massed *Kikusui* attacks, the number of fast carriers available for the direct support of the troops ashore declined from thirteen on 23 March to eight on 12 May. Eventually only one Task Group could be made available for direct support missions. The Support Carrier Group, stationed to the southward of Okinawa in a far less exposed position, suffered comparatively few losses. Control of American air operations was exercised by Commander Air Support Control Units (CTG.51.10) but later, as the troops became established ashore, control devolved to Air Support Control Units at XXIV and III Corps Headquarters.

As well as direct support missions, there was also the problem of providing CAP for the various elements of the Expeditionary Force—the radar pickets, the main attack force, the bombardment group and the fast carriers—and the islands of Kerama Retto, which were spread out over a wide area. The original plan called for one division of fighters (four aircraft) to be stationed in the south-west, six divisions over the island and a further five divisions to the north. However, on account of the damage inflicted on the carriers by the *Kikusui* attacks, it was not always possible to marshal this strength and the scheme had to be modified.

For a few days after the landing, eight divisions of fighters were maintained on station, but from L+5 onwards up to 75 aircraft were furnished by the fast carriers and Support Carrier Group. From L+7 these forces were supplemented by aircraft from the Tactical Air Force operating from recently captured airfields on Okinawa itself. This force ultimately relieved the carriers of the responsibility for providing aircraft for the air defence of Okinawa and the direct support of troops. However, the Tactical Air Force was slow in establishing itself ashore, largely owing to difficulties in setting up its communications. It was only after General Buckner had provided sufficient radio sets from his own stocks that its communications became adequate to manage its operations.

When large-scale raids were indicated, a CAP of 84 aircraft was maintained, with a further 36 machines on ground alert; this force was in addition to the CAPs that operated over the radar picket ships. On days when little enemy air activity was expected, the CAP was reduced to around 60 aircraft, with 24 on ground alert. The CAP was deployed across the main threat axes from Formosa and Kyushu, other sectors being comparatively lightly watched.

The Support Carrier Group co-operated with the British Pacific Fleet in keeping the airfields on the Sakishima Gunto under constant attack and in providing CAP for the south and south-western approaches. Most Japanese raids launched from Formosa were carried out in the late afternoon when the CAP from the Support Carrier Group had been withdrawn. In these cases Admiral Sir Bernard Rawlings (CTF.57) ordered afternoon and night strikes on the Sakishima airfields. Two night fighters were provided by TF.58. One was controlled from the Headquarters Ship of the Amphibious Support Force and the other by a battleship of the Gunfire and Covering Force. After L+13 the night CAP was increased to four aircraft, all provided by the Tactical Air Force ashore. As with so many operations, the identification of aircraft by AA gunners was a problem, and one that was never properly overcome. There were many occasions when, in the heat of the moment, 'friendly' aircraft were the victims of their own AA fire.

An important feature of the provision of air support was the build-up of the Tactical Air Force ashore. Fortunately, this was not delayed by the bloody fighting in which XXIV Corps was engaged in the south of the island after 5 April and which almost brought the American offensive to a halt. Okinawa Gunto provided twenty-six potential sites for airfields which in theory could operate five VLR Wings, two fighter Wings and numerous light and medium bombers and a depot field. A number of useful sites were captured in the initial landings and efforts were devoted to the development of facilities for fighters —even at the expense of bombers. Corsair fighters of the US Marine Corps' MAG-31 and MAG-33 squadrons under the command of Major-General Francis P. Mulcahy USMC were flown in from the transport CVEs on L+6 to the airfields at Yontan and Kadena (although it would be three weeks before they could begin large-scale operations).

In addition to the Corsairs, a flight of photo-reconnaissance Lightning aircraft arrived together with a squadron of Avengers for anti-submarine work. On 25 April a flight of B-24 Liberators began operations and would range as far afield as Chosen and Tsu-Shima. The airfield at Yontan was captured in a good condition but that at Kadena required considerable work to render it fit for all-weather work. Likewise the airfields on Ie Shima had suffered terribly in the preliminary strikes and it was not until 13 May that two strips were in operation there. Once operational, however, Ie Shima became 'home' to US Army Thunderbolts which flew in from Guam and were followed later by further Groups. The partially complete airstrip at Machinato was not captured until 29 April and that at Yonabaru a fortnight later, and the field at Naha did not fall until 6 June. These airfields could not be made ready for operations before the end of the fighting on Okinawa but additional small strips for the use of artillery spotting aircraft were commissioned on 17, 21 and 22 April.

Thus, in facing the Japanese massed *Kikusui* attacks, the Americans, though blessed with quantitative superiority in terms of aircraft available, had numerous problems in the organization of their air defence. In the early stages of the operation their 'airfields', the carriers, were extremely vulnerable to *Kikusui* attack, as were the radar pickets, the 'eyes' of the Expeditionary Force. The establishment of the Tactical Air Force ashore should have relieved the carriers of much of the burden, but this took longer than expected. Thus it was on the men of the carriers and the radar pickets that the onslaught of the *Kikusui* attacks first fell.

It was not until the sixth day after the landing that the Japanese launched their first major air attack on both the Expeditionary Force and the Covering Force. The raids, which began at about 1500 on 6 April, were principally directed against patrols and the radar pickets. The destroyers USS *Bush* and *Colhoun* were sunk. *Bush* (Commander R. E. Westholme USN) was occupying Radar Picket Station No 1 and *Colhoun* (Commander G. R. Wilson USN) was on the neighbouring Station No 2. Early in the morning of 6 April both ships were subjected to conventional bombing without success, but at about 1500 between 40 and 50 aircraft approached from the north, stacked at various altitudes, and began to orbit *Bush*, peeling off in groups to attack. Meanwhile a smaller group of twelve aircraft went after the destroyer *Cassin Young* at Station No 3.

Bush shot down two 'Vals'[1] and discouraged two more. Then a 'Jill'[2] came in low and, despite the AA fire, crashed into the ship between her two funnels, exploding in the forward engine room. Flooding started immediately and *Bush* assumed a 10-degree list and lay dead in the water. Nevertheless, the spirit of the crew was indomitable: the fires were brought under control and the wounded were gathered together and treated, and everyone felt that the ship could be saved, especially when CAP appeared overhead. *Colhoun* closed the stricken destroyer to render assistance together with *LCS64*. However, in doing so she was struck by a 'Zeke' which hit her main deck and exploded in the after fire-room. Her Engineer Officer quickly restored power by cross-connecting machinery, but the ship was again hit by a suicide plane, which tore a great hole in her side below the waterline and broke her back. At the same time a further two planes hit *Bush*, while *Colhoun* was also struck again. Each ship was now little more than a floating shambles, yet neither Commander Westholme nor Commander Wilson would consider abandoning his vessel.

As night fell a swell arose. The swell began to work *Bush*'s damaged hull, and at 1830 the ship folded up and sank. Commander Wilson judged that *Colhoun* would not last much longer either, and he gave the order to abandon ship. At 1900 *Cassin Young* came alongside to take off survivors and then sank

Colhoun with gunfire. Only 35 out of *Colhoun*'s ship's company of 307 were lost. *Bush* suffered much greater casualties: many were drowned after abandoning ship, and 94 of her crew were killed or missing.

✓ Other casualties included the high-speed minesweeper USS *Emmons*, which was sunk while at Kerama Retto. *LST447* was also sunk, and two ammunition ships which had arrived only that day were gutted by fire and were declared constructive total losses. Twenty-two other vessels, most of them destroyers, were damaged. American casualties totalled 466 killed or missing and 568 wounded. One ship, the high-speed minesweeper USS *Rodman*, was attacked by at least eleven Japanese aircraft, of which three hit home and the remainder were shot down. The Japanese made considerable use of co-ordinated attacks by pairs of aircraft: one would approach the target to distract the gunners while the other would fly down the reciprocal bearing to hit the ship. The destroyer USS *Howorth* was attacked by five aircraft simultaneously using this ploy, one of which succeeded in hitting the ship. The DE USS *Witter* was another victim of such an attack: the 'decoy' came in from dead ahead while the attacker made a simultaneous run-in from low on the port beam.

A second wave of attacks was launched just as the Night Retirement Group was forming, and the destroyers USS *Leutze* and *Newcomb* were hit and severely damaged. Both ships were part of the screen for the Gunfire and Covering Force. *Newcomb* was struck by two suicide aircraft which totally demolished the machinery spaces while at the same time spraying the main deck with gasoline which exploded, covering the ships with a thick pall of smoke so that observers on nearby vessels thought that she had sunk.

Lieutenant Leon Grabowsky USN, Commanding Officer of *Leutze*, lost no time in bringing his ship to the scene to rescue survivors. He was astonished to see that *Newcomb* was still afloat, although her main deck was a solid mass of flame. Going alongside, Grabowsky sent over damage control parties and passed fire hoses while at the same time fighting his own ship against a further attack which was developing. *Leutze* was unable to manoeuvre to save herself and a suicide plane exploded on her fantail, tearing the ship's side open and jamming the rudder. Grabowsky did his best, but, with the destroyer beginning to settle by the stern, he eventually drew away from *Newcomb*, fearing that his ship would founder. Rescue came in the shape of the minesweeper USS *Defense* (Lieutenant-Commander Gordon Abbott USNR), which towed *Leutze* to Kerama Retto while *Newcomb* was helped by the destroyer USS *Beale*.

TF.58 was also on the receiving end of these attacks. However, Mitscher had made his dispositions thoroughly and had provided for radar pickets stationed 30 to 40 miles on the flanks of the Task Force. The value of these ships was amply demonstrated when one destroyer alone shot down three suicide planes. Despite the damage inflicted on the Americans, the Japanese losses were enormous. Nearly three-quarters of their 400 aircraft were shot down, 248 of them by TG.58.1 and TG.58.3. The carrier USS *Essex* was responsible for shooting down 65 attackers.

The massed attacks continued on 12 April when all the portents pointed to another day of heavy air activity. The Expeditionary and Covering Forces adjusted their dispositions accordingly: TF.58 cancelled the strike programme for the day and placed fighters on station to the north of Okinawa; the British Pacific Fleet struck the airfields on Formosa to lessen the threat from that direction; the Support Carrier Unit, made up of lightly protected and vulnerable escort carriers, was withdrawn from Sakishima altogether; and the shore bombardment assignments were reduced to the bare minimum so that TF.54 could cruise in a compact formation designed to offer the maximum defence against aircraft.

After reports had been received that Japanese aircraft had been seen landing at Naha, it was considered that these were suicide planes topping up with fuel before their last mission. Accordingly the cruiser USS *Minneapolis* fired 100 rounds of 8-inch shell and 300 rounds of 3-inch shell on to the airfield. After 1300 a very heavy air raid developed with planes attacking in groups of ten or a dozen at heights of between 18,000 and 20,000 feet. The fighters on station over the northern islands of Kikai, Tokuno and Amami shot down nearly eighty of the attackers while CAP over Okinawa shot down another eighty and only one Japanese aircraft penetrated the transport area—a significant sucess for the air defence plan.

Again, it was the radar pickets which bore the brunt of the attacks, not only from suicide planes but also from the *Baka* piloted bomb and from the *Viper*, an unmanned version of the *Baka*. One or other of these weapons sank the destroyer *M. L. Abele*, which was subjected in Station No 14 to an intense co-ordinated attack by twenty aircraft. The destroyer shot down two, then a suicide hit was followed almost immediately by a hit by either a *Baka* or a *Viper* and the ship broke in two and sank. The destroyer *Cassin Young*, which had assisted *Colhoun* on 6 April, now came in for her own ordeal. On picket duty in Station No 1 with the destroyer *Purdy* and four LCSs, she was hit by a *Kamikaze* at 1340 which inflicted severe damage on the destroyer's machinery spaces, forcing her to retire to Kerama Retto for repairs. Her consort *Purdy* survived several attacks but was eventually hit and had to return to the Hagushi beaches.

As soon as Admiral Turner heard that Station No 1 was not covered he ordered *Stanly* and *Lang* to proceed from the adjacent Station No 2. En route *Stanly* was damaged by a *Baka* which struck the starboard side and continued through to the port side where it exploded. *Stanly* had to proceed to the Hagushi beaches and while running south she became involved in a dogfight between five 'Zekes' and the CAP, the latter assisted by Marine Corps Corsairs. One 'Zeke' peeled away and headed for the destroyer, hotly pursued by a Corsair which retired when *Stanly* opened up with her 5-inch and 40mm armament. The 'Zeke' hit the water off the destroyer's bow, the fuselage on one side and the bomb on the other. Throughout these hectic and intense engagements *Stanly*'s fighter direction team continued to control the CAP and saw their work rewarded with the shooting down of seven Japanese aircraft. Miraculously the destroyer only had three of her crew wounded and the damage to her bows was repaired in a few days at Kerama Retto.

Other ships damaged on 12 April included the destroyer *Whitehurst* (Lieutenant-Commander J. C. Horton USNR), which was attacked south-west of Kerama Retto and hit by one plane; the destroyer *Riddle*, which, south-east of Ie Shima, was hit by a bomb which passed through the ship without exploding; and the destroyer *Walter C. Wann*, over which, north-west of Kerama Retto, an aircraft passed low before exploding off the ship's port bow, showering her with debris.

During the afternoon of 12 April TF.54 came in for attention from the Japanese with little warning. Within minutes eleven different groups of Japanese aircraft were plotted on the radar and shortly after 1445 a group of three 'Jills' bore in on the destroyer *Zellars* (Commander L. S. Kinteberger) which was screening the battleship *Tennessee*. The first two 'Jills' were shot down but the third crashed into the port side near No 2 Handing Room. The impact was followed by a massive explosion and many considered that *Zellars* had been sunk. However, her crew fought the fires with what her Action Report described as 'dogged determination and an air of unfrantic concentrated effort' and at 1540 *Zellars* was under way and steaming at 15 knots, although she was of no further use to TF.54 and had to return to the United States for repairs. Casualties amounted to 29 killed or missing and 37 wounded.

A further group of five Japanese aircraft now approached *Tennessee* under cover of the pall of smoke rising from the stricken *Zellars* and the puffs of smoke from the AA fire. All five were shot down in short order but they were probably decoys because a 'Val' which had been flying off the battleship's port bow suddenly turned and came in from the starboard side, just missing the bridge and slithering aft to come to rest alongside No 3 14-inch turret, spraying burning gasoline as it went. The 250lb bomb penetrated the main deck and exploded in the Warrant Officers' quarters, causing much damage. In the same attack both *Idaho* and *New Mexico* were singled out for attention. The former shot down a 'Jill', which exploded in the water close alongside the battleship, shaking the ship but doing no damage other than ruining a store of beer kept in one of the blisters.

During a night attack on TF.54 the Japanese used flares for the first time to illuminate their targets. Admiral Deyo instantly recognized the flares as the precursor to a torpedo attack and ordered an emergency turn to avoid torpedoes. The action was justified for the destroyer *Rooks* sighted a torpedo passing astern of her and explosions were heard in the wakes of both *Tennessee* and *Idaho*.

The next massed air attack began on the night of 15/16 April with the appearance of many Japanese aircraft over the assault area, which was at once covered by smoke. There was much wild and indiscriminate AA fire in which shipping was endangered and friendly aircraft were attacked, despite the efforts of Admiral Turner to enforce a degree of fire discipline.

April 16 saw the *Kamikazes* continuing to concentrate on the radar pickets. The pickets were performing a vital duty in giving warning of the attacks and vectoring CAP on to Japanese formations, but the price they paid was high and was described by the American Official Historian as the 'finest kind of self-sacrificing service'.[3]

The destroyer USS *Laffey* (Commander Frederick J. Becton USN) was occupying the ill-fated Station No 1 when the first attacks developed shortly after 0820. *Kamikazes* approached from all points of the compass and at one time the ship's radar operator counted fifty aircraft closing from the northern quadrant. It was unfortunate that, just as the attack developed, CAP was being relieved. Nevertheless, on being appraised of the destroyer's position, CAP dealt with a number of the attackers outside *Laffey*'s gun range while some aircraft boldly flew into the destroyer's AA barrage in order to intercept others.

No other ship at Okinawa endured what *Laffey* suffered. In describing the performance of his crew as 'outstanding', Commander Becton was almost being deliberately self-effacing. Over a period of one hour twenty minutes, *Laffey* received twenty-two attacks as plotted by the ship's officers. Six suicide planes struck the ship as well as four bombs, and she was continually raked by strafing fire. Her AA armament, which had to be fired in local control after the director was destroyed, accounted for nine of her assailants. Throughout the three-hour ordeal *Laffey*'s crew demonstrated

> . . . cool-headed resourcefulness and continued to deliver accurate fire throughout the action, often in local control. Damage control parties were undaunted, although succeeding hits undid much of their previous efforts and destroyed more of their fire-fighting equipment. They were utterly fearless in combatting fires, although continually imperilled by exploding ammunition. Especially deserving of mention were the 20mm gunners, of whom at least four were killed 'in the straps', firing to the last.[4]

Thirty-one of *Laffey*'s ship's company were killed or missing in this action and a further 72 wounded. At 1247 *Laffey* was taken in tow by the destroyer-minesweeper USS *Macomb*, which was later relieved by the fleet tug *Pakana*. *Laffey*'s situation was critical, for the tug's pumps could only just keep the flooding at bay. The appearance of a second tug saved the day and *Laffey* was towed into the Hagushi anchorage before proceeding to Guam under her own power.

The attacks continued. *LCS116* was hit by a suicide plane in the same station as *Laffey* and the destroyer *Bryant* in the neighbouring No 2 position was crashed while hastening to assist *Laffey*. The destroyer *Pringle* and the high-speed minesweeper *Hobson*, which were occupying the same exposed RP position, No 14, where *M. L. Abele* had been sunk earlier, were attacked by a force of between twelve and fifteen aircraft, all of which seemed to be directed by a 'control' plane. *Pringle* was hit just aft of No 1 funnel and the resulting explosion broke the ship's back, possibly as a result of the torpedoes in her upper deck tubes exploding. She sank in less than five minutes: 65 of her crew were killed but the remainder were rescued. *Hobson* was damaged by the blast from the bomb carried by the suicide aircraft, which was destroyed just before it would have hit. She was ordered back to the Hagushi anchorage for repairs, her place being taken by the DMS USS *Harding*. The latter was en route for Station No 14 when she was attacked by two aircraft. One approached from the stern—a favourite diversionary manœuvre—while the other tore in from the starboard side and blew a hole 10 feet by 20 feet in her side and twisted the keel by 45 degrees. *Harding* managed to make a slow astern passage back to Kerama Retto having had 22 of her crew killed and another ten wounded. The destroyer *Bowers*, which was part of the A/S screen six miles north of Ie Shima, shot down two of her attackers before being hit by the third. The aircraft ploughed into the bridge, spraying it with burning gasoline. Both her Commanding Officer (Lieutenant-Commander C. F. Highfield USNR) and the Executive Officer (Lieutenant S. A. Haavik USNR) were badly wounded but *Bowers* was brought safely back to Hagushi.

This was last attack for a period of twelve days while the Japanese regrouped their forces. Their aircraft losses had been very heavy, many having been sacrificed in the first three *Kikusui* attacks. In the evening of 22 April a force of around eighty aircraft launched an attack. Only one succeeded in reaching the transport area and 54 were destroyed. However, the minesweeper USS *Swallow* was sunk in the screen, going down in less than seven minutes although only two of her crew were killed, and *LCS15* was hit so squarely that she sank immediately with the loss of fifteen of her crew. Once again the radar pickets were in the thick of things. The destroyer USS *Isherwood* was heavily damaged when there was a sympathetic detonation among the depth charges stowed on her fantail: 42 of her crew were killed or otherwise lost.

April 27 and 28 saw a change in tactics by the Japanese in that they attacked by night rather than at dawn or dusk. The raids began at 1910 on the 27th with 'conventional' bombing over the Transport Area, despite the fact that the latter was covered by smoke. The smoke proved extremely effective and no ship which was hidden was hit. Alas, the transport *Canada Victory*, loaded with small-arms ammunition, was exposed by a rift in the smoke and was hit and sunk at 2212 by a *Kamikaze*. Two high-speed destroyer-escorts, *Ralph Talbot* and *Rathburne*, were hit and damaged although both made Kerama Retto under their own power.

There was then a lull in the attacks until 1400 on 28 April, when the Japanese returned with a vengeance. From then until 0200 the next day there were forty-four attacks by over 200 enemy aircraft. One hundred and eighteen of these were destroyed by CAP and gunfire but there were more casualties among the radar pickets. In Station No 2 *Daly* and *Twiggs* were constantly engaged all afternoon. A force of over 30 'Zekes' was broken up at a distance by a flight of six Corsairs which were vectored out to them, and then at 1730 the ships were further attacked by a large force of 'Vals'. Brilliant ship-handling prevented any of the *Kamikazes* from scoring a direct hit but both vessels were badly damaged by near misses. Other casualties included the destroyer *Brown* in Station No 10 and *LCI580*, which were both damaged, as was the evacuation transport *Pinkney*.

The most serious casualty was the hospital ship *Comfort*, which was packed with wounded and heading towards Saipan, fully illuminated as required by the Geneva Convention. Fifty miles south-east of Okinawa she was circled by a Japanese aircraft which crossed the ship at mast-head height before diving into the superstructure. The point of impact was directly over the main operating theatre suite. Two sailors and 21 soldiers, including six Army nurses, were killed and a further seven sailors and 31 soldiers wounded. This was not the first time that *Comfort* had been attacked. She had been slightly damaged by a near miss from a bomb on 7 April and had suffered a lucky escape when one of *Enterprise*'s aircraft had attempted to bomb her on 9 April. It is arguable, however, that it was futile to expect that the Japanese would respect the Red Cross (their conduct in the war thus far having given no such indication) and that the illuminated markings were more of an invitation or provocation than a guarantee of security.

The Japanese night attacks increased in strength as the moon waxed, but there was such a shortage of dedicated night fighters—the maximum number employed at Okinawa was eight—that it was impossible to maintain a night fighter CAP. The night of 3/4 May saw heavy and closely co-ordinated enemy air, sea and land attacks in an attempt to land behind the American lines on both sides of Okinawa. For nearly a week thereafter Japanese air activity remained at a very low level, but on 10 May, following a major American offensive on the island by the Tenth Army, heavy *Kikusui* attacks were launched on both shipping off Okinawa and the fast carriers.

Between 0100 and 0500 and between 0800 and 0830 on 11 May some 110 enemy aircraft were over Okinawa, while off Ie Shima there were attacks by 'conventional' torpedo bombers at about 0900. The only ship damaged was the Dutch merchantman *Tjisadane*, which was hit by a *Kamikaze*. The radar pickets to the north-west of Okinawa came in for heavy attack. Station No 15 was occupied by the destroyers *Hugh W. Hadley* and *Evans* together with three LCSs and one LCS(R). From 0750 to 0930 the Japanese made a maximum effort to knock these ships out: at one stage *Hadley* had more than 150 enemy aircraft on her plot. CAPs were vectored out to break up the formations and shot down about fifty of the aircraft, but a group of fifty went after the two destroyers. *Evans* shot down fifteen but was hit by four and damaged by falling debris from four others. The four hits left the ship burning furiously and dead in the water, with her machinery spaces flooded and with thirty of her crew dead and 29 wounded. At the same time *Hadley* was attacked by groups of aircraft which came in from both bows, presenting her gunners with an interesting fire control problem. Despite the gunfire, one aircraft smashed into the ship aft, another dropped its bomb aft, a *Baka* bomb exploded amidships and a fourth aircraft brought down the halyards and aerials. The ship was badly holed, with both engine rooms and one fire room flooded. A heavy fire raged around No 2 funnel and ready-use ammunition on the main deck began to explode. Commander Mullaney ordered all but fifty of his crew to abandon ship. Those who remained on board strove to save their ship and, despite the fires and exploding ammunition, succeeded in doing so. *Hadley* had 28 killed and 67 wounded: she was eventually towed to Ie Shima for temporary repairs before going on to Kerama Retto.

Admiral Spruance's flagship, the battleship USS *New Mexico*, was damaged during the evening of 12 May when a lone *Kamikaze* penetrated the transport area, but from then until the evening of 23 May there were only isolated attacks. The construction of a radar station on Iheya Retto, north-east of Ie Shima, would, it was hoped, go some way towards giving more advanced warning of Japanese attacks. Nevertheless, in the period before the next *Kikusui* attack on 23 May two destroyers were badly damaged.

During the night of 24/25 May the invasion shipping suffered a heavy air attack, apparently in connection with a Japanese offensive ashore. Attacks continued intermittently until noon on the 25th and, with the exception of the cargo ship *W. Allison* which was damaged by an aerial torpedo off the Hagushi beaches, were confined to the pickets. The high-speed destroyer-transport *Bates* was damaged, as was the destroyer *Stormes*, which emerged from her ordeal with a hole in her hull between the propeller shafts.

The final *Kikusui* attack, the last to which the Japanese committed more than 100 aircraft, took place from 27 to 29 May. Again the radar pickets were in the thick of it. The destroyers *Braine* and *Antony* were in Station No 5 when their CAP of Army Thunderbolts had to return to Okinawa because of poor weather. Almost immediately, coinciding with the CAP's departure, a flight of three or four 'Vals' came out of the cloud. One went for *Antony* but exploded on her starboard beam after being deflected by her AA gunfire. The explosion riddled the ship with splinters and debris rained down on her, including the body of the Japanese pilot. *Braine* was hit by two aircraft: the explosions started fierce fires on her main deck which divided the ship into three sections each unable to communicate with the others. *Antony* came alongside to render assistance and take off her casualties—78 wounded—and *Braine* was eventually towed to Kerama Retto by the tug *Ute*. Sixty-six of her crew were killed in this attack.

The Japanese offensives continued in the evening of the 27th and until 0930 on the 28th. Station No 15, manned by the destroyers *Lowry* and *Drexler* (Commander R. L. Wilson USN), was singled out for attention. This was a well conducted attack by Japanese pilots of exceptional skill and determination. Despite the efforts of the CAP and brilliant ship-handling, *Drexler* was struck by two 'Frances' aircraft,[5] the second of which carried two bombs. The explosion was terrific, an oil fire shot up into the air for several hundred feet and parts of the ship were blown in all directions. The casualties were very heavy—158 killed or missing and 51, including Commander Wilson, wounded.

The last casualty of this attack was the destroyer *Shubrick* (Lieutenant-Commander J. C. Jolly USN), which was struck by an unidentified twin-engine aircraft while proceeding to Picket Station No 16. The starboard side of the ship was blown out and she began to settle by the stern. By 0130 the fantail aft of No 4 gun was awash and Commander Jolly ordered all confidential publications destroyed and sensitive electronic equipment smashed. The destroyer *Van Valkenburgh* came alongside and with the aid of portable pumps managed to bring the fires and flooding under control. At 0510 a tug arrived to tow the crippled *Shubrick* back to Kerama Retto. She had lost 32 of her crew killed or missing and 28 wounded.

From this point on, air raids on Okinawa declined considerably in intensity, although they never ceased altogether. During the remainder of the operation only eight ships were damaged and one sunk by Japanese aircraft. The massed *Kikusui* attacks had cost the Japanese 6,810 aircraft. They had succeeded, however, in sinking 28 ships and damaging a further 227 out of a total casualty list of 36 and 371 respectively. This contest between Japanese and American air power was the most hard-fought and decisive since the battles off Guadalcanal.

The *Kikusui* attacks represented the desperate measures that the Japanese High Command were prepared to resort to in the defence of the Home Islands, but, though nerve-racking and damaging, they were self-defeating. *Kikusui* represented a declining asset, for there is no such thing as an experienced suicide pilot. It was noticeable that, as the attacks progressed, the quality of the Japanese air crew showed a marked deterioration, indicative of the fact that the Japanese High Command was having problems in 'manning' such attacks and that poorly trained crewmen were having to be used. It was later noted that pilots with less than 100 hours of flying time were sometimes employed—pilots with just sufficient knowledge to take off and fly their aircraft. A total of 1,900 aircraft were expended in suicide attacks and they succeeded in sinking 27 and damaging 164 ships—roughly one success in ten.

It is difficult in a bald account of ships sunk or damaged to render a true picture of these attacks. There is something very alien to those brought up in the Western, Christian tradition about the concept of the *Kamikaze*. The spectre of these aircraft coming in relentlessly against all opposition was an unnerving one. Both Americans and British who experienced these attacks subsequently recalled that they felt that the pilot was flying straight at them—a feeling which gave such experiences a horribly personal character. Both the Americans and the British had endured massed air attacks elsewhere during the war, particularly in the Mediterranean, but nothing had prepared them for the inhuman, almost robotic way in which the Japanese just kept on coming. The noise of approaching aircraft, coupled with the din of the AA barrage put up, created an atmosphere of pandemonium: it speaks volumes for the courage of the officers and men on those ships off Okinawa that they never faltered.

Casualties of these attacks were horrifically wounded, with terrible burns caused by escaping steam or burning oil, often compounded by immersion in sea water. The Medical Officers performed wonders under conditions which must have taxed their stamina and concentration to the limit. The rear hospitals and hospital ships were packed with men so badly burned that they resembled mummies, breathing and feeding through tubes beneath their bandages. The ordeal of those confronting the massed attacks off Okinawa has no parallel in naval history. In paying tribute to his own ship's company, Commander Baron J. Mullaney USN of the USS *Hugh W. Hadley* speaks for all those who endured the *Kikusui* attacks off Okinawa:

No captain of a man of war had a crew who fought more valiantly against such overwhelming odds. Who can measure the degree of courage of men who stand up to their guns in the face of diving planes that destroy them? Who can measure the loyalty of a crew who risked death to save the ship from sinking when all seemed lost. I desire to record that the history of our Navy was enhanced on 11 May 1945. I am proud to record that I know of no record of a destroyer's crew fighting for one hour and thirty-five minutes and against overwhelming aircraft attacks and destroying twenty-three planes. My crew accomplished their mission and displayed outstanding fighting abilities . . . Destroyer men are good men and my officers and crew were good destroyer men.[6]

NOTES TO CHAPTER 6

1. 'Val' was the Allied code-name for the Aichi D3A single-engine, carrier-borne bomber.
2. 'Jill' was the Allied code-name for the Nakajima B6N single-engine, carrier-borne attack plane.
3. Morison, Samuel E., *History of United States Naval Operations in World War II. Vol. XIV: Victory in the Pacific 1945*, Little, Brown (1968), p.235.
4. Morison, p.236.
5. 'Frances' was the Allied code-name for the Yokosuka P1Y bomber and night fighter.
6. Morison, p.258.

7

Blasting Them Out

*It is going to be really tough: there are 65,000–70,000 fighting
Japanese holed up in the south end of the island. I see no
way to get them out except blasting them out yard by
yard.*—Major-General John R. Hodge, US Army

THE swiftness with which the troops had established themselves ashore came as a welcome surprise to the American
planners. General Buckner's plan called for the two corps
under his command to drive across the island to the east coast
and bisect the island. The two 'inner' divisions, the 1st Marine and
the 7th Infantry, would head for the east coast while the two outer
divisions, the 6th Marine and the 96th Infantry, would wheel
north and south respectively, tearing the Japanese forces apart.
Such was the plan.

The two Marine Divisions accomplished their task with little
difficulty. At times the Marines were hampered as much by the
terrain as by the resistance of the enemy. On 2 April the 6th
Marine Division, commanded by Major-General Lemuel G.
Sheppard USMC, advanced into the foothills of Mount Yontan
and began throwing out patrols to the north-west of the Hagushi
beaches. Two pockets of resistance were eliminated, costing the
Japanese some 250 dead. On 3 April the Marines were approaching the Nakadomari–Ishikawa position some twelve days ahead of
schedule and it was decided that they could be released from their
timetable and allowed to make an unrestricted advance. On 4
April the 1st Marine Division reached the east coast and wheeled
north, and it was hoped that a rapid advance would throw the
Japanese off balance and deny them the chance to organize and
prepare defences.

The 22nd Marines were now spearheading the advance towards
the Motobu Peninsula, with tank/infantry teams moving north
along the island's west coast while making forays inland. The

22nd stopped at the Atsubara–Kin line to allow the other battalions of the division, the 4th and 29th Marines, to catch up and by 7 April, L+6, had sealed off the Motobu Peninsula. The Marines of the 1st Division had occupied the Kachin Peninsula on the east of the island and were engaged in clearing isolated parties of Japanese resistance.

The Japanese had retreated to prepared positions among the Yaetake Hills on the Motobu Peninsula. Colonel Takehido Udo, Commander of Japanese forces there, had marshalled his men in the hills and, like General Ushido in the south, adopted a passive policy, keeping them under cover until late in the afternoon when he knew it would be too late to for the Americans to send expeditions into the the hills. Udo had a good supply of light artillery as well as mortars and heavy machine guns together with a battery of field artillery. He possessed excellent communications and his men were trained in guerrilla and mountain warfare. Udo expected to carry out a campaign of attrition on the American forces, using guerrilla tactics to exact as heavy a toll as possible.

After sealing off the Peninsula from the remainder of the island, the Marines concentrated on establishing the whereabouts of the Japanese defences and troop concentrations. Early forays into the Peninsula had shown that tanks would be useless in the rugged terrain and that clearing it would have to involve traditional infantry tactics. Early on 14 April the 4th Marines attacked Mount Yaetake. As the Marines advanced, the Japanese seemed like phantoms. They would appear from behind a clump of bushes or a rock for long enough to shoot any American they saw carrying a map or a pistol—a deliberate policy of eliminating the command—before disappearing again.

Plans for the assault on Mount Yaetake were finalized on 13 April and were to involve various battalions from the 6th Marines advancing up the hill from a variety of directions. The fact that the Americans had advanced to the north of the Peninsula meant that they could concentrate exclusively on Mount Yaetake without worrying about a counter-attack in their rear. The 1st and 2nd Battalions of the 4th Marines, together with the 3rd Battalion of the 29th Marines under Colonel Alan Shapley USMC, were to attack up the west slope while the 1st and 2nd of the 29th were to occupy the high ground north of the Itomi–Manna Road.

On 14 April Colonel Shapley's three battalions secured positions on the first ridges of the mountain while from the east the 3/29th had advanced and after some savage hand-to-hand combat had taken a ridge just below the Yaetake Heights. Twenty-two-year-old Corporal Richard E. Bush became the only Marine to win the Congressional Medal of Honor on the Motobu Peninsula when, in an act of selfless heroism, severely wounded and taking cover with other Marines behind rocks, he grabbed and held against him a Japanese grenade which landed among the wounded. Amazingly, Bush lived to receive his award. The 2/4th reached the crest only to be driven back by heavy and accurate fire. They did, however, manage to secure a long, curving ridge facing the heights while providing cover for the 1/29th advancing on their right. Thus by the evening of 15 April the Marines were well established on the mountain and ready for the final assault the next day.

The assault on 16 April called for the 3/29th and 2/4th to maintain pressure on the Japanese along a line running west of Yaetake while the 1 and 3/4th pushed north across their fronts to seize the crest itself. At the same time the remaining battalions of the 29th Marines would attack the northern part from the east. The Marines of the 1/4th advanced slowly up the mountain, supported by artillery and air strikes. When only 100 yards from the crest their advance was halted by a barrage of mortar and machine-gun fire. But, to the right, troops of A and C Companies of the same battalion had swept over the ridge and taken it after fierce hand-to-hand fighting. By late afternoon the Heights were in American hands.

The Marines could not sit back and rest on their laurels. It was clear from movement in the woods below that the Japanese were planning an immediate counter-attack. Every Marine present, including the battalion's Commanding Officer, Lieutenant-Colonel Fred T. Beans USMC, was pressed into hauling ammunition up to the ridge just in time to stop a desperate *Banzai* charge by the Japanese.

On 17 April the Marines set about conquering the rest of the mountain. Colonel Shapley's three battalions were responsible for clearing the south and western slopes while the 29th Marines, minus their 3rd Battalion, attacked the north-eastern heights. Colonel Jean Moreau of the 1/29th succeeded in clearing the

Above: Marines take cover as dynamite is used to blast a Japanese strongpoint. Rather than surrender, many Japanese, and their native Okinawan 'hostages', were entombed in their bunkers. (US National Archives)

Below: Three Japanese prisoners, closely covered by Marines, carry one of their wounded to an aid post during the fighting around the island's ancient capital of Shuri. Very few Japanese surrendered in the early stages of the campaign. (US National Archives)

Left, upper: A flame-throwing Sherman tank in action. These converted vehicles proved to be especially effective at clearing Japanese positions and were greatly feared by the defenders. (US National Archives)

Left, lower: Admiral Nimitz (left) with General Buckner (right) and Admiral Spruance (centre, looking somewhat incongruous in a pith helmet) at Yontan airfield on 20 April during Nimitz's visit to the island to express his confidence in Buckner's handling of the campaign. (US National Archives)

Above: Two Stinson L-5 spotter aircraft on the flight deck of a carrier. Dwarfed by the Avengers alongside them, these aircraft would have been assembled on board the carrier before being flown ashore. (US National Archives)

Below: Close-quarter fighting in the streets of Naha. The city fell on 29 May. (US National Archives)

Above: An L-5 flying over the ruins of the city of Naha. (US National Archives)
Below: An infantryman standing before a Japanese bunker on the Shuri line. Many of these positions were interconnected and proved resistant to anything but a direct attack. (US National Archives)

Above: Marines wander through the ruins of Okinawa's ancient capital of Shuri, which finally fell on 29 May. The city was completely devastated in the attack and nothing remained other than the ruins of these barracks. (US National Archives)
Below: The weather broke on 30 May, making conditions difficult for wheeled transport. (US National Archives)

Left: Infantrymen use a cargo net to scale the heights of Yaeju Dake in the final serious fighting on the island. (US National Archives)
Above: Marines gather supplies air-dropped to them. Waist-deep mud caused by torrential rains made air-dropping the only practical method of getting supplies through to the forward area. (US National Archives)
Below: American soldiers trudge past an assault engineering Sherman in the wet weather which characterized operations in early June. (US National Archives)

Above: Exhaustion: infantry of the 96th Division rest after the capture of a Japanese strongpoint nicknamed 'Big Apple'. The intensity of fighting on Okinawa was of a scale which the Americans had not hitherto experienced in the Pacific. (US National Archives)
Below: A Ryukuan tomb, many of which were used by the Japanese as strongpoints, now serves as an aid station for Marines. (US National Archives)
Right, upper: Surgery in progress on a wounded soldier in a cave on Okinawa. (US National Archives)
Right, lower: American wounded are flown off Okinawa to base hospitals scattered throughout the central and southern Pacific. (US National Archives)

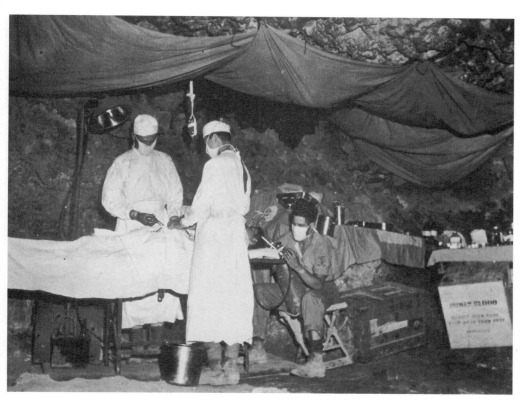

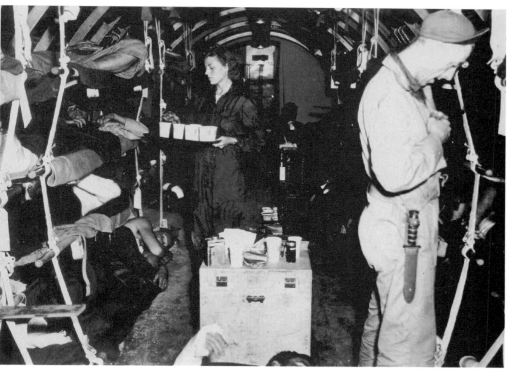

Left, upper: Medical attention for a wounded Okinawan child. The Americans tried to exploit the differences between the Japanese and the native Okinawans. (US National Archives)

Left, lower: Hearts and minds. Lieutenant Richard K. Jones gives some of his K-rations to two Okinawan children found hiding in an abandoned tomb. (US National Archives)

Right: A bulldozer prepares a mass grave for Japanese who took their own lives rather than surrender. (US National Archives)

Below: An aerial reconnaissance photograph of the airfield on Ie Shima, captured by the 77th Division after fierce fighting. (US National Archives)

Left, upper: Repair work on the airstrip on Ie Shima, which had been extensively mined by the Japanese. (US National Archives)

Left, lower: Japanese soldiers, one carrying a white flag, approach American troops to surrender. (US National Archives)

Above: Carefully covered by armed Marines, a wounded Japanese soldier emerges from his bunker following the use of white phosphorous. (US National Archives)

Right: The crew of an LCI pick up a Japanese soldier. He had swum out to them from southern Okinawa after responding to a call to surrender. As the campaign drew to a close, increasing numbers of Japanese gave themselves up instead of taking their lives. (US National Archives)

Left, upper: Japanese prisoners in a temporary cage on Okinawa. (US National Archives)
Left, lower: General Simon B. Buckner Jr lays a wreath at the grave of an unknown American soldier killed in the fighting on Okinawa. On 18 June Buckner himself was killed while observing fighting at the front line. (US National Archives)
Above: The misery and shame of defeat. (US National Archives)

Above: General Joseph C Stilwell—'Vinegar Joe'—in muddy conditions on Okinawa after taking over command of the Tenth Army following the death of General Buckner on 18 June. (US National Archives)

north side by a brilliant piece of deception. His actions gave the Japanese every indication that the attack would come from the north and it was gratifying for the Americans to observe the Japanese adjusting their dispositions accordingly. Meanwhile his Marines were scaling the almost sheer face of the south side and by noon had taken the ridge with only one casualty.

On the same day the 4th Marines swept rapidly northwards, killing over 700 Japanese as they tried to withdraw, and by 18 April organized Japanese resistance had come to an end. The elimination of the Japanese from the Motobu Peninsula and the clearing of the rest of the northern part of the island brought operations to a halt in the area north of the Hagushi beaches. The fighting had been fierce. It was estimated that 2,500 Japanese had been killed and only 46 taken prisoner. The grim implication of these figures was that the majority of the defenders were in the south of the island. In turn III Corps had lost 246 killed and over 1,000 wounded. The Marines were justly proud of their achievement, not only in terms of how they had performed on Okinawa, but in terms of the wider agenda: they had shown that they were as capable as any Army division of extended ground operations against a determined enemy.

Allied with the clearing of the northern half of the island went the successful capture of Ie Shima. For the assault a gunfire support unit (TU.52.21.1) was formed under the command of Rear-Admiral B. J. Rogers and consisting of the battleship *Texas*, the cruisers *Birmingham* (flag) and *Mobile* and four destroyers. The preliminary bombardment began on 13 April while UDT teams prepared the landing beaches. On 15 April two battalions of field artillery were landed on Menna Shima, a small island south of Ie Shima, to support the main landings the next day.

The assault troops came from the 77th (Statue of Liberty) Division which had taken Kerama Retto and which had been kept at sea pending further operations since then. At 0830 on 16 April two RCTs landed, covered by gunfire from TU.52.21.1, which had now been augmented by the battleship *West Virginia*, the cruisers *Tuscaloosa* and *Portland* and two destroyers for the operation. Resistance was light on the beaches but stiffened as the troops progressed inland. The Japanese fought with fanatical resistance to deny the Americans the use of the airfield. Civilians, including women, some armed only with wooden spears, joined the troops in the defence of the island, but to no avail. By 21 April resistance was at an end and the 77th moved to southern Okinawa.[1] The Americans counted 4,176 Japanese dead, 208 prisoners and 1,586 civilians to be interned, a total of nearly 6,000 persons. There was amazement amongst the US personnel: air reconnaissance had indicated that there were no more than five people on the small and relatively open island, and this was simultaneous proof of the Japanese skill at camouflage and of the limitations of aerial reconnaissance.

In contrast to the operations in the north, General Hodge's XXIV Corps endured a grim battle of attrition in the south—a battle in which literally every yard of ground had to be contested against an enemy who was well armed, well-positioned and determined to sell his life dearly. On 4 April XXIV Corps began to wheel south, with the 7th Infantry Division taking the left flank (the east coast) and the 96th taking the right. As they moved south both divisions encountered small, well-positioned pockets of resistance which had to be rooted out individually. There was a sharp and noticeable rise in casualties. The first major obstacle encountered by the Americans was known as The Pinnacle, a 30-foot coral spike on a 450-yard ridge 1,000 yards east of Arakuchi. This position was defended by the 1st Company of the 14th Infantry Battalion, commanded by 1st Lieutenant Seiji Tamagawa. Tamagawa had plenty of heavy machine guns and mortars and his position was within the field of fire of the 62nd Division's field artillery. An attack by B Company of the 184th Infantry was repulsed but on 6 April the assault was renewed by B and C Companies of the 184th. Their first attack was thrown back but their second succeeded: Tamagawa allowed his men to concentrate exclusively on repulsing B Company, which was making a frontal attack, while ignoring C Company, which made a flanking movement and took the Japanese by surprise. For some reason all of Tamagawa's appeals to the 62nd Division went unheeded and his position was taken. The 96th Division encountered a similar position called Cactus Ridge. The rugged terrain meant that no armour could be used. The Japanese were well positioned and only an old-fashioned bayonet charge by the 2/383rd Infantry on 6 April succeeded in taking the position.

As XXIV Corps moved south they encountered a series of such positions. On the 7th Division's front the 184th Infantry took the lead and in heavy fighting cleared three of them, Red Hill, Tombstone Hill and Triangulation Hill. All had to be cleared using the bayonet since armour was of little use in the rough country. When tanks were employed, more often than not they were quickly destroyed by very accurate Japanese artillery or satchel charges and their crews were bayoneted; moreover, if the tank were sufficiently battleworthy, it was turned around and used against the Americans.

In an attempt to break the deadlock, the 7th Division attempted a large-scale outflanking movement to the centre of the island but found that they were confronting a defensive perimeter which stretched across it. Faced with this seemingly impenetrable barrier, the Division halted and waited for the 96th to catch up before launching a combined attack.

On the other side of the island the 96th Division had run into a series of Japanese positions around Kakazu. These positions were deceptively strong and two battalions, the 1st and 3rd of the 383th Infantry, were ordered to seize them. The attack got off with some companies pinned down under a withering hail of fire from the defenders. L Company, however, commanded by Lieutenant Willard E. Mitchell, reached the crest after a bayonet charge. However, his one company could not hope to hold the crest unsupported, and after beating off a series of counter-attacks aimed at cutting his men off Mitchell was forced to retreat. For their gallantry in reaching the crest and their subsequent defence of it, L Company were awarded the Distinguished Unit Citation. The 96th Division's planners now decided to employ two regiments, the 381st and 383rd Infantry, to attack the position, hoping that this 'powerhouse' move would succeed. The attack began after a two-hour barrage and the Japanese were gradually forced back.

In the fighting up to 12 April XXIV Corps had suffered 451 dead and over 2,000 wounded. Little ground was being taken and it was now evident to the Americans—whose intelligence about the nature of the Japanese defence was very hazy despite the resources expended on air reconnaissance—that the Japanese were established in strength along a line which ran the whole width of the island starting some four miles north of the capital, Naha. This was referred to as the Machinato Line. Behind it lay the inner defence ring around the ancient capital of Shuri,

Machinato airfield on the west coast and Yonabaru airfield on the east coast. Defending these objectives was the bulk of the 32nd Army, including the crack 62nd Division, with the 24th Division held as a reserve in southern Okinawa.

Until 19 April there was little or no activity on the front. General Buckner, who had established his headquarters ashore on the 18th, used this time to conduct a thorough reconnaissance of the Japanese line and to bring in reinforcements. Replacements were introduced to fill the ranks of the 7th and 96th Divisions, and the 27th Division, which had been held as a floating reserve, was brought ashore on the 18th/19th and inserted into the line on the right of the 96th Division.

Buckner planned an attack by all three divisions for 19 April. The 27th Division, acting on intelligence from captured Japanese documents, sought to pre-position troops before the assault by crossing the Machinato inlet during the night of the 18th/19th. Engineers succeeded in bringing up Bailey bridges under cover of darkness and the troops were successfully moved across.

The assault opened in the morning of 19 April with a bombardment by the greatest concentration of artillery employed by the Americans in the Pacific. On Okinawa twenty-seven artillery units, including 8-inch howitzers, were used, while off-shore six battleships, six cruisers and six destroyers were deployed, supported by over 600 land-based and carrier aircraft. The bombardment opened at 0600 with twenty minutes of fire on the 62nd Division's front line positions, switching to their rear positions for twenty minutes before returning to the forward area. It is estimated that 19,000 shells were fired in forty minutes.

The aim was to tease the Japanese out from their caves and bunkers, but it was not achieved. The Japanese remained dug in and only emerged when the bombardment lifted in time to repulse the attack. Lieutenant Hidara recalled that:

> We were quite safe in our caves, which were all inter-connected by underground passages, so that we could move from one to the other without exposing ourselves. The American artillery was very fierce but, because their fire was spread out over a large area, it did very little damage to our bunkers.[2]

The American attack failed to break the Japanese line at all points on the front. Fierce fighting followed from 20 to 24 April, particularly in the area where the 27th and 96th Divisions met.

Between the two Divisions was the Kakazu Ridge. The 27th was badly mauled trying to take this area, which included the Japanese strongholds named Item Pocket and the East and West Pinnacles. By 21 April the 27th Division was in a serious position. It was fully committed to battle and had no reserves, its lines had been infiltrated by the Japanese and an ominous gap was opening between its front and that of the 96th Division. The Division was suffering a large number of casualties and, in particular, a large number of non-battle casualties. On 20 April the Division suffered 506 casualties, more than any other division engaged on Okinawa.

Drastic action was required. General Griner was relieved of command while his Assistant Divisional Commander, Brigadier William Bradford, put together a Task Force consisting of four battalions of infantry from the 7th and 96th Divisions, with the 102nd Engineer Battalion from the 27th Division acting as riflemen. This unit attacked Japanese positions on Kakazu Ridge on 24 April, only to find that the Japanese had disengaged and conducted a skilful withdrawal.

In the centre of the island the 96th Division had pushed forward hard and managed to place four battalions atop the Nishibaru Ridge. A final push was planned to clear the Japanese from the remainder of the Ridge on 24 April but, once again, the Americans found that the Japanese had simply melted away. During the night of 23/24 April General Ushijima had ordered a withdrawal to the main defensive position around the town of Shuri. At the same time he moved troops up from southern Okinawa to fill the gaps in the ranks of the 62nd Division caused by the heavy fighting. The 44th Independent Mixed Brigade was deployed west of Shuri while the 22nd Infantry Regiment from the 24th Division was moved into the line east of Shuri.

By the end of the April the American advanced had slowed almost to a halt. Gains were measured in yards; the Divisions were exhausted and their casualties were rising. General Buckner, too, was regrouping his forces. Since Phase II of Operation 'Iceberg' (the conquest of Miyako in the Sakishima Gunto) had been cancelled, he was free to redeploy the Marines of III Amphibious Corps. Accordingly the 1st Marine Division relieved the battered 27th Division, which would be assigned to security duties in northern Okinawa. The 96th Division was relieved by the

77th, which, although it had seen hard fighting and suffered casualties on Ie Shima, was still relatively fresh. Once the 96th had been rested and the gaps in its ranks filled, it would relieve the 7th Division.

Time, however, was on the Americans' side. The gaps in their ranks could be filled and their losses in *matériel* could be made good. For Ushijima there were no reinforcements and his losses in *matériel* could not be made up other than by using captured US equipment. It could only be a matter of time before the Japanese were ground down. However, there were those in the American camp who felt that General Buckner could be setting about the destruction of Japanese forces with a little more imagination. Criticism came from the Marine Corps. Lieutenant-General Alexander Vandegrift, the Commandant of the Marine Corps, visited Okinawa and urged Buckner to recall the 2nd Marine Division (which had conducted the feint landings off Okinawa on L-Day) and land it behind enemy lines. Vandegrift was supported by Vice-Admiral Turner, General Hodge and General Geiger of III Corps, but to no avail: Buckner considered such a move inappropriate and one which might well result in a stalemate such as had happened at Anzio in the Italian campaign.

Buckner's traditional tactics of frontal assault began to be the focus of some sharp criticism in the American press, with observations that they were 'a worse example of military incompetence than Pearl Harbor' and 'ultra conservative. Instead of an end run, we persisted in frontal attacks.'[3] It is easy to say with hindsight that Buckner's tactics lacked imagination. Perhaps Buckner was the wrong man to command the forces on Okinawa: his previous post had been Commander of the US Army in Alaska and perhaps he was not *au fait* with the mobility and flexibility of thought which the American amphibious campaign required. However, it was well known that the Japanese were at their most formidable in defence when confronting assault. Such tactics required little more than blind obedience to the dictum that a position should never be given up. The Japanese military were adept at carrying out carefully prepared orders but when confronted with a rapidly developing situation which required fast thinking and quick decision-making their command structure often fell apart. It is impossible to say whether or not a landing in the rear of the Japanese positions around Shuri would have hastened the end of the fighting. However, the suggestion was a valid one and Buckner's refusal to consider it condemned the American soldiers and Marines on Okinawa to another two months of attrition.

Nimitz was furious about the leaks, which he blamed on Vandegrift. At this stage in the war, with the Navy taking huge losses off Okinawa, the last thing Nimitz wanted in his command was an incestuous feud between the Army and the Marines. On 20 April he paid a well-publicized visit to Yontan airfield to signal his confidence in Buckner. Privately, though, he too wanted a speedy conclusion to hostilities on the island.

If the Americans were dissatisfied with the way things were going, so were the Japanese. Ushijima's defensive posture was working brilliantly, but such tactics were alien to the *Samurai* spirit which motivated the Japanese officer corps. In particular, Lieutenant-General Isamu Cho, Ushijima's Chief of Staff, wanted a counter-offensive launched. Cho felt that the defensive posture was undignified and was having a detrimental effect on morale. Colonel Hiromachi Yahara, an officer on Ushijima's staff, was violently opposed to such a move. It would, he argued, permit the Americans to bring their greater firepower to bear on troops in the open and bereft of cover. Moreover, the preliminary bombardment necessary for such an attack would give away the locations of most of the Japanese heavy artillery and probably result in their destruction. There was a stormy meeting on 2 May at which a considerable amount of alcohol was consumed, and in the heat of the moment Ushijima agreed to an offensive on 4 May in combination with air and sea units.

The fate of the air and naval components of the operation has already been dealt with. The land offensive faired no better. During the night of 3/4 May the Japanese began the attack with a tremendous artillery barrage—the heaviest encountered by the Americans in the Pacific War. They attacked through their own barrage but, apart from making local gains in one sector, were unable to breach the American line. Yahara's prophecy came true: the Japanese troops were cut down in hundreds by the Americans' firepower. Yet they kept on coming. Undeterred by the failure of the first offensive, Lieutenant-General Tatsumi Amamiya, Commander of the 24th Division, ordered another attempt on 4/5 May—which was also beaten back.

On 5 May Ushijima called the offensive off. It had cost the Japanese over 5,000 dead and the loss of much equipment. Moreover, the Americans had located, and destroyed, nineteen of Ushijima's heavy guns. Significantly, there was a marked decline in American 'battle fatigue' casualties after this date.

Following the failure of the Japanese offensive, General Buckner began the planning for a renewed push south, heartened by the fact that his forces had held firm against the Japanese offensive. On 9 May he took control of operations himself and carried out a further reorganization. The 27th Division were engaged in security duties in northern Okinawa so the 6th Marine Division and the Corps HQ of III Amphibious Corps were brought south, reunited with the 6th Marine Division and brought into the line on the right of XXIV Corps. In effect Buckner had doubled his forces to conquer the southern part of the island and would attack on a four-division front comprising, from west to east, the 6th and 1st Marines of III Corps and the 77th and 96th of XXIV Corps. The 7th Division were out of the line, having a hard-earned (but brief) rest.

Buckner's plan called for XXIV Corps to envelope Shuri from the east and III Amphibious Corps to do likewise from the west, with a holding attack proceeding in the centre. Buckner's staff recognized that the terrain was easier on the right flank, and this was therefore allotted to the Marines on the grounds that they were the freshest troops and because intelligence indicated that Japanese forces were weaker on that side of the island. On this occasion the Americans dispensed with the usual massed barrage from ships, aircraft and shore-based artillery in favour of directed fire on specific targets. Belatedly, the Americans had accepted that a general bombardment was little more than a waste of ammunition against the Japanese positions. This change in practice was noticed by the Japanese:

The Americans now started to target specific bunkers with phosphorous and flame throwers rather than merely firing massive blind barrages. This was more effective and it certainly imposed a greater strain on the troops. In particular the flame throwers were greatly feared.[4]

The attack was launched on 11 May and almost immediately disintegrated into a series of bitterly contested struggles for ground across the whole width of the island. Ushijima had anticipated the American offensive and, correctly, reinforced his line in the sector facing the Marines. It took ten days of bitter fighting before the Japanese line broke, allowing Shuri to be enveloped.

The most ferocious fighting took place to the north of the town of Asato around Sugar Loaf Hill, a group of three peaks with mutually supporting artillery positions. The veteran Marines of the 6th Division regarded this battle as the fiercest in which they had been engaged and the Division was badly mauled. On 15 May the 2nd Battalion had to be pulled out of the line after suffering 400 casualties in three days while trying to take the crest of the hill. Despite concentrated naval gunfire support, air strikes and armour and artillery support, each time the Marines took the crest of the hill they were driven back by the Japanese, who had chosen to make their stand on the reverse slopes rather than on the the the crest. An assault by two regiments on 16 May was repulsed and it was not until 18 May that the hill was finally taken.

No sooner had Sugar Loaf Hill fallen than the Marines were confronted with an equally formidable defensive position— Horseshoe Hill and Crescent Hill. The Marines were exhausted: Sugar Loaf Hill had cost 2,662 casualties plus a further 1,289 from combat fatigue. The 29th Marines had to be relieved by the 4th Marines. However, just as the relief had taken place the Japanese launched a battalion-size raid which would have broken the line but for the Marines' calling on every man who could wield a weapon to hold his position. And there the 6th Marine Division stayed. Any progress on the front was dependent upon the activities of the 1st Marine Division which was engaged on the Shuri Heights.

The 1st Division had been struggling to take the areas around Dakeshi Ridge, Wana Ridge and Wana Draw but without success. The Japanese positions were mutually supporting and the defenders' clever use of the reverse slopes caused heavy losses. Dakeshi Ridge fell on 11 May after an ingenious outflanking movement using armour had caught the Japanese exposed on the reverse slopes—evidence that the frontal assault favoured by the Tenth Army was not always the best way of beating the Japanese. Thereafter Japanese resistance stiffened and the

Marines' casualty figures rose. Despite tanks, self-propelled artillery, naval gunfire support and air strikes, the 7th Marines lost 1,000 casualties and had to be relieved by the 1st Marines; the regiment was subsequently awarded a Presidential Unit Citation for the bravery and determination shown by its officers and men in this fighting. The problem facing the Americans was that the Japanese were well positioned in the sheer rock face of Wana Draw. The Marines were having to pay for every yard of ground gained and their hard-won but tenuous holding positions were acutely vulnerable to sudden, savage Japanese counter-attacks.

The same problem was faced by XXIV Corps in the centre of the island. Here two regiments of the 77th Division were edging slowly down a long valley east of Route Five. The 305th and 306th Infantry Regiments encountered fierce resistance and rough terrain, the former losing 75 per cent of its strength during this period.

The breakthrough finally came on the left of the Tenth Army alongside Nagagusuku Wan in the sector occupied by the 96th Infantry Division. The key to the Japanese defence in this area was a position known as Conical Hill. It was the usual warren of caves, bunkers and artillery strongpoints, but on 14 May elements of the 383rd Infantry, to the complete surprise of their Divisional, Corps and Army commands, managed to seize and hold the eastern slopes of the hill. This development meant that, with their left flank covered by bombardment from the sea and with US infantry digging in on the east slopes of Conical Hill, the 7th Division, returning to duty, could pour down a narrow corridor in the centre. General Buckner was optimistic, remarking that 'if the 7th can swing round, running the gauntlet, it may be the kill.'[5]

The 7th began their attack on the 19 May at night and in foul weather, moving quickly through the town of Yonabaru. The American attack, using unsupported infantry, took the Japanese—evidently used to more sophisticated American assaults—completely by surprise. The 184th Infantry tore a gap 2,000 yards wide in the Japanese line which was left to the 32nd Infantry to exploit. However, the weather took a hand in proceedings: torrential rain turned such roads as existed into quagmires, making it impossible for the Americans to use tanks or self-propelled artillery. The infantry encountered heavy and accurate Japanese fire and their advance slowed and, on 26 May, halted.

Nevertheless, the American breakthrough, stalled as it was, caused Ushijima to reconsider his position. He had been told by Lieutenant-General Miyazaki Suichi, at IGHQ in Tokyo, that there would be no reinforcements and no shipments of supplies. Ushijima now considered the three options open to him. The first was to gather all his troops and make a last-ditch stand at Shuri. This he rejected on the grounds that such a course would end in swift defeat and thus drastically shorten the time available to those preparing the defence of the Home Islands. Secondly, he could retreat to the Chinen Peninsula, but this course was also rejected because the area was insufficiently prepared for defence. Lastly, there was a retreat to the Kan Peninsula, an area which had already been prepared by the 24th Division and where stocks of supplies and ammunition already existed. This was the course he chose. Orders were given for core elements of the 62nd and 24th Divisions and the 44th Independent Mixed Brigade to fall back to the positions on the Yaeju Dake–Yuza Dake Ridge line, leaving skeleton formations to defend Shuri. After that there could be no more retreat. At the same time, units of the Japanese Navy holding the Oroku Peninsula in the west of the island were ordered to fall back and join the co-ordinated defence.

The Americans assumed all along that Ushijima would make a last stand at Shuri. Thus when, on 26 May, large numbers of personnel and trucks were seen heading south, it was considered that these were civilians being evacuated. Despite reports of evacuated Japanese positions facing the 7th Division, Buckner still considered that Shuri held the key to the Japanese defence and even contemplated the possibility that the Japanese were massing for a counter-offensive. He therefore gave no orders to exploit the Japanese withdrawal, allowing Ushijima precious time to slip away once again.

Suddenly, at the end of May, Japanese resistance around Shuri crumbled. The Americans began to advance swiftly—so swiftly that the 1st Marine Division moved into the sector occupied by the 77th Infantry Division and narrowly escaped an air strike called down in support of the latter. On 1 June Shuri fell to the 1st Marine Division, although its capture was hardly a cause for celebration. The town was a mass of rubble strewn with rotting corpses—a 'crater of the moon landscape', in the words of the US Army's Official History.

In the two months since the Americans had landed on Okinawa the cost in lives and equipment had been immense. They had lost 26,044 killed, wounded or missing, with nearly 15,000 cases of combat fatigue. Forty-three per cent of US armour had been destroyed as well as twelve of the armoured flame-throwers—immensely valuable in flushing out defenders from their caves. However, the American figures pale into insignificance when considering the Japanese casualties. The Americans stated that 62,548 Japanese had been killed and counted on the island, with at least another 10,000 killed. Yet the number of prisoners taken in this period was less than 200—proof of the determination of the Japanese defenders.

Buckner was confident that the fall of Shuri meant the end of organized Japanese resistance on the island:

> . . . it's all over now but cleaning up pockets of resistance. This doesn't mean there won't be stiff fighting, but the Japs won't be able to organize another line.[6]

However, he reckoned without the skill and determination of Ushijima and his staff who, aided by the foul weather, had withdrawn to their positions four miles south of Shuri. Accordingly, when Buckner launched his next offensive, which was a circling movement designed to link up XXIV Corps and III Amphibious Corps at Chan, south of Shuri, and destroy the Japanese forces to the north, he found that the enemy had escaped. Buckner had no more imaginative plan than to resume the advance south on a two-corps front. His advance was also being frustrated by the weather. The island's inadequate roads could not cope with the mass of American wheeled and tracked traffic and, after heavy rain, had dissolved into quagmires reminiscent of the Western Front in the Great War. Despite herculean efforts by Army and Marine engineers to stabilize the roads with hardcore and the use of amphibious vehicles and coastal transport, only a trickle of supplies made their way south.

While XXIV Corps and the 1st Marine Division pressed southwards, the 6th Marine Division swung round to seal off the Oroku Peninsula. The assault was made by sea across the Kokuba River south of Naha. The Peninsula had originally been evacuated by

Japanese Navy forces under the command of Rear-Admiral Ota Minoru. However, on reaching their assigned defensive positions in the Kan Peninsula, Ota's men found them unprepared and lacking in weapons—and they had destroyed theirs in the evacuation of Oroku. Ota pleaded with Ushijima to be allowed to return to Oroku and make a final stand there. Ushijima felt that he could not refuse Ota's request and so the sailors returned to Oroku. The to-and-fro movements of these men undoubtedly confused the Americans as to the Japanese' intentions.

Again the Japanese had chosen not to make a stand on the beaches, and the 4th Marines were soon well established ashore. In the interior of the Peninsula the fighting was bitter. Private Robert M. McTureous of H Company, 29th Marines, was posthumously awarded the Medal of Honor after making two lone grenade attacks on Japanese bunkers after which he died of his wounds. McTureous was a battle casualty replacement who had been with the company only seven days—proof that 'uncommon valour was a common virtue'.

By 9 June the Marines had squeezed the Japanese into a small pocket and on 12 June the final stronghold was taken. Thereafter individual Japanese parties were pursued until the Peninsula was declared secure on 14 June. More than 4,000 Japanese had been killed, including Ota and his staff, who had committed suicide. American casualties, at 1,608, were greater than those suffered in the taking of Shuri. The sailors, only partly trained in infantry tactics and lacking heavy weapons, had managed to conduct a successful delaying action, fully in accordance with their code of resistance to the end.

In the main portion of the island, Ushijima had deployed the 8,000 remaining men of the 24th Division across his centre and west flank, its line stretching from the town of Itoman on the west coast to Yaeju Dake. The remaining 3,000 men of the 32nd Division were in reserve, while the 44th Independent Mixed Brigade held the right flank facing the US 7th Division. Ushijima had managed to hold his forces together, preventing their disintegration and a collapse of morale, in preparation for one last stand. His troops knew that there could be no further retreats and that they would fight to the end and die where they stood.

June 1 found the 96th and 7th Divisions trudging south through thick mud which made a nonsense of their orders to advance. Even so, it was apparent that the Japanese forces ranged against them were not of the calibre of those encountered earlier in the campaign. The Japanese would increasingly evacuate positions in the face of an American attack and were mown down by superior US firepower.

From 3 June it became clear that the Chinen Peninsula would not have to be cleared as there were no concentrations of Japanese forces there. However, on the west coast a 3,000-yard gap had opened up between the 1st Marine Division and the 96th Division on account of the Marines' being delayed. Hodges ordered the 305th Infantry to close the gap and protect the right flank of the 96th Division. At the same time the boundary between XXIV and III Corps was shifted westwards, so that the whole of the Japanese position around Yaeju and Yuza Dake fell within XXIV Corps' front.

Yaeju Dake fell during the night of 11/12 June after an assault in the darkness by the 17th Infantry (7th Division). Yuza Dake fell to the 96th Division on 16 June after a stout defence. From Yuza Peak to the sea ran Kunishi Ridge. On 10 June this position was attacked by the 1st Marine Division. Three days and some fierce fighting later, the Marines had three companies established on the seaward end of the ridge but were pinned down. Supplies were running short and air drops had to be made, while tanks made the dangerous journey to evacuate the wounded. Further assaults proved equally unsuccessful: an initial advance would grind to a halt in the face of machine-gun fire. But the final outcome was inevitable: on 17 June the defence began to disintegrate and, as the ground dried, more use could be made of armour in supporting the Marines and in ferrying supplies up to the line and taking the wounded out.

June 17 marked the end of organized resistance by the 32nd Army on Okinawa. The Japanese had been ceaselessly pounded by artillery and naval gunfire, and from the air, and under this onslaught, together with the continual infantry attacks, their line began to give way. Not even the stoutest of defences could withstand such a violent assault indefinitely. The officers and men of the 24th Division maintained their cohesion for four more days before they too broke up into individual groups. Ushijima had anticipated this trend when on 18 June he ordered his men to disperse and form guerrilla units. Formal opposition to the

Americans was now useless: Japanese casualties were running at 4,000 killed per day and guerrilla warfare seemed to be the only method by which the campaign of attrition could continue.

That Japanese resistance was crumbling was shown in the increasing number of those surrendering: 50 between 12 and 18 June, 343 on 19 June and 997 on 21 June—the largest number of Japanese taken prisoner in the Pacific on a single occasion. Not all Japanese chose captivity. Many killed themselves, some flinging themselves over the cliffs into the sea. General Ushijima and General Cho chose to take their own lives in the traditional bloody fashion rather than surrender. Both men had rejected an appeal by Buckner to save their lives:

> The forces under your command have fought bravely and well, and your infantry tactics have merited the respect of your opponent . . . like myself you are an infantry General long schooled and practiced in infantry warfare . . . I believe, therefore, that you understand as clearly as I that the destruction of all Japanese resistance is merely a matter of days.[7]

The note was contemptuously rejected. Even as American troops massed outside their command 'cave', Ushijima and Cho disembowelled themselves before being decapitated by their aides. The wily Colonel Yahara became a prisoner of war, as did Lieutenant Hidara:

> Quite simply, I had had enough. All around me, soldiers were throwing themselves over cliffs and shooting themselves. Others were taking their lives in the more traditional and ritualistic way. I was too tired to even consider it as an option. I had been continuously in action since the beginning of April and all I wanted more than anything else was sleep, some hot food and a chance to rest. Consequently when an American patrol of Marines came my way, I gave myself up. Contrary to my expectations I was treated well.[8]

Buckner did not live long to savour his victory. While visiting a forward observation post on 18 June in the 1st Marine Division's sector, a Japanese shell exploded near the OP, spraying it with pieces of razor sharp coral. One of these pieces pierced Buckner's chest, wounding him fatally. Nimitz immediately appointed Major-General Roy Geiger USMC, Commander of III Amphibious Corps, as Acting Commander of the Tenth Army—the first occasion on which a Marine General held command of an army in the field. Geiger led the Tenth Army in the final days of the campaign on Okinawa until 23 June, when General Joseph ('Vinegar Joe') Stilwell USA assumed command.

Before Stilwell arrived, the Tenth Army conducted mopping-up operations against the Japanese forces, which now consisted of little more than a mass of armed men milling about the southern part of the island. On 22 June formal resistance was declared to be at an end.

NOTES TO CHAPTER 7

1. Intensive mining by the Japanese meant that the airstrip was not ready for use until 13 May 1945.
2. Tomiichi Hidara to author, 29 September 1993.
3. Moskin, J. Robert, *The US Marine Corps Story*, Little Brown (1992), p.383.
4. Hidara to author, 29 September 1993.
5. Gow, Ian, *Okinawa 1945: Gateway to Japan*, Grub Street Press (1986), p.160.
6. Gow, p.171.
7. Gow, p.188.
8. Hidara to author, 29 September 1993.

The Battle of the East China Sea

*If you are asked what is the heart of Yamato, reply that it is
the scent of the wild cherry in the Rising Sun.*—Japanese
proverb.

D URING the consolidation of the beach-head and the
subsequent advance inland, the fast carriers had played
a defensive role by protecting the troops ashore and the
shipping anchored around Okinawa with an umbrella of aircraft.
As Admiral Spruance subsequently wrote:

> The achievement of Task Force 58 (and Task Group 52.1 composed
> of CVEs) in staying within easy aircraft range, under almost
> constant Japanese aerial reconnaissance, for a period of more than
> 70 days while furnishing direct air support to the landings on
> Okinawa, target CAP, own CAP, aerial interdiction of Japanese
> suiciders en route to Okinawa, plus several strikes on Kyushu
> itself, all without losing a single ship sunk, is one which needs no
> comment.[1]

While it is true that the no ships in TF.58 were sunk, the price paid
for this achievement was heavy. Eight carriers, four battleships,
four cruisers and sixteen destroyers suffered damage while out on
the left flank all four British carriers of TF.57 were damaged. But
if, in the parlance of the day, the carriers had to stand and take
it, they also gave as good as they got. The landings were not
a week old when the opportunity came to perform an operation in
keeping with their proper function of reaching out across the
ocean to deliver heavy, co-ordinated air strikes. The great Japanese air strikes of 6 April had just finished when word was
received that capital ships of the Japanese fleet were heading
south.

The Japanese plan for the defence of Okinawa, *Ten-Go*, directed
the remaining surface forces of the fleet to make use of favourable

opportunities to penetrate the Okinawa anchorage using suicide tactics if required. Following the successful landings on Okinawa, IGHQ was requested by Ushijima to strike back at the Americans and in particular to do something to compensate for the loss of the airfields at Yontan and Kadena. Acting on this request, Admiral Soemu Toyoda, Commander-in-Chief of the Combined Fleet, resolved to launch a combined air–sea offensive against the invaders using VI Air Army and all naval forces under his command together with such surface forces which could be gathered together.

Accordingly, on 4 April Admiral Toyoda directed Vice-Admiral Ito Seichi, Commander-in-Chief Second Fleet, to prepare for the operation. Ito's first plan had been to lure the American carriers to within range of land-based aircraft, but this was abandoned after heavy American air raids on southern Kyushu. Ito then changed the plan to a swing to the west away from the American carriers, followed by a high-speed dash down the west coast of Okinawa so as to be off the Hagushi beaches by dawn on 8 April. It was hoped that the battleship *Yamato* and her consorts would be able to finish off the few surviving ships after the mass air attacks which preceded the sortie. After firing off all their ammunition, the crews were to beach the ships and make their way ashore and join the island's defenders as naval infantry. There was no question of *Yamato* or any of her consorts returning from this operation.

The chances of success were not considered high, but the spirit of the operation, known as *Ten-Ichi* ('Ten One'), was in keeping with the Japanese tradition of the last desperate charge. Before the ships sailed Admiral Toyoda issued the following message:

> . . . The fate of our Empire depends on this one action. I order the Special Attack Force to carry out on Okinawa the most tragic and heroic attack of the war. We shall concentrate our Imperial naval forces on this action and give full play to the brilliant tradition of the Imperial Navy's Sea Force and make its glory remembered for ever.[2]

Although Ito had a large number of ships at his disposal, the crippling fuel shortage meant that he could only take a small number to sea. He chose to fly his flag in *Yamato* (Rear-Admiral Ariga Kosaku IJN), which would be escorted by the light cruiser *Yahagi* and the destroyers *Fuyutsuki*, *Suzutsuki*, *Isokaze*,

Hamakaze, *Yukikaze*, *Asashimo*, *Hatsushimo* and *Kasumi*. Two and a half thousand tons of fuel would be needed to take these ships on the one-way trip to Okinawa, and this requirement strained the resources of the Japanese Navy to the limit. The war of attrition waged on Japanese tanker traffic by American submarines meant that fuel oil, especially the heavy furnace oil required by warships, was in very short supply. The Imperial Navy's fuel depot at Tokuyama in Tokyo Bay was ransacked and eventually the great tanks were drained by chain gangs of sailors using buckets passed from hand to hand.

Yamato and her sister ship *Musashi* (the latter was sunk on 24 October 1944) were the world's largest battleships. *Yamato* displaced 62,315 tons standard and 69,990 tons at full load. Everything about her was superlative. Her main armament consisted of nine 18.1-inch guns disposed in three triple turrets, each barrel firing a 3,219lb shell at a muzzle velocity of 2,575 feet per second to a range of 45,960 yards. Her vitals were protected by an armour belt 16 inches thick and by a 9-inch thick armoured deck. She was powered by four steam turbines developing 150,000 horsepower. Despite her great bulk, her top speed was 27.5 knots and she was an extremely handy ship with a very small turning circle. One of the most notable features of *Yamato*'s design was that her displacement-to-length ratio was great and that her speed-to-length ratio small in comparison with other battleships. Moreover her block coefficient was 0.612, perhaps the highest figure among all the battleships of the world. This produced a ship which had immense beam and shallow draught for such a large displacement. Considerable attention was paid to eliminating water resistance around the hull by the construction of a large bulbous bow and by improving the fitting of shaft brackets and bilge keels. The savings achieved by these measures represented the equivalent of 15,820shp. Above all, *Yamato* was a stunningly attractive ship, with a sharply raked bow dominated by a rosette depicting the chrysanthemum, the Imperial emblem, and with the upper deck sweeping aft without a break. Unlike the ungainly pagoda-like superstructures of other Japanese capital ships, *Yamato*'s bridge was streamlined and compact.

The major handicap under which the ships sailed was that they had no air cover. All available aircraft were required for the strikes on the American carriers and none could be spared for providing

CAP over *Yamato*. Other than the appearance of one or two seaplanes on anti-submarine patrol and of fighters sent between 0630 and 1000, the Special Attack Force could count on seeing no friendly aircraft.

The ships sailed on 6 April at 1520 accompanied for an hour by the destroyers *Hamatsuki, Kaya* and *Maki* as an anti-submarine screen. Rear-Admiral Ariga (*Yamato* was unusual in that she was commanded by a Flag Officer) had cleared lower decks on sailing and explained the operation to the crew. Morale was high, and during the voyage through the Inland Sea the crew were occupied in throwing overboard any superfluous items or fittings which would burn in the event of a fire.

At 2010 on the 6th the American submarine *Threadfin* reported the ships emerging at high speed from the Bungo Suido, the narrow channel between Kyushu and Shikoku. A second submarine, the USS *Hackleback*, gained contact shortly afterwards and stayed in touch despite some half-hearted attempts by one of the escorting destroyers to force her down. Although the range was too great for a torpedo attack, *Threadfin* remained in contact until 2345, by which time her commanding officer had accurately assessed the force as two large ships escorted by six or more destroyers steering 215° down the east coat of Kyushu at a speed of 22 knots. Both submarines were hampered by a restriction requiring them to report large surface contacts to Pearl Harbor before attacking. Much time was lost waiting for an acknowledgement to their reports, and when at 2300 this restriction was belatedly lifted, the feelings of the submarines' commanding officers can be imagined

On hearing of the sortie of the Japanese ships, Admiral Spruance ordered Rear-Admiral Deyo to form a task group from his bombardment battleships and be ready to take on *Yamato*. At this stage Spruance made no move to alert Mitscher's carriers, preferring to see them continue with their opwerations against targets on Okinawa. Accordingly, Deyo formed a line of battle using the six most modern battleships under his command—*Idaho, New Mexico, Tennessee, West Virginia, Maryland* and *Colarado*—screened by the Right Flank Forces (three cruisers and eleven destroyers) and the Left Flank Forces (four cruisers and ten destroyers). The battleships hurriedly embarked supplies of armour-piercing ammunition as opposed to the HE they had been using for shore bombardment, and at 1530 on 7 April Deyo took his ships to sea for a position north-west of Okinawa and began practising line-of-battle tactics. The more perceptive gunnery officers noted that, although the Americans possessed greater numbers, the *Yamato*'s 18.1-inch guns had a range of 45,000 yards as against 42,000 yards for the 16-inch gun ships in Deyo's force and 37,000 for *Tennessee*. The possibility existed that *Yamato* could hold the American ships off at extreme range and still get in amongst the transports. While these exercises were in progress, the ships were attacked by a lone Japanese aircraft which, braving the AA barrage put up by the cruisers and destroyers of the Right Flank Force, dropped a bomb on *Maryland* which put one of her 14-inch turrets out of action.

The three Task Groups of TF.58 were operating in their usual position to the east of Okinawa; the fourth group, TF.58.2, was absent fuelling from the tankers of TG.50.8 and, after completing fuelling early in the morning of 7 April, headed at high speed to rejoin the rest of Admiral Mitscher's carriers but arrived too late to take part in the subsequent action. Mitscher was obviously privy to the signal traffic concerning *Yamato*'s sortie and had no intention of letting the battleships claim the credit for sinking her. While his intelligence officers offered predictions of likely Japanese intentions—which, in the event, concurred entirely with the Japanese' plans—Mitscher's ships raced northwards ready to launch a strike during the morning of the 7th.

In the event, Deyo's preparations proved unnecessary. After passing through the Bungo Suido, Ito headed west through Van Diemen Strait, separating Kyushu from the island of Tanega Shima, hoping to put as much distance as possible between his ships and the American carriers. In this he was unsuccessful, for at 0815 on 7 April his ships were sighted by a reconnaissance aircraft from the carrier USS *Essex*, the flagship of TG.58.3 commanded by Rear-Admiral F. C. Sherman USN.

Sherman had ordered a Special Tracking Team launched at dawn consisting of sixteen Hellcats with four Marine Corps Corsairs to act as communications links between the ships and the aircraft, to shadow and report the movements of the enemy. The Tracking Team picked up *Yamato* at 0815 and remained in contact despite drawing heavy gunfire, including some blind-barrage salvoes fired from the battleship's 18.1-inch guns using

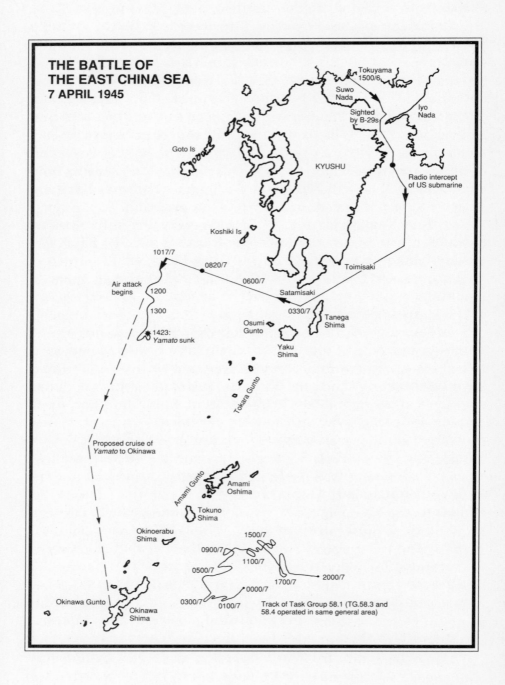

**THE BATTLE OF
THE EAST CHINA SEA
7 APRIL 1945**

Tokuyama
1500/6

Suwo
Nada

Sighted
by B-29s

Iyo
Nada

Goto Is

KYUSHU

Radio intercept
of US submarine

Koshiki Is

1017/7

0820/7

Toimisaki

Air attack
begins

1200

0600/7

Satamisaki

1300

0330/7

Tanega
Shima

1423:
Yamato sunk

Osumi
Gunto

Yaku
Shima

Tokara Gunto

Proposed cruise of
Yamato to Okinawa

Amami Gunto

Amami
Oshima

Tokuno
Shima

Okinoerabu
Shima

1500/7

0900/7

1100/7

0500/7

1700/7

2000/7

0000/7

Okinawa Gunto

0300/7

0100/7

Okinawa
Shima

Track of Task Group 58.1 (TG.58.3 and
58.4 operated in same general area)

the *San-Shiki* anti-aircraft shell (a modern form of grapeshot). The enemy were reported as one battleship with one or two light cruisers escorted by seven to eight destroyers in 30°44'N 129°10'E, proceeding at 12 knots. This position was too far to the south. A second report at 0823 gave their position as 31°22'N 129°15'E., but this was too far to the north, the actual position of *Yamato* at 0600 having been 31°00'N 129°51'E, course 290°.

The weather over *Yamato* was poor, with a ceiling at 3,000 feet and visibility 5 to 8 miles with occasional rain squalls. At 1017 Ito suddenly swung his ships to the south to 240° to head for Okinawa. The alteration of course was noted and confirmed that Okinawa was where the Japanese force was heading rather than towards Sasebo for a change of fleet base as had been thought.

Now that his ships' aircraft were in contact with *Yamato*, Mitscher felt it safe to reveal his intentions. At 1045 he signalled to Spruance that he was in position and proposed to launch a strike to attack *Yamato* at 1200 and asked, 'Will you take them or shall I?'

The sighting of the Japanese ships by *Essex's* aircraft placed Admiral Spruance in something of a dilemma. Japanese intentions were not clear, and he had the choice either of releasing Mitscher's aircraft to attack and sink the ships, with no guarantee that the reconnaissance aircraft could maintain contact with the Japanese ships or that the strike aircraft would find her, or of waiting until *Yamato* was within range of Deyo, knowing that she was faster and possessed of superior armament and that Deyo's ships were not properly worked-up in surface combat tactics. However, Spruance was never a man to shirk a decision and he signalled to Mitscher, 'You take them'.

Mitscher wasted no time. From 1000 onwards his carriers launched a massive strike of 380 aircraft of all types—fighters, fighter-bombers, torpedo bombers and bombers. At the time of launching the enemy bore approximately 345°, distance 250 miles from TG.58.1 and TG.58.3 and 273 miles from TG.58.4. Mitscher ordered the aircraft from TG.58.1 and 3 to attack first, in co-ordinated fashion, followed by the aircraft from TG.58.4 which had launched at 1045.

The first aircraft from TG.58.1, the carriers *San Jacinto*, *Bennington*, *Hornet* and *Belleau Wood*, found *Yamato* shortly after midday. The strike was under the command of Commander

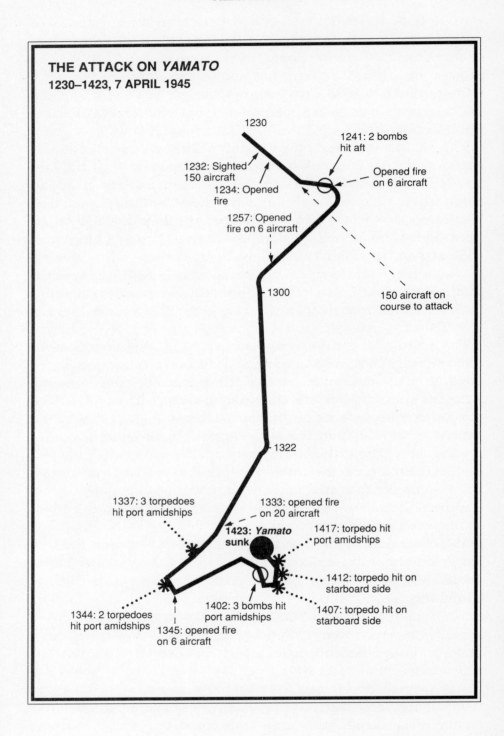

THE ATTACK ON *YAMATO*
1230–1423, 7 APRIL 1945

1230

1232: Sighted
150 aircraft

1234: Opened
fire

1257: Opened
fire on 6 aircraft

1241: 2 bombs
hit aft

Opened fire
on 6 aircraft

1300

150 aircraft on
course to attack

1322

1337: 3 torpedoes
hit port amidships

1333: opened fire
on 20 aircraft

1423: *Yamato*
sunk

1417: torpedo hit
port amidships

1412: torpedo hit on
starboard side

1344: 2 torpedoes
hit port amidships

1345: opened fire
on 6 aircraft

1402: 3 bombs hit
port amidships

1407: torpedo hit on
starboard side

Edward G. Konrad USN from *Hornet*, who, together with his three wingmen, was flying an unarmed Hellcat. Konrad's job was to ensure that the aircraft were properly allocated amongst the targets and that the pilots did not succumb to the perfectly natural desire to concentrate on the battleship. The strike force included almost every aircraft in service during the Pacific War: F4U Corsair fighters which could also carry a 2,000lb bomb load, SB2C-1 Helldiver dive-bombers, F4F Wildcat fighters, F64 Hell-cat fighters and TBMF-1 Avenger torpedo bombers. The attack on the Japanese ships would see dive bombers coming in first to distract the AA gunners while the torpedo bombers made their long approach at 300 feet to drop their torpedoes, 1,200 yards from the target and in a spread which the target could not evade, whatever tactics might be employed.

The Japanese ships were disposed in three groups. To the north was the destroyer *Asashimo*, apparently deployed as a radar picket but stopped with engine trouble. The cruiser *Yahagi* together with *Hatsushimo*, *Isokaze* and *Fuyutsuki* were streaking ahead of *Yamato* in an attempt to divide the attackers. The AA barrage put up by the Japanese ships was heavy and consisted of blind, predicted concentration and continuously pointed fire. Again *Yamato* used her main armament, and great bursts of black smoke from the explosion of the *San-Shiki* shells followed the aircraft on retiring out to a distance of 12 to 14 miles.

In the accounts of the attacks which followed there are consid-erable differences in the numbers of bombs and torpedoes which hit *Yamato*. This is inevitable given the circumstances under which the attacks were conducted, with air crews operating under some pressure and at great speed. The simultaneous detonation of bombs and torpedoes is another factor likely to mask the true number of hits. There is equal confusion on the Japanese side, particularly as so many of *Yamato*'s crew, including most of the command, did not survive the sinking of the ship.

The first attack was made by a group of four Helldivers from *Bennington* which went in at 1241 and scored two hits aft with bombs. Konrad sent the remaining six Helldivers from *Bennington* after the escorts, and these aircraft sank the stationary *Asashimo* and damaged *Kasumi*. A lone Corsair pilot, Lieutenant Kenneth E. Huntingdon USMC, hurtled after *Yahagi* and dropped his bomb on her forecastle. Huntingdon was awarded the Navy Cross for his almost suicidal bravery. Another pilot, Lieutenant-Commander E. W. Hessel, found that the bomb on his Hellcat was hung up after his first strafing run, but, undeterred, he went around for a second time, only to see the bomb fall alongside a destroyer without exploding.

The fighters from *Hornet* were busy with flak-suppression runs over the escorts before beginning their bombing runs on *Yamato*. They scored four hits on the battleship, two on the superstructure, one on the bow and the last on the flight deck aft. Elsewhere three hits were claimed on *Yahagi* and one each on the four destroyers. At 1243 *Hamakaze* rolled over and exploded.

The first torpedo bomber strike, mounted by Avengers from *Bennington*, found that they could not attack *Yamato* because their torpedoes were set to shallow and thus would be wasted against the massive side armour of the battleship. Since in nearly all the aircraft the radio operator had been left behind in order to increase the weight of fuel that could be carried, there was no one who could adjust the setting in mid-air. Three of the Avengers, led by the Squadron Commander, Lieutenant-Commander Ed de Garno USN, went after and scored one hit on her starboard bow and a second on her port quarter.

Avengers from *Hornet* scored another two hits on *Yamato*. By now *Yahagi* was immobilized and *Hamakaze* had sunk. The last attack from TG.58.1 was by aircraft from *Belleau Wood*, since *San Jacinto*'s aircraft were occupied elsewhere, finishing off *Asashimo*. The destroyer was sunk in less than three minutes. The results of this attack were that at 1241 *Yamato* was struck by three torpedoes all on the port side, two between Frames 125 and 150 and the third at frame 190. The ship was also struck by four bombs, all around 'Y' 18.1-inch turret. She assumed a 5–6-degree list to port, which was almost immediately corrected by counter-flooding. Two of the four bombs hit the top of Frame 150 on the starboard side of the weather deck, destroying the 12.7cm HA mounting and blowing a large hole (some accounts say as big as six metres in diameter) in the flying deck. Many of the 25mm close-range guns were knocked out in this blast. The other two bombs followed the first pair after about five minutes. One of them passed through the after 15.5cm fire control station, wrecking the director. Both penetrated the flying and upper decks and exploded above the main armour belt. The after 15.5cm turret was destroyed with only one survivor and a fire was started which was never extinguished and which may well have been the cause of the explosion which subsequently sank the ship. Fire-fighting and damage control were haphazard and ineffective.

The aircraft from TG.58.1 had been in action over the Japanese ships for a little over twenty minutes. Now Konrad handed over control to Commander Harmon G. Utter USN of the USS *Essex*, leading in the second strike from TG.58.3, the carriers *Essex*, *Bataan*, *Bunker Hill*, *Cabot* and *Hancock*. In the event, the aircraft from *Hancock* were not engaged since, having launched later than the others, they failed to find the target. Both Konrad and Utter found it hard to direct attacks on to *Yamato* since frequent squalls often hid the ship from view, but there were some breaks in the murk. Utter ordered in the first strike of torpedo bombers from *Essex* against the battleship. The aircraft attacked in three waves and, as they made their approach, *Yamato* began to swing to starboard, presenting the entire length of her port side to her attackers. As before, the Americans found the AA fire put up by the Japanese to be intense and accurate. Utter recalled that

> Bomber pilots rushed about in all sorts of crazy dives. fighter pilots used every maneouvre in the book, torpedo pilots stuck their neck out, dropped right down onto the surface and delivered their parcels so near the ships that many of the planes missed the ships' superstructures by inches.[3]

Aircraft from the other three carriers delivered equally devastating attacks, claiming another six hits between them—a figure which was somehwat exaggerated, if understandable given the confusion of the action.

In the second attack *Yamato* was hit by three torpedoes on her port side, on Frames 143, 124 and 131, and one on the starboard side, on Frame 124; there was a further, unconfirmed hit on the port side on Frame 148. The three hits on the port side caused Nos 8 and 12 boiler rooms, the port outboard engine room and the port hydraulic machinery room to flood immediately. Again, the ship assumed a list to port, which was corrected by further counter-flooding. All the compartments on the starboard side which could be flooded to correct the list had now been flooded, and the ship's speed fell off to 18 knots. There were a number of hits by bombs which did negligible damage.

No sooner had the aircraft from TG.58.3 finished their attacks —thirty minutes was all they spent over the area—than the aircraft from TG.58.4 (*Intrepid*, *Yorktown* and *Langley*) were circling, waiting to pounce. They had had the furthest distance to come and, as a result, their formations had become confused, with several groups failing to make contact. Commander W. E. Rawrie USN, the strike controller, found it impossible to rally his forces in the foul weather and with poor radio and radar communications. Consequently he presided over what amounted to a final free-for-all over *Yamato*—which was none the less effective for that. Despite Nimitz's stringent orders banning target controllers from participating in strikes, Rawrie found himself lining up with other pilots for an attack on *Yamato*. However, Lieutenant-Commander Herbert N. Houck USN, from *Yorktown*, gathered together a miscellany of aircraft from the different groups of TG.58.4, sent them against the crippled *Yahagi* and sank her.

Intrepid's fourteen dive-bombers headed for *Yamato*, which was now moving at slow speed though her AA armament was still firing accurately. Conditions were appalling, but a number of hits were observed on the battleship's upper deck.

Lieutenant-Commander Tom Stetson's torpedo bombers from *Yorktown* had been assigned to *Yahagi*, but she had sunk by the time they reached the target. Instead, Stetson went after *Yamato*. He noticed that the battleship was listing further and further to port, so much so that her red underbelly was clearly visible on her starboard side. Stetson realized that torpedo hits on her vulnerable starboard side would tear the bottom of out of the ship, so, while his aircraft cirlced overhead, observers fantically altered the depth settings on their torpedoes from 10 feet to between 18 and 22 feet. *Yorktown*'s aircraft made two approach runs before Stetson was satisfied. Four of the six aircraft went in line abreast with the other two following behind, and at least two hits were observed.

This attack was the *coup de grâce*. Three hits were scored on the port side at Frames 135, 154 and 164 and one on Frame 150 to starboard. Admiral Ariga ordered the starboard machinery spaces flooded to counter the list, but the flooding only served to reduce the ship's speed and make her lower in the water. The hit on the starboard side had caused a leak in the starboard outboard engine room and those on the port side had flooded the inboard port boiler room and port inboard engine room. The list began to increase and it became impossible for the armament to be worked. *Yamato* was steaming in a large circle, and shortly after 1400 all power was lost.

Conditions on board the huge vessel at this stage were horrific. The upper deck was a shambles of twisted metal and disabled gun positions. Below decks things were even worse, with smashed and flooded compartments packed with dead and wounded. One survivor spoke of seeing the large communal baths favoured by the Japanese filled with dead bodies. Shortly after 1400 Admiral Ariga gave the order to abandon ship, although he remained on board together with Admiral Ito. The Navigating Officer lashed himself to the binnacle on the bridge while many others took their own lives in a final gesture of defiance. Shortly after the order to abandon ship was given *Yamato* began to sink by the head with a list of 90°. When she reached an angle of 120° a gigantic explosion tore her apart, the consequent huge cloud of smoke reaching a ceiling of 6,000 feet and being seen by sentries on Kagoshima, more than 120 miles away:

> In the sea a cone formed 160 feet deep and boiled around the battleship as she settled heavily. The big shells, escaping from their racks, fell into the magazines with a dull rolling sound. Bulkheads burst in, and explosions sounded in the depths of the vessel like the last beatings of an injured heart. Suddenly came a convulsive swirl, and a tongue of flame licked high into the sky, announcing to Kagoshima that the *Yamato* was no more. With her died the Imperial Navy.[4]

Three thousand and sixty three officers and men went down with her, leaving only 269 to be rescued. All the survivors came from positions on the upper deck. There are two theories as to the cause of the explosion. First, the *San-Shiki* shells may have rolled over when the ship capsized and struck the deck, the impact setting off their fuzes. However, post-war tests conducted by the Americans showed that this would have been unlikely. The second, more likely hypothesis is that the fire at the after end of the ship spread to the magazines via the hoists, which could have been opened by the weight of falling projectiles and other debris as the ship rolled over.

The destroyer *Kasumi*, which had been damaged in the first attack, sank at 1657 and *Isokaze* had to be scuttled at 2240 after her crew had been taken off. Thus, of the force which had made the forlorn sortie, only *Fuyutsuki*, *Yukikaze*, Suyutsuki and *Hatsushimo* returned to Japan.

There was much criticism in Japan after the war of the decision to send *Yamato* and her escorts on the operation without air cover. Admiral Toyoda, then Commander-in-Chief of the Combined Fleet, justified the operation:

> I knew very well what the fate would be of warships without air cover, and that the probability of success would be very slight. For all that we had to venture this recklessness. I thought that if there was slim chance of success, we had to do everything to help our troops on Okinawa.[5]

At 1340 Mitscher ordered that no further strikes be made against the enemy force and that the carriers revert to their planned operations against installations on Amami Oshima. American losses were very light—nine aircraft, the pilot of one being rescued by a PBY. In the meantime, before the aircraft returned to the carriers, the Japanese launched a heavy air attack against TF.58 at noon. Eighteen of the attackers were destroyed, fifteen by CAP and three by AA fire. However, at 1211 one aircraft managed to penetrate the defences and headed for *Hancock*. The pilot came over the flight at a height of 50 feet, releasing his bomb on to the flight deck before crashing into a group of aircraft ranged at the after end of the deck. A large hole was blown in the flight deck, the forward lift was buckled upwards by 18 inches and the hangar deck was dished. Twenty-eight men were killed and 52 wounded. Once again, the American passion for damage control paid off: fires were extinguished and at 1615 the ship was able to recover her aircraft by manual operation of the barriers. *Hancock* remained with TF.58 until the next replenishment period, when she was detached to Ulithi for repairs.

* * *

In August 1985 the wreck of *Yamato* was surveyed. The great ship lies in position 128°04'W 30°43'N in 200 fathoms of water. Her stern section lies upside down, with the midships portion horribly twisted and distorted. The bow section lies on its starboard side, with 'B' turret still in its mounting. A large mass of twisted wreckage, possibly the bridge structure, lies off the port side of the wreck, while either 'A' or 'Y' turret lies upside down off the stern. most of the ship is now embedded in the sandy bottom but some parts of her hull protrude 50 feet above the bottom.[6] There she lies, the last battleship to be sunk in combat: a victim of air power, the weapon which had supplanted the capital ship as the dominant naval force.

NOTES TO CHAPTER 8

1. Commander Fifth Fleet: Action Report, Ryukus Operations, p.IV-B-2.
2. Miyo, Captain Kazunai, 'Death of a Behemoth', *History of the Second World War*, Vol. 6 No 12, Purnell, p.2561.
3. Spurr, Russell, *A Glorious Way to Die*, Sidgewick anhd Jackson (1983), p.264.
4. D'Albas, Captain Andrieu, *Death of a Navy*, Devin-Adair (New York, 1957), p.348.
5. Miyo, p.2563.
6. Skulski, Janusz, *Anatomy of the Ship: The Battleship Yamato*, Conway Maritime Press (1988), p.192.

9

Mitscher's Long Arm

WHILE the fierce fighting continued on the island of Okinawa and in its surrounding waters, far out at sea were the fast carriers and battleships of Admiral Mitscher's TF.58. They, too, were playing an essential role in the battle for Okinawa in that, until shore-based aircraft were established on the island, they constituted the main tactical air component of the Joint Expeditionary Force. From 1 April, when TF.58 began launching almost continuous strikes in support of the landings, the records of Mitscher's carriers show for each of them an almost continuous pattern of two to four days of operations in support of ground troops, broken by a day for replenishment and refuelling.

The main tasks for Mitscher's aircraft were to neutralize the Japanese coastal and AA guns which could impede the landings; to destroy buildings and obstructions near the beaches which might provide cover for the defenders; to destroy any surviving beach defences; to prevent the movement of enemy reserves; to furnish CAP and anti-submarine patrols over the entire force; to provide reconnaissance and air spotting for bombardment vessels; and to provide photo-reconnaissance. Other operations were as directed by the Force Commander. This would be an ambitious flying programme for any land-based air force, but for a carrier-based group which was operating thousands of miles from its land base, it represented a very tall order indeed.

One of the best examples of ground support furnished by TF.58 occurred on 20 May when a number of Avengers were detached from the carrier group to operate from Kadena airfield on Okinawa. Their objective was a Japanese position which had defied all efforts to take it for nearly a week. After being carefully briefed on the objective and with a Marine observer flying with the strike leader—essential because US soldiers were dug-in only fifty yards

Above: The battleship *Yamato* under air attack and on fire aft on 7 April during her one-way mission. This sortie effectively marked the end of the Japanese Navy as a sea-going force. (US National Archives)

Below: TF.58 at sea. The fast carriers occupied a position north-west of Okinawa, from where they launched ground-support missions and strikes on southern Kyushu. (US National Archives)

Above: A Japanese suicide plane makes its final dive over an *Essex* class carrier of TF.58. In this case the plane was shot down by AA fire. (US National Archives)
Below: The scene on the flight deck of the carrier *Hancock* after she was struck by a suicide plane on 7 April. (US National Archives)

Above: Mitscher's flagship *Bunker Hill*, on fire after the devastating suicide attack on 11 May. A destroyer closes to render assistance. (US National Archives)
Below: The USS *Bunker Hill* wreathed in flames and smoke after being struck by two *Kamikaze*s with very little warning. (US National Archives)

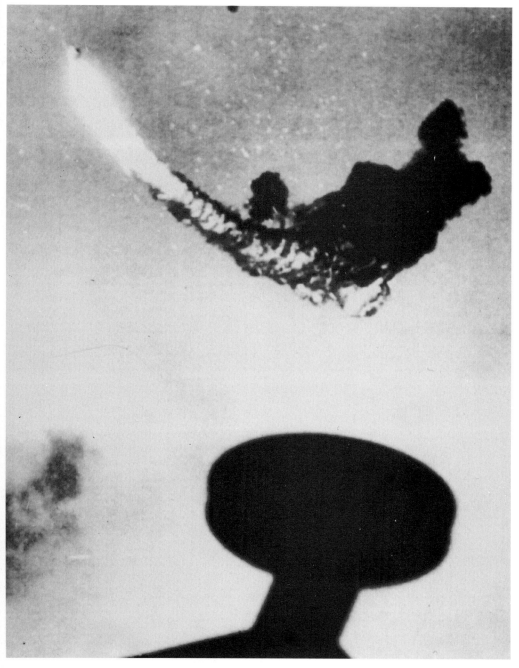

Left, upper: The scene on *Bunker Hill's* flight deck. The fire burned throughout the entire after section of the flight deck. (US National Archives)
Left, lower: The hole in *Bunker Hill's* flight deck and side caused by the second suicide aircraft. (US National Archives)
Above: A 'Judy' crashes in flames after being hit by AA fire from TF.58 during the strikes on southern Kyushu in late May 1945. (US National Archives)

Left, upper: A 'Judy' falls short of its target and crashes into the sea during an attack on TF.58 on 23 May 1945. (US National Archives)
Left, lower: The cruiser USS *Pittsburgh*, safely secured alongside at Guam following the loss her bow in the typhoon of 5 June. (US National Archives)
Above: Admiral William Halsey, who assumed command of the Anglo-American forces off Okinawa on 28 May 1945. (US National Archives)

Above: The British battleship HMS *King George V*, flagship of Vice-Admiral Sir Bernard Rawlings, CTF.57. (US National Archives)

Below: TF.57 at sea: a view looking aft from the flight deck of HMS *Victorious*, showing a Corsair and three Avengers, with HMS *Formidable* and HMS *Indomitable* astern. (US National Archives)

Right, upper: Admiral Sir Bruce Fraser, Commander-in-Chief of the British Pacific Fleet, with his American liaison officers. Fraser was a passionate advocate of Anglo-American co-operation in the Pacific and was determined that the British would play as full a role as possible. (US National Archives)

Right, lower: An airfield on Sakishima Gunto under attack by aircraft of TF.57, the British Pacific Fleet. (US National Archives)

Above: Vice-Admiral Sir Bernard Rawlings (right), CTF.57, with his Flag Captain, Captain T. Halsey RN. (US National Archives)
Right, upper: A suicide plane explodes in the water alongside HMS *Victorious* on 1 April. (US National Archives)
Right, lower: HMS *Formidable* on fire and blowing off steam after being hit by a suicide plane on 4 May. (US National Archives)

Left, upper: The scene on *Formidable*'s flight deck on 4 May, showing damage control teams at work clearing the wreckage. One hour and twenty-three minutes after the attack the ship was ready to operate aircraft. (IWM A.29312)

Left, lower: The remains of the *Kamikaze* which smashed into HMS *Formidable*'s island. (US National Archives)

Above: Burnt-out aircraft and wreckage litter the flight deck of HMS *Formidable* after a *Kamikaze* had ploughed across the after end of her flight deck, May 1945. (US National Archives)

Below: Avengers from 857 Naval Air Squadron approaching an island in Sakishima Gunto for a bombing operation on 23 May 1945. (US National Archives)

Left, upper: HMS *Argonaut*, a *Dido* class AA cruiser of the BPF, refuelling from a tanker during one of TF.57's frequent withdrawals to replenish. *Argonaut* is fuelling by the abeam method, unusual in the Royal Navy at that time, while the aircraft carrier from which the photograph was taken is fuelling by the more tradtional astern method. The inability of the British ships to fuel quickly while at sea was a severe handicap to their operations. (US National Archives)

Left, lower: An American battleship in a floating dock for routine bottom-cleaning and maintenance. Such repair facilities were essential for ships operating at such great distances from their forward bases. (US National Archives)

Above: A 'type-loaded' LST supplying 14-inch cordite charges to a battleship at the Kerama Retto anchorage. (US National Archives)

Above: The harbour at Guam, showing the immense storage facilities available. (US National Archives)

Left: The explosion of the second atomic bomb on Nagasaki on 9 August 1945. The dropping of the two atomic bombs drove the Japanese into surrender and thus ended the planning for the final invasion of Japan, a campaign in which the newly captured Ryukus would have played a vital part. (US National Archives)

from the target—the twelve Avengers roared in in pairs at heights of between 200 and 400 feet to deliver two 500lb bombs each. As the last pair of aircraft pulled away, the ground artillery began firing and the American troops stormed the ridge. It was a text-book example of air support of ground forces.

No less important were the fighter sweeps flown daily over Okinawa, the neighbouring islands and southern Kyushu. These were mounted to prevent the Japanese' constant and aggressive attacks against the American ships off Okinawa. These strikes were only partially successful in that the Americans never managed to destroy Japanese air bases in these areas. However, the constant attrition meant that the Japanese were hampered in their efforts to use these fields as bases from which to attack the Task Force.

At the beginning of the landings TF.58 was operating with only three groups since TG.58.2 had been dissolved after the attacks on *Franklin* during the preparatory operations. However, TG.58.2, now consisting of the carriers *Randolph, Enterprise* and *Independence*, re-joined on 8 April. The scale and ferocity of the Japanese attacks on TF.58 meant that the force was quickly reduced to three groups once again, so rapid was the rate of attrition amongst the carriers. Between 23 March and 27 April there were, on average, seven carriers and seven light carriers; from that time until 12 May there were five and four respectively; and between 12 and 18 May there remained four of each type.

After the air attack of 7 April in which *Hancock* had been damaged, the Japanese lost little time in mounting a second attack on Mitscher's ships. During the morning of the 11th all the indications pointed to a major Japanese operation. Additionally, a Japanese pilot shot down on 7 April and picked up by *Hancock* was confident enough to crow that they would all be dead after 11 April since a massive attack was in preparation. Mitscher there-fore cancelled the day's close-support programme and instead mounted heavy CAP over Okinawa and the islands of Amami, Kikai and Tokuno as well as over TG.58.2, TG.58.3 and TG.58.4 (TG.58.1 had retired out of the area to fuel), which were operating to the east of Okinawa in the approximate area of 27°N 130°E.

The weather, which had been dull and overcast, began to break up around midday. The attack was detected at 1330 and at once the force adopted cruising dispositions and began evasive

129

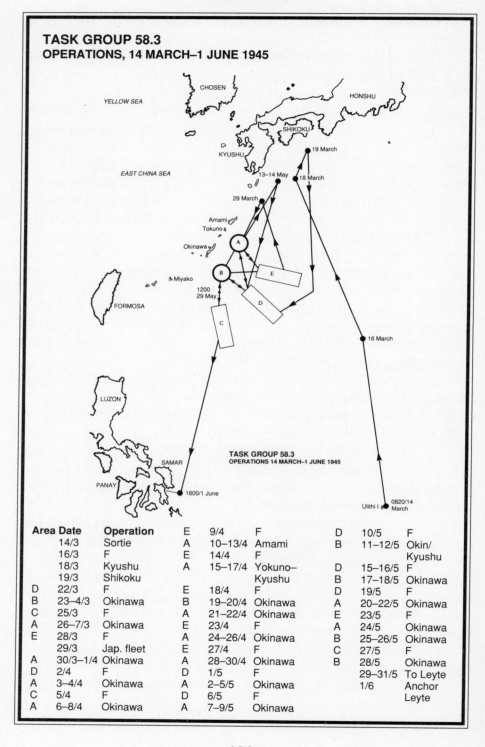

**TASK GROUP 58.3
OPERATIONS, 14 MARCH–1 JUNE 1945**

Area	Date	Operation		Date	Operation		Date	Operation
	14/3	Sortie	E	9/4	F	D	10/5	F
	16/3	F	A	10–13/4	Amami	B	11–12/5	Okin/
	18/3	Kyushu	E	14/4	F			Kyushu
	19/3	Shikoku	A	15–17/4	Yokuno–	D	15–16/5	F
D	22/3	F			Kyushu	B	17–18/5	Okinawa
B	23–4/3	Okinawa	E	18/4	F	D	19/5	F
C	25/3	F	B	19–20/4	Okinawa	A	20–22/5	Okinawa
A	26–7/3	Okinawa	A	21–22/4	Okinawa	E	23/5	F
E	28/3	F	E	23/4	F	A	24/5	Okinawa
	29/3	Jap. fleet	A	24–26/4	Okinawa	B	25–26/5	Okinawa
A	30/3–1/4	Okinawa	E	27/4	F	C	27/5	F
D	2/4	F	A	28–30/4	Okinawa	B	28/5	Okinawa
A	3–4/4	Okinawa	D	1/5	F		29–31/5	To Leyte
C	5/4	F	A	2–5/5	Okinawa		1/6	Anchor
A	6–8/4	Okinawa	D	6/5	F			Leyte
			A	7–9/5	Okinawa			

130

manœuvres at 25 knots. The raid was conducted with great determination by the Japanese and it was clear that a higher 'grade' of suicide pilot was being employed against the carriers than against the less manœuvrable targets off Okinawa itself. First, one or two Japanese aircraft approaching singly, making considerable use of radar countermeasures. Gradually the number of aircraft employed was increased, with pilots making maximum use of the sun and the five-tenths cloud cover in making their dives. The aircraft were also attacking with one flying directly behind the other, the logic being that the AA gunners would be so occupied with the 'front' aircraft that the second would be 'ignored'. All the aircraft pressed home their attacks with self-destruction as their aim. Against their elusive preliminary manœuvres, their straight, high-speed dives and their persistence, any form of defence was very difficult.

At 1410 *Enterprise* was struck a glancing blow by a *Kamikaze* which approached in a shallow glide from dead astern—the arc in which few of the ship's guns could be brought to bear. Its bomb exploded under the ship's port quarter, lifting her three or four feet into the air and causing extensive shock damage to her machinery. At 1501 a second *Kamikaze* crashed close to the starboard bow, causing further damage.

TG.58.3 was the next to be attacked. Again the attack developed from astern. One Japanese aircraft flew through the AA barrage and dropped a bomb which fell close alongside *Essex*, causing minor damage. No other ships in the group received a direct hit, but the battleship *Missouri* and the destroyer *Kidd* received minor damage.

Fighters had shot down seventeen of the attackers and AA fire from the ships had accounted for another twelve, but it was very clear from the day's action that no successful method of defence against the *Kamikaze*s had been found. The enemy renewed his attack during the evening of the 11th but was less successful: no attackers managed to approach the ships, and eleven were shot down by fighters and another seven by AA fire.

In an attempt to reduce the weight of the Japanese air attacks against the American forces on or around Okinawa, Admiral Spruance requested, through Admiral Nimitz, that B-29 bombers of XXI Bomber Command be directed against airfields in southern Kyushu. At the same time, the first shore-based aircraft began operating from captured airfields on Okinawa. This meant that there were fewer demands on TF.58 to provide direct air support for the troops and thus aircraft could be released for other operations.

At noon on 15 April an order was received to cancel the day's programme of strikes on Okinawa. Instead, TG.58.1, 58.2 and 58.3 were ordered to preapre 125 aircraft for a sweep against Kyushu that afternoon. Admiral Mitscher was not in favour of the operation. He believed that the Japanese suffered greater losses when forced to send their aircraft against targets off Okinawa. By attacking the Japanese in their well-defended and well-camouflaged lairs, Mitscher felt strongly that he was risking the lives of his air crews unnecessarily. In view of the work which still had to be done by TF.58, Mitscher could not afford to squander pilots on sweeps over Kyushu. In the event the operation clearly took the Japanese by surprise. Many aircraft were discovered and destroyed on the ground, while a further 29 were shot down in the air.

The next day, 16 April, TG.58.4 returned from having fuelled and relieved TG.58.2. During the morning another sweep was launched against Kyushu in order to break up a heavy Japanese air attack, for which aircraft had been seen massing by photo-reconnaissance. More than fifty aircraft were destroyed on the ground, together with another seventeen in the air. However, the sweep did not prevent the Japanese from launching massed air attacks against Okinawa and the carriers. Once again, ground support operations for the day were cancelled as the carriers concentrated on protecting themselves.

During the afternoon of the 16th, TG.58.4, which had so far escaped the attentions of the Japanese, was attacked by several aircraft. At 1336 one suicide plane crashed on to *Intrepid*. The engine and part of the body of the plane, including the bomb, crashed through the flight deck into the hangar. The resulting explosion dished the hangar deck by four inches, raised the flight deck by twelve inches and damaged No 3 lift beyond repair. A number of large fires were started among the parked aircraft, fuel and ammunition adding to the blaze. Yet by 1615 *Intrepid* was able to fly-on 26 of her aircraft and the remainder an hour later. Nevertheless, the damage was considered so severe that Mitscher decided to send her back to Ulithi the next day and thence to a

Navy yard for permanent repairs. No other ships were damaged in the attack, and TF.58 reported shooting down 155 enemy aircraft for the loss of nine of their own.

In view of the damage to *Enterprise* and *Intrepid*, Mitscher decided to reorganize his ships into three groups. TG.58.2 was disbanded: *Enterprise* was sent back to Ulithi, *Independence* took the place of *Intrepid* in TG.58.4 and *Randolph* joined TG.58.3. On 24 April the new carrier *Shangri-La* joined TG.58.4 and while the rest of the group was fuelling blooded her air crews with a strike against Okino Oagari Shima.

Dissolving TG.58.2 meant extra fire support for the remaining three groups since the battleships, cruisers and destroyers formerly assigned to TG.58.2 were now redistributed. The Japanese launched another series of attacks on the 17th with the express intention of disabling the carriers. Fifty-five Japanese aircraft were shot down in this attack and the only damage was caused by a near miss on *Bataan*.

On 27 April TG.58.1 (*Hornet*, *Bennington*, *Belleau Wood* and *San Jacinto*) was ordered to return to Ulithi for ten days of replenishment, repair and recreation. Since leaving Ulithi on 14 March TG.58.1 had endured 105 enemy air attacks. Fifty-one of the attackers had been shot down by the ships' gunfire and one had destroyed itself by crashing into the destroyer *Sigsbee* on 14 April. On that day the three radar picket destroyers *Sigsbee*, *Dashiell* and *McKee* shot down ten out of fifteen attackers in half an hour. Against the concentrated fire of the Task Group whilst disposed for air defence, no Japanese suicide pilot was able to effect his mission and no Japanese aircraft got away. The ammunition expended by TG.58.1 was prodigious. During the period 59 rounds of 6-inch, 13,658 rounds of 5-inch 38-cal, 52,536 rounds of 40mm 60-cal and 90,266 rounds of 20mm were expended; thus the amount of ammunition required to destroy each aircraft was 1.2 rounds of 6-inch, 268 rounds of 5-inch 38-cal, 1,030 rounds of 40mm and 1,770 rounds of 20mm. The consumption of ammunition at such high levels had important implications for the logistics chain.

In addition to mounting a heavy attack on the Expeditionary Force shipping during the night of 28/29 April, the Japanese also found the resources to launch another attack on TF.58 on the 29th. No serious losses were inflicted until the afternoon, when

133

the destroyer *Haggard*, a radar picket, was struck by one suicide aircraft and missed by a second. The destroyer *Hazelwood*, sent to assist, was also hit: fires on this ship burned for more than eight hours before being extinguished. Both ships were seriously damaged and had to be sent back to Ulithi for repairs.

There were no attacks for nearly a week while the Japanese regrouped and tried to make good their losses. Then, during the night of 10/11 May, there was another simultaneous attack on the Expeditionary Force and the carriers. During the night of 10 May, TF.58 was constantly shadowed and in the morning a major air battle developed overhead. The attack began very quickly. The destroyer *Ault* reported aircraft overhead at 1009 and within minutes two suicide planes had crashed into Mitscher's flagship, the USS *Bunker Hill* in TF.58.3. There had been no warning of this attack by either visual sighting or radar other than a report from TG.58.4 that their CAP had shot down a shadowing aircraft seventy miles from TG.58.3. Action stations were sounded in *Bunker Hill* as the first suicide plane ploughed into the flight deck. It was thought that the two aircraft which attacked the carrier had come in at low level and, on sighting the group, had climbed rapidly into the clouds over the ships and went undetected amongst friendly aircraft circling overhead either because of the limitations of American IFF equipment or because the Japanese aircraft were emitting signals similar to American IFF.

Whatever the reason, the first of the suicide planes crashed on to *Bunker Hill*'s flight deck just aft of No 3 lift, released a 500lb delayed-action bomb, skidded across the deck into a group of parked aircraft, setting them on fire, and finally crashed over the port side into the sea. The bomb penetrated the flight deck, burst through the side of the ship above the waterline and exploded just before it reached the water, riddling the sponsons and the ship's side. The second aircraft approached the ship in a very steep dive from astern. The pilot released his bomb before he crashed his aircraft at the intersection of the flight deck and the island. The bomb went through the flight deck, exploded on the gallery deck and started large fires which became continuous from No 2 lift to the fantail. It seemed as though the whole ship was engulfed in smoke and flames. The ship's own damage control parties were swiftly on the scene, aided by men from the cruiser *Wilkes-Barre* and a number of destroyers. Nevertheless, 404 officers and men of *Bunker Hill* were killed or reported missing in this attack. Most were asphyxiated by the thick black smoke which was spread throughout the ship by her ventilation fans, which were running when the suicide planes hit. Admiral Mitscher reluctantly transferred his flag to *Enterprise* since his own flagship required the services of a Navy yard.

By 12 May sufficient numbers of aircraft were operating from airfields on Okinawa to release TF.58 from its role of supporting the troops ashore. Mitscher wished to use the opportunity to take his entire force back to Ulithi for some well-earned rest before the invasion of Japan proper. Moreover, he considered that TF.58's work off Okinawa had been completed: the airfields ashore were providing support for the troops and CAP for the Expeditionary Force ships, and all TF.58 was doing was acting as a stationary target for the training of Japanese pilots. Spruance felt otherwise: he considered that the air defence of Okinawa was not yet secure and that the resources of TF.58 were still required. Accordingly, on 12 May TF.58 was ordered to cease operations against Okinawa and set course for a position south of Kyushu for a third series of strikes against Japanese airfields there. TG.58.4 was detached to Ulithi for maintenance, her place being filled by the rejuvenated TG.58.1.

This third series of strikes allowed *Enterprise* to demonstrate her capabilities as the Task Force's only dedicated night-flying carrier to superb effect. The scope of operations for her air crews covered the entire island of Kyushu, and during the night of 12/13 May her aircraft attacked every airfield on the island with incendiary rockets and cannon fire. The long list of raided airfields included Kushira, Shibushi, Kokubu, Kagoshima, Chiran and Inujo in the south, Miyazaki, Nigattahara and Tomitaka on the east coast and Kumamoto, Omuta and Sasebo in the middle west. Numerous fires and explosions were reported and twelve enemy aircraft were destroyed in the air. Particular satisfaction was felt at the attack on the airfields at Kanoya and Kanoya East, where exhaust flames showed that aircraft were being prepared for operations.

The night raids were followed by a dawn fighter CAP over the area to keep Japanese aircraft grounded until the strikes from the 'day' carriers arrived. The first daytime strikes were launched at 0500, and over 700 sorties were dispatched before night fell.

Opposition both in the air and from ground fire was minimal and not a single attack was made on the Task Force, although the northern radar pickets broke up an attack which closed to a distance of nine miles.

During the night of 13/14 May *Enterprise* repeated her attacks on Kyushu and extended her operations to cover the island of Shikoku. Despite the attacks, the Japanese still managed to mount an air raid against the Task Force on the 14th.

Japanese aircraft had been tracked by the carriers throughout the night of 13/14 May, and soon after 0600 on the 14th the attacks commenced. They continued without respite for over four hours. A group of around 26 enemy aircraft passed the force well to the west at low altitude and then approached from the south-west, thus neatly side-stepping the radar pickets which were disposed to the north-west of the carriers. At 0658 four of these aircraft penetrated the CAP and were over TG.58.3. Three were shot down by AA fire but the fourth dived out of the cloud on to *Enterprise* and crashed into the flight deck just aft of the forward elevator. The 500lb bomb, fitted with a delayed-action fuze, penetrated the flight deck and the decking of the elevator pit and exploded on a 6-foot thick layer of rags in a store room, demolishing the lift and blowing the flight deck upwards to a maximum of three feet. Fortunately the ships was at Action Stations and it took less than an hour to bring the fires under control. Thirteen of the 'Big E"s crew were killed and 58 injured in this attack. For the second time in a week Mitscher had to move his flag since *Enterprise* needed the services of a dockyard. He moved to *Randolph. Enterprise* was the only casualty of this attack: CAP had accounted for nineteen of the enemy and AA fire for another six.

The sweeps over Kyushu had gone ahead in the face of minimal opposition, and, after the aircraft had been recovered, the remains of TF.58 retired towards Okinawa. In two days of strikes off Kyushu, 72 Japanese aircraft had been destroyed in the air and more than 200 on the ground. Seventeen Japanese airfields had been attacked, many of them having already been pounded by B-29s. The American losses for the day were fourteen aircraft. On 24 May a clean-up sweep was flown over the airfields on southern Kyushu. At Kanoya a group of 70 enemy aircraft, many with *Baka* bombs under their wings, were destroyed on the ground but little activity was noticed on other fields—the result of the previous strikes on the area. A total of 84 Japanese aircraft were destroyed in the air and on the ground in return for three aircraft shot down over Kanoya.

On 27 May TG.58.4 rejoined from Ulithi to relieve TG.58.3 for a maintenance period. At the same time Vice-Admiral Mitscher was relieved by Vice-Admiral J. S. McCain, flying his flag in the USS *Shangri-La*. On 28 May more important changes in command were afoot when at 0000 all units of the Fifth Fleet passed under the command of Commander Third Fleet, Admiral William 'Bull' Halsey. All unit designations were therefore changed: TF.58 became TF.38 and so on. Admiral Spruance returned to Ulithi in order to commence planning for the invasion of Japan.

TF.38 launched further long-range sweeps against Kyushu on 2 and 3 June, but the bad weather made operations very difficult. The briefing period was very short and the lack of an alternative approach track from the flying-off point made detection of the sweep very easy for the Japanese. As a result, American losses were very heavy—sixteen aircraft shot down and twelve air crew lost. It was doubly unfortunate that on these sweeps the Americans encountered some Japanese pilots who were a cut above the average.

The next morning all flying was cancelled and TF.38 was ordered to steer eastward to avoid a typhoon approaching from the south-west. TG.38.1 and TG.38.4 rendezvoused at 2006 and proceeded in company with the Logistic Support Group. At 0505 on 5 June TG.38.1 became separated from the main body in an attempt to avoid the centre of the typhoon which was nearer to them than to TG.38.4. The manoeuvre backfired, for an hour and a half later TG.38.1 sailed straight through the centre of the typhoon, with serious results.

The cruiser *Pittsburgh* received the worst damage. A 100-foot section of her bow broke away, and this was subsequently taken in tow by the tug *Munsee*. Two other cruisers of the same class, *Baltimore* and *Duluth*, suffered similar structural damage. The carriers *Bennington* and *Hornet* sustained damage to their flight decks when the forward sections collapsed in heavy seas. Other ships which suffered that day included three battleships, two light carriers, three escort carriers, one heavy cruiser, four light cruisers, twelve destroyers, two destroyer-escorts, two oilers and one ammunition ship. Twenty-nine aircraft were lost as a result of storm damage. The typhoon had blown itself out by the morning of 5 June, and after *Pittsburgh*, *Duluth*, the destroyer *Blue* and the tug *Munsee* with *Pittsburgh*'s bow in tow had been sent to Guam for repairs, TG.38.1 re-formed for further operations.

For 8 June TF.38 intended to make a final sweep against the airfields on Kyushu. The attack was planned with the specific intention of avoiding the mistakes made during the attacks on the 2nd and 3rd of the month. The launching point was much closer in than before and the attack was concentrated on installations around Kanoya. The strike was composed of 200 fighters divided into four groups, each with a specific objective. Although the enemy were found to be alert, the defences were completely saturated by the American aircraft, all of which attacked in less than five minutes. One Japanese aircraft was shot down and 29 destroyed on the ground. The Americans lost four aircraft, but all of their pilots were rescued.

On the same day Cruiser Division 16, consisting of the large cruisers (in reality, small battlecruisers) *Alaska* and *Guam*, the light cruisers *Flint* and *San Diego* and the 107th Destroyer Division, was detached to carry out a bombardment of Okino Oagari Shima on 9 June. The bombardment was conducted as planned, with cover provided by CAP from TF.38. During the afternoon of the 9th TG.38.1 launched a strike against the island to test the effectiveness of napalm against certain targets. The pilots returned and were enthusiastic about the use of the weapon, claiming 75 to 90 per cent effectiveness. However, it must be said that the targets had been so worked over by bombardment and air strikes that any form of damage assessment was very difficult.

On 10 June the battleships *Massachusetts*, *Indiana* and *Alabama*, screened by five destroyers, were detached from TG.38.1 and formed TG.30.2 for the purpose of bombarding Minami Ogari Shima. As on the previous day, the island was also attacked by aircraft from TG.38.1 and TG.38.4 in order to obtain further information on the use of napalm. Similar results were reported to those achieved the previous day. This was the last sortie conducted by TF.38 during Operation 'Iceberg'. On 10 June, once the bombarding ships had rejoined the main body, the carriers turned towards Leyte for rest, voyage repairs and replenishment. Their part in the operation was over, for they were still at Leyte when organized resistance on Okinawa was declared at an end on 21 June.

While the fast carriers of TF.58/38 had been engaged north and east of Okinawa, the escort carriers of the Support Carrier Group (TG.52.1), commanded by Rear-Admiral C. T. Durgin, had been doing much the same sort of work but with considerably less publicity. The escort carriers carried out the same ground support operations as TF.58 but also alternated with the British TF.57 in the suppression of airfields on the Sakishima Gunto while the British ships were fuelling.

The Support Carrier Group was the 'Cinderella' of the Joint Expeditionary Force. Its pilots were called upon to do all the odd jobs required of naval aviation but with little public acknowledgement. However, one British observer noted that the Support Carrier Group

. . . was the backbone of the attacks against the defence installations, and provided the close support for the assault of the western islands and the UDT operations. It was apparent that this force realised what was required of it far better than did the fast carrier force, and its pilots were far more assiduous in engaging concealed defences.[1]

The escort carriers suffered far less severely from enemy action than did the fast carriers, for none was sunk and their numbers did not drop below the fourteen ships which made up the Group at the beginning of the operation. During April their numbers varied between seventeen and eighteen. Including the two escort carriers of the anti-submarine warfare group (TG.50.7) and the six escort carriers of the Logistic Support Group (TG.50.8), a total of nine ships were damaged, mainly from the weather and only three from enemy action, and all the latter as a result of suicide attack.

The Support Carrier Group was completely isolated from the rest of the Joint Expeditionary Force. Orders were issued that the escort carrier groups were to keep clear of all others in the operating area. Consequently the Carrier Group Commander was often faced with the possibility of having to land-on his aircraft at night and with the wind line fouled by another Group which could have avoided him by a small change of course: 'With planes low on gas and with darkness approaching, it is not a pleasant picture to dwell on,' wrote Rear-Admiral Henderson, Commander of Carrier Division 25.[2] The rationale behind these orders was to keep the Japanese ignorant of the escort carriers' presence on the grounds that the lightly built CVEs were not at all well equipped to survive massed suicide attacks. However, it did little for the morale of the carriers' crews!

Between 23 March, when TF.58 commenced its strikes on Okinawa, and 13 June, when the ships dropped anchor in San Pedro Harbour, Leyte, the aircraft of the fast carriers had flown 29,949 sorties. They had expended 7,639 tons of bombs, 34,003 rockets, 624 napalm tanks, 178 torpedoes and 31 'Tiny Tims'. One of the Task Groups, TG.58.3, was at sea for 79 consecutive days, on 52 of which offensive missions were flown. The flagship of the Group, the USS *Essex*, was present for the entire operation. In TG.58.1 some pilots were averaging 100 hours of combat flying per month.

In 81 days of operations, 1,908 Japanese aircraft were reported to have been destroyed, 1,352 of them in the air. Intelligence estimated that at least 50 per cent of these were either suicide planes or aircraft fitted to carry the *Baka* or the *Viper*. Had these aircraft succeeded in getting through to the landing beaches or the ships anchored off Okinawa, then the American losses there would have been much greater than they were. In addition, 188 Japanese ships and 283 small craft had been sunk and 437 ships and 769 small craft damaged. American losses were 195 aircraft in combat, 246 aircraft operationally and 188 air crew. A notable feature of these operations was that 60 per cent of the air crew were rescued by aircraft or submarines.

Suicide attacks were the most serious problem with which the fast carriers had to contend. Eighteen ships were damaged by suicide weapons, although the Americans gradually mastered the threat—as shown by the fact that only two of the eighteen were damaged after the end of April. Instances of damage by more conventional means were few. The destroyer *Murray* was struck by an air-dropped torpedo which went straight through her hull without exploding. Four other destroyers were damaged by enemy attack, while the battleship *North Carolina* was hit by a shell which wrecked one of her directors.

The other problem suffered by the US carriers was an acute shortage of manpower—other than air crew. During April the USS *Hornet* was short of 175 seamen—a serious problem for a ship engaged in twenty-four-hour flying operations. This shortage reduced the efficiency of flight deck and hangar parties and meant that gunners had to spend longer periods at their posts. When *Hornet's* Group arrived at Ulithi on 30 April for replenishment, it needed 500 seamen, 250 firemen and 50 stewards: this, moreover, was before large numbers of men left the Group on drafts to other assignments or courses, with the prospect of returning to the forward area for operations in ten days' time.

Nevertheless, the achievement of TF.58/38, and of TG.52.1, was stupendous. Operating thousands of miles from their base, they had provided an umbrella over the landing force until aircraft could be established ashore, and had reached out and struck at the Japanese in their homeland. The operations of these carriers are a potent illustration of the flexibility and striking power of carrier Task Groups.

NOTES TO CHAPTER 9

1. Admiralty, Naval Staff History, Battle Summary No. 47: 'Okinawa: Operation Iceberg, March–June 1945' (London, 1950), p.92.
2. Admiralty, Battle Summary No. 47, p.92.

10

Logistics

Logistics is the most important aspect of the war at sea in the Pacific.—Commander Harold Hopkins RN, British Liaison Officer to CINCPAC.

IN the course of three years of hostilities in the Pacific the Americans had developed and perfected an entirely new form of warfare. They had mastered the art of deploying and maintaining large formations thousands of miles from their home bases and the tactical control of such formations at previously unheard of distances from their most advanced base. To achieve this, a new kind of fleet was required: fast aircraft carriers supplied with inexhaustible numbers of aircraft and munitions; a stream of air crew to replace those worn out by intense operational activity (whole Air Groups were replaced at intervals of between four and six months); and a fleet of supply ships which could keep pace with the warships so that there would be no operational delays caused by failures in the supply line.

The great numbers of troops, ships and assault craft involved in the landings on Okinawa together with the vast distances involved across the Pacific created problems of supply, maintenance and repair greater than those encountered in any previous amphibious landing operation undertaken by the Americans; one British observer compared the Okinawa landings with conducting operations off the west coast of Canada from a base in the Eastern Mediterranean. Moreover, these operations took place at a time when the American supply organization was strained to the utmost: the Philippines were not yet liberated, while in Europe General Eisenhower's forces were still engaged in the final drive on Berlin.

The Joint Expeditionary Force (TF.51) was composed of over 1,200 ships and landing craft of all types while TF.58, the Carrier Force, added a further 88 ships with an entirely different set of requirements. The landings called for the embarkation of 182,821 sailors, Marines and soldiers together with 746,850 tons of cargo in 433 assault transports and landing ships organized by eight different embarkation authorities at eleven different ports ranged 6,000 miles across the Pacific from the American West Coast to the Philippines.[1] Between 1 April and 21 June 1945, 1,921,955 tons of cargo were discharged on Okinawa.

Logistics planning for 'Iceberg' began in the autumn of 1944 and the threads gradually came together at a series of meetings around Christmas that year. Admiral King believed that the appointment of an officer of some seniority on the West Coast was essential to ensure the smooth organization and flow of supplies from the United States to the operational areas. Accordingly, Admiral Royal E. Ingersoll took up the appointment of Commander Western Sea Frontier.

Initially all ships were loaded with ammunition, fuel and lubricants to their authorized capacity but they also stowed as much fresh food as could be safely taken on board. Sufficient clothing, dry provisions, general stores, ship's stores and medical supplies were embarked to last for 120 days, thus obviating the need to have victualling stores ships present in the assault phase—one less target for the Japanese to attack. Embarked troops carried sufficient supplies for 60 days.

The administration of the tremendous quantities of fuel, stores, food and ammunition required for the Okinawa operations involved two Task Groups and a multiplicity of other authorities. Commander Service Squadron 10 (CTG.50.9) was responsible for supplying the ships of the fleet at forward area bases and with organizing the sailing and routing of supply ships required by forces in the combat area. Commander Service Squadron 6 (CTG.50.8), Rear-Admiral Donald Beary, commanded the fleet supply ships in the combat area. He was also responsible for the organization of the fuelling programme for the Fast Carrier Force and the Amphibious Force and exercised direct command of the replenishment forces at sea, under the command of Rear-Admiral D. B. Beary USN, flying his flag in the cruiser USS *Detroit*. His formal remit was to 'furnish direct support to Fifth Fleet units in and near [the] combat zone', and to do this he had a miscellaneous group of ferry carriers, fleet oilers, rescue tugs, ammunition ships, general stores ships and a hospital ship. Beary's ships supplied the carriers and their escorts with everything from fuel to the latest offering from Hollywood. His tankers were nothing if not versatile: in addition to fuelling the carriers they would also supply aircraft drop tanks and lubricating oil and provisions for the destroyers and would, in return, accept empty ammunition cases for 'recycling'. Dry provisions were issued at every replenishment period, but the supply of fresh food was erratic in the first days after the landing. An innovation developed by Beary's ships was the transfer of ammunition at sea. Rear-Admiral J. J. Clark, commanding CTG.58.1 aboard the USS *Hornet*, wrote after the operation that

> It is considered that the complete servicing of Task Groups at sea is not only feasible but also marks a definite forward step in Fleet operations.[2]

Fuelling the armada of ships involved in the Okinawa operation was a major concern. Commodore A. H. Gray, 'the oil king of the Pacific', was responsible for the smooth supply of fuel oil. His estimates provided for a monthly consumption of six million barrels of all types of fuel, which was met by commercial tankers on charter bringing the fuel from the West Coast to Ulithi. There a floating reserve of 100,000 barrels was maintained while a shuttle service of 40 fleet tankers operated between Ulithi and Okinawa. In addition, a reserve of 900,000 barrels was divided among Saipan, Guam and Kwajalein while at Pearl Harbor a further 5,000,000 barrels were stored. The tank farm at Pearl which had escaped the attentions of Admiral Nagumo's carrier pilots on 7 December 1941 was now playing a vital role in the downfall of Japan.

Heavy oil was required for the larger warships and transports while diesel was required for landing craft and some auxiliary vessels. The ships of the Joint Expeditionary Force replenished either at Kerama Retto or at anchorages in or close to Okinawa Shima. Screening and fire support ships could fuel at Kerama Retto or from oilers or tankers near the landing beaches at Okinawa which were refilled from fleet oilers or Liberty tankers detached from the Logistic Support Group. Screening vessels could also take the opportunity to replenish while under way from tankers en route to Kerama Retto to replenish the station tankers there. The only ships not to use these facilities were those of the

Support Carrier Group (TF.52.1), which fuelled every nine days at sea in their operating area from tankers of the Logistic Support Group.

The planners had assumed that transports and landing ships using heavy oil which had been in the forward area since L-Day (1 April) would not need to fuel again until L+16 (17 April). This estimate proved considerably wide of the mark largely because the ships which had been involved in the seizure of Kerama Retto on L–6 (26 March) needed to fuel again on L+2 (2 April) on account of the heavy demands made upon them prior to the arrival of the first fleet oiler. Consequently, by L+2 the consumption of heavy oil was running at 8,500 tons a day, although it did fall to 4,250 tons a day by L+16. The consumption of diesel fuel for the landing craft also exceeded estimates and by L+15 major deliveries were required to keep the landing craft running. During the period 4–24 April a daily average of 167,000 barrels of fuel oil and 385,000 barrels of avgas were issued to the Fifth Fleet.

As well as fuel, water was required in huge quantities for the troops ashore until distilling plants could be established. It had been assumed by the planners—correctly as things turned out—that the Japanese would poison the wells. Four fleet oilers were converted to water carriers, but even then supply remained a problem since Ulithi, Saipan and Iwo Jima also needed water.

One other vital but unsung function of the oilers and water carriers was the delivery of mail. The prompt arrival of mail was a major factor in ensuring the high morale of the men in the ships off Okinawa. Since the oilers were the most travelled of the supply ships, it was natural that they should carry out this task, and 24 million letters were safely delivered during 'Iceberg'.

The carriers had special needs, particularly in respect of the rapid replacement of aircraft and aircrew. Commander Air Pacific had representatives at each forward area base who channelled supplies through to to the forward area, where they were distributed under the ægis of Commander Logistic Support Group within CTG.50.8.

The Fast Carrier Force was replenished at sea in an area southeast of Minami Oagari by the Logistic Support Group (TG.50.8). Sometimes the carriers would close the tankers to fuel but usually a group of oilers with the appropriate screen would be dispatched to rendezvous with TF.58. *Ad hoc* service groups were formed each evening and the rendezvous was made at daybreak so that fuelling could begin as soon as light permitted and finish early. Every few days empty oilers were returned to Ulithi to be replaced by laden ones.

However, the carriers suffered from two chronic shortages. The first involved certain aircraft spares, the supply of which was the responsibility of an officer with the awesome title of ComAirPacSubComFwdArea. However, the ferry carriers and the tankers did their best in distributing these parts around the carrier force so that the situation never got out of hand. The other shortage concerned replacement aircraft for those shot down or written off by suicide attacks or accidents. There were never enough replacements, and supply only managed to meet demand because so many of the carriers were inoperable on account of battle damage. Aircraft which were flying when 'mother' was damaged were recovered to another ship, where they were re-tained in order to augment the new vessel's Air Group. The shortage of personnel which affected the carrier Group has already been referred to.

As well as fuel, the ships of TF.50.8 transferred a wide miscel-lany of general stores. For example, in a two-day period, 64,000 tons of cargo were transferred to the fast carriers—more than the port of Boston handled in a week. During the Okinawa camapign it became possible for the first time to transfer general stores at sea. The cargo vessel *Mercury* became a mobile general stores issue ship while *Aldebaran* dispensed chilled and refrigerated stores.

Ammunition was also high on the list of TF.50.8's priorities. The planners had estimated that three times the amount of ammuni-tion used to subdue the Marianas would be required for 'Iceberg'. This estimate, based on consumption at Iwo Jima, was slightly exceeded before the island was secured. Shortages did develop of particular items (reduced charges for 8-inch bombardment shells being one problem), but these were never acute enough to affect gunfire support.

At sea the aircraft carriers would replenish with ammunition while refuelling. While one carrier was fuelling, her consorts would go alongside the ammunition replenishment ships, *Shasta* or *Wrangell*, and take on ammunition by jackstay transfer. TF.58 received a huge quantity of ammunition: 77,582 rounds of 5-

OKINAWA OPERATION:
AMMUNITION EXPENDITURE (ROUNDS)

	Before 2/4	2–30/4	1–10/5	10–20/5	Total
16in HC	1,500	1,000	400	800	3,700
14in HC	4,600	5,500	1,800	650	12,550
12in HC	750	1,600	350	0	2,700
8in HC	5,800	11,000	4,300	4,700	25,800
6in HC	7,200	18,000	6,400	5,100	36,700
5in HC	5,000	9,000	2,000	1,600	17,600
5in AAC	50,000	115,000	40,000	42,000	247,000
5in Star	1,500	18,000	6,000	6,000	31,500
5in 25 AAC	9,000	27,000	9,000	11,000	56,100
5in 25 Star	500	8,870	3,000	3,200	15,570
Total (in tons)	**7,417**	**11,870**	**4,052**	**3,651**	**26,990**

inch; 34,773 5-inch rockets; 19,297 500lb bombs; 18,579 100lb bombs, 3,671 250lb bombs, 798 GP, AP and SAP bombs from 500lb to 250lb, 83 torpedoes and 810 depth charges. For the ships engaged in shore bombardment the statistics are even more impressive, as shown in the accompanying table.

For the ships of TF.51 and the troops ashore, ammunition went straight to Kerama Retto from the United States. Two of these ships, *Hobbs Victory* and *Logan Victory*, were sunk by *Kamikaze*s. Together with the unexpectedly high use of ammunition ashore, the loss of these two ships meant that there was a shortage of phosphorous (essential for flushing the Japanese out of their caves on the island) and 81mm mortar rounds. Supplies of both had to be flown up from Guam. Another innovation in terms of ammunition supply for Okinawa was the 'type loading' of ships, i.e. each carried only ammunition for one type of vessel. Nine LSTs were 'type loaded' in this fashion and proved very effective in the speedy replenishment of warships.

TG.50.8 employed five ammunition ships (*Shasta, Lassen, Mauna Loa, Wrangell* and *Vesuvius*) and between them they dispensed a daily average of 243 tons between 22 March and 27 May for a total of 15,169 tons. Ammunition transfer posed no difficulties, but problems arose in another area. Each ammunition ship carried over 150 different items ranging from 16-inch shell to small-arms rounds. Occasionally stocks of some of these items would become exhausted and the ship's load become unbalanced from the point of view of issue. In these circumstances the ships could not supply the requirements of a large unit like a battleship. Consolidation of cargo at sea in the forward area was not safe, but as an experiment it was decided to send *Shasta* to Kerama Retto to discharge the remnants of her cargo. Since TG.50.8 was thereby left with only four ammunition ships, the experiment was not repeated.

The Kerama Retto group of islands, fifteen miles west of Okinawa Gunto, provided a number of secure and sheltered anchorages which proved invaluable as forward supply bases during the assault phase. The bases were originally viewed as temporary until a proper base could be established on Okinawa. However, the number of ships requiring urgent attention to battle damage necessitated the stationing there of a number of repair vessels since the land-locked anchorages offered good protection. A number of oilers, water carriers, ammunition ships and stores ships were also stationed there for the use of vessels in the Expeditionary Force. Between 28 March (the islands were seized on 27 March) and 8 April, the immediate assault phase of the operation, seven fleet tankers and three station tankers based at Kerama Retto issued 940,000 barrels of fuel oil, 203,000 barrels of diesel and large quantities of lubricants and aviation spirit to over 270 ships.

Supply ships were routed direct to Kerama Retto by Commander Service Squadron 10 from his base at Ulithi. It says much for his organization that the flow was not disrupted even though his own headquarters was in the process of moving from Ulithi to Leyte in the Philippines, which was 300 miles closer to the operational area. The responsibility for the ships at Kerama Retto was divided between Senior Officer Presently Afloat at Kerama Retto, who could vary as ships moved in and out of the area, and the Commander Joint Expeditionary Force, who arranged supply schedules at Hagushi, Ie Shima and Nagagusuku Wan and who was also responsible for calling supply ships into the forward area as and when necessary. However, on 17 March 1945 a representative from Commander Service Squadron 10 assumed responsibilty for all logistic operations in the Okinawa area.

The importance of Kerama Retto to the operation cannot be overemphasized, and it was certainly a brilliant thought of Admiral Kelly Turner's to take the island in advance of the main assault. In a sense the assault on Kerama Retto showed just how far the Americans had travelled in their amphibious warfare techniques since the first operations undertaken in 1942. Kerama Retto was quickly seized by the 77th Infantry Division in what, by 1942 standards, would have been considered a major operation but which by the standards of March 1945 was little more than a diversion. The Official US Navy Historian described Kerama Retto as giving a feeling of security 'like having a roof over your head in an air raid',[3] while Rear-Admiral Allan Smith described the islands as giving

> . . . a firmness to the Okinawa tactical situation . . . We were there to stay with a place to tow damaged ships, look after survivors, replenish and refuel, drop an anchor.[4]

Supplying the naval forces off Okinawa was a daunting enough prospect for any commander. However, an army marches on its stomach and the soldiers and Marines ashore on Okinawa required food, ammunition, medical supplies and all the other materials needed by any large force enagaged in extensive operations. There were a score of provisions and general stores ships serving the men of the Joint Expeditionary Force. To begin with there were the 'Reefers', general cargo ships carrying fresh and frozen food. On 1 March nine of these ships were supplying foodstuffs to ships about to sail for Okinawa. A month later they had all returned to Pearl Harbor or New Zealand for restocking or repair. By 1 May five ships from the *Adria* class, which had loaded at Mobile, Alabama, were discharging cargo in the forward area. A further five vessels, chartered for the operation and loaded at San Francisco and Seattle, were discharging cargo in the Marianas and at Ulithi.

The islands in the Marianas chain occupied an important position in the supply of fresh and frozen provisions. A good proportion of fresh meat, dairy produce and vegetables came from New Zealand. However, the ships which had been loaded with provisions in New Zealand were not prepared for issuing such supplies to the Fleet or ashore. Accordingly, a considerable number of refrigerated stores were constructed on Guam into which fresh provisions from New Zealand would be discharged. Ships would then be 'combat loaded' for supply to the Fleet. For the issue of dry provisions there were thirteen Navy cargo ships and a number of ships from the War Shipping Adminstration (WSA). As the operation progressed it became clear that the planners had overestimated the tonnage of dried provisions required (no bad thing in itself) and so some ships were released from 'Iceberg' while others were redeployed to General MacArthur's command and the Seventh Fleet. There was never any shortage of dry provisions during the entire operation: on 1 June there were still over 65,000 tons available for issue. The overestimation irritated the WSA, some of whose ships were left riding at anchor for weeks unemployed, but the factors responsible for the overestimate were beyond the Navy's control. First, the Navy supplied far more fresh produce than anyone anticipated. Since ships will always take fresh produce in preference to dry, there was less demand for dry goods. Secondly, over 100 ships were sunk off Okinawa or returned to the West Coast for repairs, so there were fewer mouths to feed.

Medical supplies were another factor in the supply chain. In addition to preparing a number of LSTs with the wealth of instruments, bedding, drugs and blood required, to act as hospital ferries, a large amount of anti-venom serum had to be obtained from Calcutta and stored correctly to counteract the particular poison of the vipers with which the island was infested.

Another complication in the logistic chain was the prodigious amount of supplies consumed by the B-29 bombers based at Tinian and Guam. Each aircraft flew an average of eight operations a month, and each mission required 6,400 gallons of gasoline and eight tons of munitions per aircraft. That was not the end of the story, for the maintenance requirements and supplies for the ground crews meant that over 100 ships were engaged solely in keeping the Strategic Air Force running. Proponents of air power would do well to remember the logistic chain stretching back behind the runway.

Logistics also included the vitally important task of repairing battle-damaged ships. Three supply ships were sunk and eighteen damaged during the operation, along with ten landing ships and craft sunk and fifty damaged by enemy action. Ideally, no more supply ships should have been in the forward area than could be continuously unloaded. However, with the move of Commander Service Squadron 10's headquarters from Ulithi to Leyte it was necessary to send forward more ships than could be discharged immediately on arrival or worked continuously. To a certain extent this proved beneficial to the Americans since the consumption of ammunition and other stores proved higher than estimated, but it did mean that that there were more ships within striking distance of Japanese aircraft than necessary. Another seven ships and 43 landing craft and ships were damaged in the storm during the night of 4/5 April, although, considering the violence of the storm, casualties were surprisingly light—testimony to the efficiency of the salvage operations—so that there were none of the scenes of devastation which had characterized the landings on Iwo Jima.

Nevertheless, from L+2 (3 April) the repair facilities included in the original Task Force were severely overtaxed and substantial reinforcement was required. At the beginning of the operation TG.51.6, the Service and Salvage Group, comprised three landing craft repair ships and one battle-damage repair ship. To these were subsequently added four mobile floating docks, four repair ships, two destroyer depot ships and a radar maintenance vessel. However, before these ships could begin work at Okinawa a considerable backlog of work had accumulated and it would be some time before the work was cleared. Lightly damaged ships were dealt with first, so as to ensure their speedy return to operations. In particular the salvage and towing work of TG.51.6 exceeded that undertaken in any other Pacific operation and is proof of the ferocity of the Japanese attacks. The Task Group included three salvage vessels, five fleet tugs and two rescue tugs and during times of heavy enemy air activity twice this number of ships could have usefully been employed.

For the effective landing of supplies, good harbours were essential once the initial assault was over. Fortunately, the physical characteristics of Okinawa Gunto lent themselves fairly well to the development of good harbours. The overall operational plan called for two harbours to be developed, with certain other additional waterfront facilities, for the unloading of cargo vessels.

Commander Service Squadron 12 (TG.99.4) was appointed to develop the harbours and waterfront facilities up to the pierhead or beach line and his responsibilities included survey, ordnance clearance, dredging, blockship placing and salvage. His was a formidable task. The existing harbours in Okinawa Gunto had suffered heavily from American bombing and bombardment. In the harbour at Naha 146 wrecks were examined: 33 were disposed of by beaching and burning, seven were raised, towed out to sea and sunk and two were broken up on the spot. The entire north slip, including the area once occupied by the marine railway, was completely cleared. In Buckner Bay, the name given by the Americans to Nagagusuku Wan after 5 July, some 89,000 cubic yards had to be removed by dredging before the harbour was usable, but at Baten Ko, in the south-west corner of Buckner Bay, surveys revealed that even more extensive dredging would be necessary.

The task of transforming open anchorages into secure harbours was complicated by heavy ground swells which rendered work impossible on many days. Time was also lost through air raids, air alerts and warnings of typhoons which failed to materialize. As a result, port construction lagged behind schedule, through no fault of those involved, and in June 1945 there were considerable delays in discharging ships of their cargo. It was not until July that the position improved, and in the first ten days of that month 350,000 tons of cargo were unloaded.

The logistics aspect of 'Iceberg' was remarkable in that a huge fleet and land force were sustained, thousands of miles from their base, in the face of fierce opposition.

NOTES TO CHAPTER 10

1. The ports were San Francisco, Roi, Seattle, Hawaii, Saipan, Tinian, Guam, Guadalcanal, Espiritu Santo, Russell and Leyte.
2. CTG.58.1 Action Report, 14 March to 30 April 1945, M.07523/45, p.55.
3. Morison. Samuel E., *The Two Ocean War: A Short History of the United States Navy in the Second World War*, Little, Brown (1963), p.530.
4. Morison, p.530.

11

Guarding the Left Flank

*When a Kamikaze hits a US carrier, it's six months repair at
Pearl. In a Limey carrier it's a case of 'Sweepers, man your
brooms'.*—US Navy Liaison Officer aboard HMS *Indefatigable*.

THROUGHOUT the Okinawa campaign, the left flank of the
Joint Expeditionary Force was covered by TF.57, the battleships and carriers of the British Pacific Fleet. The British
contribution to 'Iceberg' was a result of political pressure from the
British Government, particularly Prime Minister Winston Churchill, who wished to see Britain participate in the defeat of Japan
partly to avenge the humiliation of the campaign of 1941–42 and
partly to ensure that Britain had a voice in deciding the post-war
political order of the area.

The British Pacific Fleet (BPF) could best be compared to an old
prize fighter who was still capable of landing the occasional heavy
punch but whose legs were weak and whose endurance was very
much on the short side. Even to describe the BPF as a Task Force
was a concession to Anglo-Saxon sensibilities: the carriers and
battleships of TF.57 equalled only one of Mitscher's Task Groups.
The British were operating with an American fleet whose ships
had been specifically designed for a form of warfare which was
new to the Royal Navy; moreover, the US Navy had had nearly
three years of experience in their specialist operations.

The dispatch of the BPF was politically motivated and the ships
had arrived in-theatre before their 'advanced' base at Australia
was ready to receive them. Essential fleet support was therefore
nearly always achieved on an improvised basis, and it says much
for the resourcefulness of the officers and men of the BPF that the
Fleet was able to participate in operations. The United Kingdom,
the main rear base of the Fleet, lay 12,000 miles from the forward
base at Sydney, which was itself 2,000 miles from the advanced
anchorage at Manus and 3,500 miles from the anchorage at Leyte

used during 'Iceberg'. Leyte itself was 800 miles from the combat area. At no time in the campaign was the BPF self-sufficient, and without the goodwill of the Americans it would not have remained operational for long.

The BPF was commanded by Admiral Bruce Fraser, a gunnery specialist who had commanded the Home Fleet and presided over the sinking of the German battlecruiser *Scharnhorst* on 26 December 1943. Fraser had a relaxed and easy-going style which belied a tough temperament and a keen, incisive mind. Moreover, he had a good deal of personal charisma which soon won over the respect and trust of the Americans, particularly Admiral Nimitz—no small thing considering the extent to which the BPF depended on the Americans for assistance. However, since Fraser was senior to both Halsey and Spruance, he did not fly his flag at sea but exercised command from Australia. At sea the BPF would be commanded by Vice-Admiral Sir Bernard Rawlings, an officer of some distinction but whose quiet and reserved manner meant that he was little known outside the Service. Rawlings, too, enjoyed the confidence of the Americans, particularly as he made it clear that he would do everything to ensure that the Royal Navy honoured its obligations to them in full. The third British commander, Rear-Admiral Sir Philip Vian, who commanded the aircraft carriers, made no effort to establish good relations with anyone. Described as 'an awkward bastard', Vian believed that people could take him as they found him. Yet, despite his abrasive manner and his dislike of staffwork and administrative trivia, Vian came to the Pacific with a fighting record second to none, and he inspired all those who served with him.

It must be said that the US Navy regarded the ships of the BPF as something of a liability. They were 'unable to look after themselves'.[1] Standards of AA gunnery in the BPF were poor since the ships' lack of training facilities and targets had been a problem in the Royal Navy throughout the war. In retrospect, it was fortunate that TF.57 faced a scale of aerial assault from the Japanese which was, by Pacific standards, weak. British carriers sustained more hits than did their American counterparts—five hits among four carriers as opposed to the same number of hits among fifteen American carriers. The anti-aircraft armament of British carriers was weak. The standard AA weapon was the 20mm Oerlikon, which had proved satisfactory in Europe against dive bombers and torpedo bombers; however, the Americans considered that suicide planes were invulnerable to anything smaller than 40mm.

Nothing in the design of the American carriers was permitted to interfere with their function of launching and recovering aircraft. Ship for ship, the British carriers embarked fewer aircraft than their American counterparts, largely because of restrictions on storage space caused by higher safety precautions, particularly the closed hangar design. However, the British carriers had one outstanding feature which was to stand them in good stead throughout the campaign—their armoured flight decks. Every American carrier struck by a *Kamikaze* had to return to a Navy Yard for repairs, while the British vessels could remain operational. In terms of personnel, the British carriers worked at a disadvantage to their American counterparts, being designed, on the whole, for operations in northern latitudes: in the Pacific they were almost uninhabitable, with consequent reductions in efficiency. The BPF was also less flexible in its use of manpower. The Americans would replace an entire Air Group on a ship after a period of extensive operations and replace it with another; the British lacked such flexibility. The Americans used large numbers of men on the flight deck to ensure the efficient launch and recovery of aircraft; for a comparable British carrier to operate successfully, it meant stripping other departments in the ship of officers and men to form Aircraft Handling Parties (AHPs).

The list goes on. Damage control was another area in which the BPF was deficient. Although the Royal Navy was used to air attack on a large scale in the Mediterranean, nothing in this experience would prepare them for the ferocity of the Japanese off Okinawa. Some British officers, however, had done their homework, or, perhaps, had taken notice of the reports submitted by various RN liaison officers to the US Navy, all of which stressed the importance of damage control. While the British carrier HMS *Formidable*, commanded by Philip Ruck-Keene, was at Sydney, her officers and men had had the opportunity to see the American film *Fighting Lady*, a story about a US carrier in the Pacific. Geoffrey Brooke was *Formidable*'s Fire and Crash Officer:

> I came to the unapalatable conclusion that our fire-fighting equipment was totally inadequate and was shocked to discover that there

was no more left in the dockyard store . . . In some trepidation I went and bearded Captain Ruck-Keene, who, hardly looking up from his papers, said 'Are you sure? Then buy some!' Knowing better than to ask how, I took myself off to the laregst store in Sydney and asked for the fire-fighting department. To my surprise, there was an excellent one, full of the latest American gear. I ordered a variety on approval, had a field day testing them on the flight deck and invited the Skipper to witness a demonstration of the chosen items. On completion he said, 'Come ashore with me in half an hour', and I found myself the rather embarrassed third party to a verbal meal, with much table thumping of the unfortunate Captain of the Dockyard. By the end of it he was only too glad to get rid of us by underwriting the expenditure of many thousands of pounds.[2]

Ruck-Keene's determination to ensure that his ship was as well equipped as possible would pay dividends. *Formidable* would need her fire-fighting equipment more than most.

The BPF's aircraft left a great deal to be desired. There were six types employed by the Fleet, Seafires, Corsairs, Hellcats, Avengers, Fireflys and Walruses, but one or more of each type were excluded from one or other of the carriers. The Seafires, which were the principal fighters of the BPF, lacked sufficient range to reach their targets and so were employed almost exclusively in CAP. Moreover the Seafire, which was an excellent fighter, was unfortunately not suited to the rough nature of carrier operations, and it had the most appalling deck landing accident rate. Though the Fleet was well supplied with American-designed aircraft—Corsairs, Hellcats and Avengers—these had been so altered 'to bring them up to British standards' that it proved impossible to pool resources with the US Navy. The lack of aircraft spares came nearer to causing the breakdown of BPF operations than any other factor.

The fact that the ships of TF.57 barely approximated to one American Task Group caused more problems. The absence of sufficient ships resulted in a higher ratio of defensive to offesnive sorties compared with US operations: 65 per cent of American sorties were offensive as opposed to the BPF's 42 per cent; in other words, the BPF spent more time and resources simply looking after itself. But the greatest disadvantage of only having one Group was that it was uneconomic: the entire force had to be withdrawn after two months at sea for necessary repair and replenishment and its place had to be taken by the escort carriers of the Support Carrier Group (TF.52.1).

Lastly, the BPF lacked an efficient fleet train. Following the capture of the Marshall Islands in 1943, Commander Harold Hopkins RN, Liaison Officer on CINCPAC's staff, had written:

> . . . it will be appreciated that the fleet requires a large and efficient fleet train. Logistics is the most important aspect of the war at sea in the Pacific.[3]

Instead of dedicated tankers and supply ships equipped and practised in the difficult art of refuelling at sea, the BPF had a rag-tag collection of whatever could be scraped together from other duties manned by a motley collection of merchant seamen stiffened by Royal Navy liaison parties. Many ships were entirely foreign-crewed, which posed huge problems of administration. It must also be said that some crews were not possessed of the qualities of self-discipline and urgency required in a naval auxiliary ship at war. In the case of the cargo transport *Denbighshire*, the NAAFI Officer noted that, during the working of cargo, the ship's officers and crew 'confined their assistance to standing about and criticising'.[4]

It was in refuelling at sea (RAS) that the deficiencies of the fleet train were most obvious. The tankers (three at first, the number later rising to five) lacked pumping capacity, while the method of fuelling, the 'receiving' ship steaming astern of the tanker, was slower than the abeam method used by the Americans. The British lacked practice in RAS, which resulted in bad station-keeping and a large number of broken hoses. Indeed, at one time Vice-Admiral Rawlings was concerned that the shortage of hoses might limit the time his ships could spend on operations. Despite these problems the Fleet always managed to meet its obligations—though only just.

That was the British Pacific Fleet—small, ill-equipped, under-armed and suffering from the deficiencies arising from having been at war for over five years. No wonder the Americans had qualms about its participation in the Pacific Campaign. In particular, Admiral Ernest King, Chief of Naval Operations, was decidedly against its employment, and it took the combined representations of Admiral Sir Bruce Fraser, Commander-in-Chief BPF, and Admiral Kincaid, Commander Seventh Fleet, to make King change his mind.

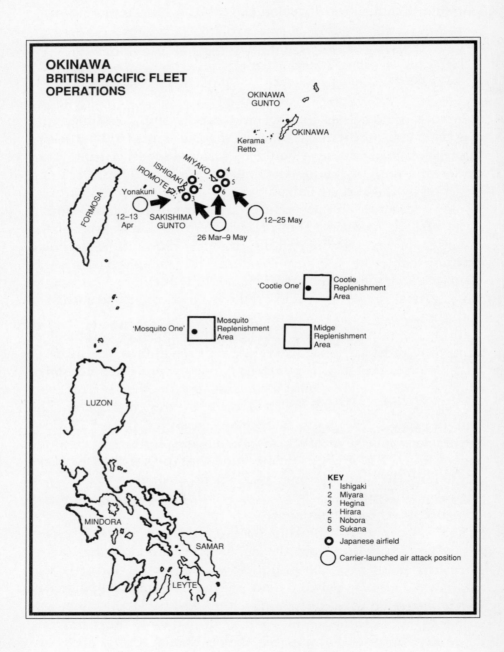

**OKINAWA
BRITISH PACIFIC FLEET
OPERATIONS**

OKINAWA
GUNTO

OKINAWA

Kerama
Retto

MIYAKO

ISHIGAKI

IROMOTE

Yonakuni

FORMOSA

12–13
Apr

SAKISHIMA
GUNTO

26 Mar–9 May

12–25 May

'Cootie One'   Cootie
Replenishment
Area

'Mosquito One'   Mosquito
Replenishment
Area

Midge
Replenishment
Area

LUZON

MINDORA

SAMAR

LEYTE

KEY
1   Ishigaki
2   Miyara
3   Hegina
4   Hirara
5   Nobora
6   Sukana

⊙   Japanese airfield

◯   Carrier-launched air attack position

The main BPF strike force, TF.113, had arrived at Sydney from the Indian Ocean on 10 February 1945. On 28 February the ships sailed for their advance anchorage at Manus, from where they moved to Ulithi on 18 March on receipt of orders to join the Fifth Fleet in preparation for 'Iceberg'. At 0715 on 23 March the BPF formally came under Spruance's command, and after the usual polite exchange of signals customary on these occasions was redesignated TF.57. It consisted of the battleships *King George V* (flag; Vice-Admiral Sir Bernard Rawlings) and *Howe* and the four fleet carriers *Indomitable* (flag; Rear-Admiral Sir Philip Vian), *Victorious*, *Illustrious* and *Indefatigable*, together with a cruiser squadron and a destroyer screen.[5] The carriers had 218 aircraft embarked, as follows:

Indomitable: 29 Hellcat, 15 Avenger
Victorious: 37 Corsair, 14 Avenger, 2 Walrus
Indefatigable: 40 Seafire, 20 Avenger, 9 Firefly
Illustrious: 36 Corsair, 16 Avenger

Admiral Rawlings sailed from Ulithi on 23 March at 0630 and on the 25th he fuelled from the tanker group which had been sent on ahead. David Divine was a correspondent for Kemsley Newspapers and was embarked in the British ships:

I had just come from the USS *Lexington*, the second *Lexington*. I'd been living in her for a long time. *Lexington* would fuel willingly in a wind of Force 6 provided the sea wasn't up to the wind yet. The American tankers would take a ship on either side in that sort of weather. They would have everything aboard, three lines pumping, in twenty minutes . . . KGV went up astern of one rusty old tanker, which appeared to be run by two Geordie mates and twenty consumptive Chinamen and it took us, I think, an hour and a half to pick up a single buoyed pipe-line, fiddling around under our bows.[6]

It was hardly surprising that, in these circumstances, refuelling took longer than expected—over six hours longer—so that the Fleet had to press on through the night of the 25th at 23½ knots in order not to be 'late' for its first assignment. Even so, the destroyers sailed only 70 per cent complete with fuel.

The role of the BPF during 'Iceberg' was to crater the airfields on the islands of the Sakishima Gunto, in particular the islands of Ishigaki and Miyako, on which were three airfields apiece: Ishigaki, Miyara and Hegina on the former and Hirara, Nobora and Sukama on the latter. Two of these fields, Ishigaki and Hirara, were heavily defended and a substantial effort had to be devoted to neutralizing the AA fire from the ground. However, after the fields had been strafed and bombed, the BPF's work consisted in the main of making sure that the Japanese did not recommission the fields and of destroying camouflaged aircraft on the ground. It was thankless work, with few targets of opportunity. Generally, the force would fly off aircraft at a distance of between 80 and 100 miles from the target and then withdraw at night.

During the first strike period, which lasted twenty-six days (from 26 March to 20 April), the force completed twelve days of sorties, usually in periods of two days interpersed with an interval of between three and five days for fuelling and replenishment. Nineteen aircraft were destroyed in combat and 28 in accidents. Enemy aircraft destroyed in the air numbered 28, with a further 34 destroyed on the ground. Subsequent analysis indicated that many of the latter were either dummies or non-operational.

The Japanese were not slow to respond to the activities of the BPF. At 0650 on 1 April the first air raid was detected at a range of 75 miles. The CAP was vectored on to the intruders but some Japanese planes managed to penetrate the fighter screen. One dived into the base of *Indefatigable*'s island, causing a number of casualties and putting the flight deck out of action. At about 0755 a 'Zeke' dropped what appeared to be a 500lb bomb very close to the destroyer HMS *Ulster*. The destroyer was holed and the flooding collapsed the bulkhead between the after boiler room and the engine room. *Ulster* could still fight but was unable to steam so had to be towed to Leyte by HMS *Gambia*. In the evening of 1 April a force of four bombers slipped past the CAP and one of them dived on *Victorious*. Her Commanding Officer, Captain Michael Denny RN, was confident that he could outmanoeuvre the aircraft by vigorous handling of the ship under full helm, and he was successful for the aircraft plunged into the sea alongside the ship. Among the debris blown up on to the flight deck was a sheaf of notes giving target priorities and other instructions for suicide pilots which was eagerly received by Naval Intelligence.

On 2 April TF.57 withdrew to fuel. Replenishment lasted three days, a prolonged experience in bad weather. There were numerous delays caused by breaking hoses and other problems so that when the ships returned to the Sakishima Gunto the capital ships were nearly 50 per cent short of their capacity while the carriers had sufficient fuel for only two days of operations. Rawlings could have asked for more time to complete replenishment, but he was determined to keep his promise to Spruance: the BPF would be back on station on time, even though a change of programme or action damage might leave the ships in a very awkward situation.

Further strikes on Ishigaki and Miyako were carried out on 6 April. The lack of night fighter and intruder aircraft was keenly felt, for the Japanese had carefully filled in all the craters. In effect, the BPF had to start the same job all over again. A response to the raids materialized at about 1700 when a group of four aircraft was detected, one of which dived on *Illustrious*. The aircraft missed the ship—though its wing clipped a radar lantern above the compass platform—and exploded in the sea alongside the starboard side. The blast wrecked two Corsairs on the flight deck but caused no casualties. One revolting after-effect of this attack was that pieces of the Japanese pilot were found decorating the wireless aerials.

April 7 amounted to a routine day for TF.57. Once again the Japanese had repaired the runways on Ishigaki and Miyako, so three Avenger strikes were launched. The runways were left severely cratered and all visible aircraft on the ground were strafed and destroyed. In the evening TF.57 withdrew to fuel. Good weather enabled this to be completed without too many problems and by 9 April the Fleet was heading back for two more strike days on the Sakishima Gunto.

Events now intervened because Nimitz was dissatisfied with the attention directed towards the airfields in Formosa, which were supposed to have been neutralized by the South-West Pacific Air Force—which came under the control of General MacArthur. Despite a number of appeals from Nimitz, little had been done to prevent the Japanese from staging aircraft from China through the island. Spruance agreed with Nimitz's proposal that TF.57 be deployed against targets on Formosa. The change was welcomed by the British air crews, who by now were heartily sick of Ishigaki and Miyako.

Rawlings made every effort to meet Spruance's request, although his air crews were showing signs of exhaustion, as were the maintenance and handling parties. Strikes were carried out using every available aircraft from a point 50 miles off Formosa. The Japanese response took the form of some half-hearted attacks, all of which were dealt with, although on 13 April *Indomitable* had a near miss.

The Fleet then withdrew to fuel, and at this stage the carrier HMS *Formidable* joined the force, replacing the damaged *Illustrious*. On 16 April the British ships were back off the Sakishima Gunto, pounding the familiar airfields on Ishigaki and Miyako. By 17 April it would have been reasonable for TF.57 to withdraw. The air crews were quite exhausted and the Fleet was running low on supplies. However, both Rawlings and Vian were keen to show the Americans that the BPF was a worthy partner and after a fuelling period on the 18th and 19th offered Spruance one more strike day on the 20th—an offer which was gratefully accepted. That was as much as the BPF could do, and in the evening of the 20th its ships withdrew to Leyte for replenishment, where they arrived on 23 April.

It was a bad time for the BPF to leave the operational area. The Americans were hard-pressed off Okinawa with the repeated *Kikusui* attacks and were losing almost one ship a day in this way. On land the American advance had ground to a halt against desperate Japanese resistance. But there was no alternative. There was just one British carrier squadron and it had shot its bolt. No replacement aircraft had been supplied since 9 April, and although there had been no dramatic loss of aircraft, there had been a steady daily wastage: for example, *Victorious* had left Ulithi with 43 Corsair pilots and seventeen Avenger crews; now she had but 31 and fourteen respectively.

Since leaving Ulithi TF.57 had been at sea for 32 days and had spent 26 of those off an enemy coastline. Twelve strike days had been completed and 2,444 sorties had been flown, during which 412 tons of bombs had been dropped and 325 rocket projectiles fired. Twelve enemy aircraft on the ground and 33 in the air had been destroyed, for the loss of nineteen aircraft to AA fire and further 28 to other causes. Sixteen pilots and thirteen air crew had been killed or missing.

The few days' stand-off at Leyte was less of a rest than had been anticipated. The Fleet found itself miles from the shore with few boats. In order to replenish fully, all shore leave was stopped and the Americans had to supply nearly half the harbour craft required for loading supplies. Moreover, the Fleet had arrived a week late, thanks to the extension of operations, and all the perishable foodstuffs had rotted in the heat. It was at this time that three Wings of experienced air crew were relieved, having reached the end of an operational tour of accepted limits, and had to be replaced with newcomers.

Rawlings sailed again on 1 May, and on 4 May the ships were back in their old positions off Miyako. Rawlings ordered a bombardment of Miyako by the capital ships and cruisers. The fine weather favoured such an operation, but, more importantly, it would do something for the morale of the men on the battle-ships, who had seen no action other than providing AA fire for the carriers. Such an operation meant taking the risk of leaving the carriers without most of their AA defence, and although the Fleet had been detected by a snooper, this was no indication that a *Kamikaze* attack would be forthcoming.

The bombardment force, consisting of *King George V*, *Howe*, *Gambia*, *Uganda*, *Swiftsure*, *Black Prince* and *Euryalus*, screened by the 25th Destroyer Flotilla, left the Fleet at 1000 and steamed northwards toward Miyako Shima at 24 knots. *King George V* and *Howe* bombarded the airfield at Hirara while the cruiser *Uganda* bombarded the field at Sukana. *Swiftsure* and *Gambia* bombarded Nobora together with *Euryalus* and *Black Prince*, the latter firing 5.25-inch shell fuzed to burst above the heads of the defenders.

No sooner had the bombardment begun than a signal was received in *King George V* from Admiral Vian to the effect that the carriers were under attack. David Divine observed:

> As we turned on the bombardment run, I was sweeping the horizon on the starboard quarter and I saw a dirty great mushroom of blue smoke, and this was the first of the *Kamikaze* hits ... Rawlings came out from behind the screen almost immediately afterwards and joined us. Rawlings was in a considerable state. There he was and there they were, being hit, and he wasn't there. He was very sober and quiet about it but you could see he was deeply moved by the whole thing.[7]

Rawlings ordered the bombardment to be speeded up and at 1247 the fleet altered course towards the carriers at 25 knots. The Japanese had taken advantage of the absence of the heavy ships to launch a series of attacks by between fifteen and twenty aircraft accompanied by decoys. Admiral Vian had concurred with the decision to go ahead with the bombardment but he subsequently regretted it:

> I was not sufficiently alive to the effect on our defensive system which would be caused by the temporary absence of radar sets and [the] anti-aircraft armament of the battleships. The Japanese were.[8]

Formidable was the first to be hit. From nowhere, at 1131, a 'Zeke' came plummeting out of the sky. Despite being enaged by the carrier's AA battery, the suicide plane ploughed into the flight deck near the island, denting it to a depth of two feet (but not holing it) and wrecking one Corsair and ten Avengers. At the time the ship had been about the launch aircraft, so the flight deck was crowded with aircraft, air crews and handlers. Eight personnel were killed and 47 wounded, many horribly burned. Geoffrey Brooke was *Formidable*'s Flight Deck Fire and Crash Officer:

> It was a grim sight. At first I thought that the *Kamikaze* had hit the island and those on the bridge must be killed. Fires were blazing around several piles of wreckage on deck a little aft of the island and clouds of dense black smoke billowed far above the ship. Much of the smoke came from fires on deck but as much seemed to be issuing from the funnel, which gave the impression off damage deep below decks.[9]

To those watching it seemed as though *Formidable* had been mortally hit. She was shrouded in smoke and steam, and to the sound of the fires burning was added the noise of ammunition 'cooking off' on the flight deck. The ship's company worked like trojans, carrying wounded below, clearing the flight deck and ditching damaged aircraft over the side. Fortunately, only days before the attack the ship's Medical Officer had decided to move the location of the flight deck sick bay from the Air Intelligence Office at the base of the island. If he had not changed his arrangements, the first casualties would have been the flight deck medical team; as it was, two officers were killed in the AIO and all the other occupants badly burned.

Amidst all the chaos, Captain Ruck-Keene signalled to Vian in *Indomitable*, referring to the *Kamikaze*, 'Little Yellow Bastard' and received the reply 'Are you addressing me?' There were few men who could take such liberties with Vian, but Ruck-Keene was a fighting sailor after Vian's heart.

Three minutes after *Formidable* was hit, another 'Zeke' struck *Indomitable* but this time the aircraft merely bounced over the side, doing no damage other than wrecking some radar aerials. However, one of the sets damaged was an American-made air warning receiver—the only one carried in the British carrier force. A third 'Zeke' was shot down and plunged into the sea only ten yards away from the carrier. By 1450 the heavy ships had rejoined and thereafter the attacks were all broken up and the aircraft shot down.

On 5 May the airfields on Ishigaki and Miyako were bombed again but there were no attacks on the Fleet. The following day TF.57 withdrew to replenish and embark replacement aircraft. Rawlings had intended to return to Sakishima on 8 May for further bombardment and air strikes. This time the carriers would remain with the battleships during the bombardment, though keeping just out of radar range from the shore. However both Formosa and the Sakishima islands were closed in with fog and the day's operations were cancelled.

The following day saw an improvement in the weather so air strikes were launched against the two islands. The force was detected by a Japanese reconnaissance plane, which the CAP drove off. Later that afternoon a group of five low-flying Japanese aircraft was detected coming in from the west. *Victorious* was the first ship to be hit. A 'Zeke' dived over her starboard quarter and crashed on to the flight deck near the forward lift, wrecking it. Though the fire was quickly brought under control, the explosion had holed the deck. Moments later a second suicide plane approached in a shallow power glide and stuck the stern a glancing blow, wrecking four Corsairs, before passing over the side.

Formidable was hit again during the evening of 9 May. A *Kamikaze*, either a 'Zeke' or a 'Jill', dived on to the after end of the flight deck and ploughed into the aircraft ranged there. The explosion blew out a rivet in the deck and burning petrol poured down to the hangar below, starting a fire which was only extinguished by spraying the hangar—which did nothing for the electrics of aircraft parked there. Seven aircraft were wrecked on deck and twelve more in the hangar, and *Formidable* had only four bombers and eleven fighters left out of her Air Group.

Clearly, the enemy had changed his tactics to very low-level approaches in the hope of staying undetected. As a result of these attacks Rawlings moved the flying-off position further eastward. The change proved to be effective and no more attacks were made on the force. Rawlings had also ordered the deployment of radar pickets, each consisting of a 6-inch gun cruiser and a destroyer, in order to give warning of the low-level approaches by *Kamikaze*s which had been a feature of the recent raids, and he ordered a destroyer to be stationed astern of each carrier since *Kamikaze*s had shown a marked tendency to approach from that direction.

After a period of replenishment, more strikes were flown on 12 and 13 May before, once again, the Fleet retired to refuel. Rawlings now began to look ahead to the participation of his ships in the invasion of Japan. However, in order that they could spend another prolonged period at sea, they would need a time for repairs—major repairs in the case of the carriers—some of which could only be carried out at Sydney. He therefore proposed that TF.57 complete operations against the Sakishima Gunto on 25 May but that, provided battle damage remained light, he could offer a further two days of strikes on 28 and 29 May. Spruance agreed but indicated that there was no need for further strikes after the 25th. Morale in TF.57 rose accordingly, for everyone had a date that they could look forward to. The air crews in particular were feeling the strain of extended operations: some of *Indefatigable*'s airmen had been in the ship since the spring and summer of 1944 and had flown in strikes against *Tirpitz* before going out to the Far East.

TF.57 was back on its usual beat off the Sakishima Gunto on 16 May and there were signs that Japanese resistance was crumbling. Air activity was light or non-existent, though the ground flak was as intense as ever. In addition to the airfields, which were a mass of craters and burnt-out aircraft, shipping was strafed and an ammunition dump in Ohama on Miyako attacked, with spectacular results. The strikes continued on 17 May, when *Victorious* was put out of action by a series of crashes which wrecked her barriers. Her aircraft had to be distributed among the other carriers, but by the evening jury barriers had been rigged and the ship was a going concern again.

Formidable had borne the brunt of the *Kamikaze* attacks but her misfortunes were compounded when, on 18 May, while refuelling and receiving replacement aircraft, she suffered a serious accident. An armourer working on a Corsair in her hangar was unaware that the aircraft's guns were armed and accidentally fired into an Avenger, which exploded. There was a fierce fire in the hangar, fuelled by kerosene, ammunition and the 'dope' used for preserving the aircraft. About 30 machines were destroyed, although by the evening the ship was operational once more.

Two days later, on 20 May in dense fog, the destroyer HMS *Quilliam* steamed straight into the stern of *Indomitable* owing to the faulty calibration of a PPI:[10]

> None of us on the bridge that day will ever forget what our eyes told us was happening. We saw our stem cleave straight into *Indomitable*'s side and bury itself back to the muzzle of 'A' gun.

Quilliam was a lucky ship: her bows had struck the carrier on her side armour and the flare of her side had deflected them downwards and to port. The carrier was unscathed. *Quilliam* had to be towed away to the fuelling area and thence to Leyte for repairs.

After a final round of strikes on the Sakishima Gunto on 25 May, the Fleet returned to Manus for replenishment prior to the invasion of Japan proper. Two days later Admiral Spruance hauled down his flag as Commander Fifth Fleet, being relieved by Admiral William 'Bull' Halsey. On leaving his command he signalled to Rawlings:

> I wish to express to you and to the officers and men under your command my appreciation of the fine work you have done and the splendid spirit of co-operation in which you have done it. To the American portion of the Fifth Fleet, TF.57 has typified the great traditions of the Royal Navy.[11]

Over the whole period of its deployment during 'Iceberg', the BPF was at sea for 62 days, broken by an eight-day period of replenishment at Leyte, strikes being flown on 23 days, with 4,691 sorties, 927 tons of bombs dropped and 950 rocket projectiles fired. It was estimated that over 100 Japanese aircraft were destroyed, although this figure was a little optimistic—75 was the figure eventually allowed by Commander Fifth Fleet. More aircraft would have been destroyed had the BPF had a suitable night fighter, since it was evident that the Japanese were using the cover of darkness to effect repairs to the runways and to stage aircraft through the islands on their way to southern Kyushu.

Aircraft losses included 26 shot down in combat, 72 destroyed operationally (61 of which were wrecked while landing-on, most of them Seafires with their fragile undercarriage), 32 wrecked as a result of suicide attacks while parked on flight decks and 30 lost in *Formidable*'s hangar fire. However, if the number of aircraft rendered non-operational is included, the figure is far higher: 203 aircraft were replaced out of a total Air Group of 218—a 93 per cent replacement rate. Air casualties numbered 41 killed or missing, while non-flying casualties numbered 44 killed and 83 wounded. Proportionately, British aircraft losses were nearly double those of the American TF.58—72 and 218 in 54 days on station as opposed to 231 and 919 in 80 days.

These figures suggest that TF.57 won something of a Pyrrhic victory over the Japanese. Nevertheless, the role of TF.57 in denying the Japanese the use of their airfields on Miyako and Ishigaki was an important, though often overlooked, aspect of the Okinawa campaign. The massed *Kikusui* attacks on the US fleet off Okinawa would have been infinitely greater had it not been for TF.57.

NOTES TO CHAPTER 11

1. Report of Experience of the British Pacific Fleet, January–August 1945. Quoted in Naval Staff History of the Second World War: *War with Japan. Vol. VI: The Advance on Japan* (London 1959), p.197.
2. Brooke, Geoffrey, *Alarm Starboard: A Remarkable True Story of the War at Sea*, PSL (1982), pp.232–3.
3. Hopkins, Captain H., *Nice To Have You Aboard*, George Allen & Unwin (1964), p.94.
4. Report of Fleet Train NAAFI Officer. Quoted in Naval Staff History of the Second World War: *War with Japan. Vol. VI: The Advance on Japan* (London 1959), p.120.
5. The 4th Cruiser Squadron and the 4th, 25th and 27th Destroyer Flotillas.
6. Winton, John, *The Forgotten Fleet*, Coward McGann (1970), p.114.
7. Winton, p.141.
8. Vian, Admiral Sir Philip, *Action this Day*, Muller (1960), p.140.
9. Brooke, p.244.
10. Plan Position Indicator, an early form of radar scope.
11. Vian, p.202.

12

Conclusions

*The strength and willpower, devotion and technical resources
applied by the United States to this task, joined with the
death struggle of the enemy . . . place this battle among the
most intense and famous in military history. We make our
salute to all your troops and their commanders
engaged.*—Winston Churchill

THE Ryukus operation was at an end. In 81 days of combat the American Tenth Army, supported by the Fifth Fleet, had landed on an fortified, strongly garrisoned island within 350 miles of the enemy's homeland and had captured or destroyed the defenders to the last man. The Japanese 32nd Army had ceased to exist. The price, however, had been high. The Tenth Army lost 7,032 officers and men killed, 181 missing and 31,081 wounded. The US Navy and associated forces, including the British Pacific Fleet, lost 22 ships, with a further 254 damaged. Amongst landing craft and auxiliary vessels, fourteen were sunk and 117 damaged, while 539 aircraft were lost in support of the operation. The US Navy had 4,907 officers and men killed and 4,824 wounded—the first occasion on which the number of dead exceeded that of the wounded, and mute testimony to the ferocity of the fighting.

In no previous operation had American losses been so high, both in themselves and in relation to the ground forces. The figures assume an even starker significance when it is considered that nearly all these casualties were inflicted by Japanese air power: their submarines played no part in the fighting around Okinawa, and the one sortie by the remnants of the surface fleet was swiftly dealt with by the fast carriers. Three factors, however, must be considered when discussing the US casualty figures: first, the proximity of the scene of the action to the Japanese homeland and the enemy's main resources in air power; secondly, the effort which the enemy put into air attack, particularly suicide attack; and thirdly, the length of time ships had to remain in the forward area, either to provide cover or while they waited for their cargo to be discharged.

The manner in which Okinawa's proximity to the Home Islands made the Japanese task easier cannot be stressed too much. The shorter the distance, the greater the intensity of attack which can be delivered at the other end. Another allied factor is that the span of the Okinawa campaign was much longer than that of any other amphibious operation in the Pacific. Thus while the operation was in progress the Allied ships were deprived of their most positive safety measure against air attack—the ability to retire out of the forward area.

This dangers faced by the ships off Okinawa caused the only disagreement in the American command during what was otherwise a well-conducted campaign. The delay in launching the southern offensive in April exasperated the Navy and it was felt that Army incompetence was costing the Navy lives. As Nimitz testily remarked, 'I am losing a ship and a half a day. So if this line isn't moving in five days we'll get someone up here to move it so we can all get out from under these damn attacks.'

The situation was not improved by vigorous lobbying from the Marines to the effect that a landing in southern Okinawa would have shortened the campaign considerably, with a commensurate saving in lives. Buckner, of course, rejected such an option, believing that it would result in another Anzio. Sadly, Buckner never lived to consider his decision in the light of hindsight, but, in retrospect, he was probably right. The terrain in southern Okinawa did not offer a suitable landing site and another landing on the island would have given the Japanese even more targets to aim at, with the resulting casualties and losses.

The nub of the disagreement was the excellent and skilled defence conducted by General Ushijima and the 32nd Army. It is difficult to envisage what more Ushijima could have done to prolong the defence of the island. He was outnumbered and without hope of reinforcement. His forces made good use of the terrain to site their artillery, mortars and machine guns to maximum effect. Moreover, Ushijima managed to suppress the traditional Japanese desire for a make-or-break charge to repulse the Americans on the beaches. Ushijima, though a traditionally minded Japanese officer—as shown by the manner of his death—was a realist. Unlike his Chief of Staff, General Cho, who believed that the inherent spiritual qualities of the Japanese soldier more than compensated for any deficiencies in *matériel*, Ushijima wanted to make the Americans pay for every yard of ground. The high American casualty figures show just how effective his strategy was. It would be easy to argue that Ushijima had been ill-served by his superiors in that they constantly removed with one hand what they had just given with the other. However, IGHQ had the total picture to look at and were desperately trying to react to a strategic situation which was constantly changing as the Americans swept towards Japan.

The Japanese' use of the suicide attack was an outstanding feature of the Okinawa Campaign It assumed a critical importance for a variety of reasons. First, air power gave the capacity to convey the suicide pilot and his 'bomb' over great distances and at high speed. Secondly, modern technology had made it possible to combine considerable destructive power with relatively small amounts of explosive. Thirdly, ships were particularly vulnerable to this form of attack. Nevertheless, the use of suicide attacks by the Japanese was a tacit admission of their deteriorating position and of their belief that traditional Japanese values could compensate for any shortcomings in other areas.

The real losers of the campaign were the native Okinawans. In their preliminary operations the Americans had sought to exploit the differences between the Japanese and the Okinawans and to stress that they came as liberators rather than conquerors. It is difficult to find words to describe the plight of the islanders. In a war which was not of their making, their land was devastated and over 160,000 died in the fighting, many entombed with Japanese soldiers who refused to surrender. Many important and irreplaceable monuments of Ryukuan culture were destroyed. All that remained of the southern half of the island was rubble and devastation. In the post-war settlement the islanders faired even less well. For many years Okinawa was an American base and did not benefit from the startling resurgence of the Japanese economy; only recently has Okinawa established an uneasy relationship with the government in Tokyo.

For the Americans, the conquest of Okinawa was a vindication of the amphibious techniques evolved at such cost during the earlier stages of the Pacific War. The Fifth Fleet performed superbly, providing everything from air cover and gunfire support to the latest films from Hollywood and mail from home. The Okinawa Campaign created new problems of morale and with the well-being of the crews of the ships involved. For months they were at sea, subjected to daily suicide attacks and night nuisance raids while always having to guard against submarines and suicide boats. Good, fresh food and regular deliveries of mail were two of the factors which helped to maintain morale throughout what must have been a very testing time.

Ashore, the American Marines and soldiers behaved with conspicuous gallantry. This was a campaign where traditional American attributes such as mobility, firepower and quantitative superiority were replaced by traditional infantry tactics requiring immense reserves of human courage against an enemy who was positioned and prepared to die where he stood.

Once the islands had been secured, attention moved on to planning for Operation 'Olympic', the invasion of southern Kyushu. It was not a prospect which the American planners approached with levity. The Japanese resistance on Okinawa had been intense, yet Okinawa, though nominally a prefecture of Japan, was not one of the Home Islands. In Kyushu the Americans could expect significantly tougher resistance, with the added problems of a hostile civilian population. The cost in American, and Allied, lives would be immense. There were those who argued that a better option would be to stand off and bomb the Japanese into surrender from bases in the newly acquired Ryukus while maintaining the submarine blockade. That argument, though a worthy one, and advanced with Allied casualties in mind, gave no guarantee that the Japanese would surrender. It was accepted that there was no alternative but to plan for a fully fledged invasion.

In the end, the decision was taken out of the planners' hands. President Truman resolved to use the atomic bomb as a means of compelling Japan to surrender or forcing her to the conference table, and thereafter events moved swiftly. On 6 September the Americans dropped the first A-bomb on Hiroshima; on 7 September the Soviet Union finally declared war on Japan; and on 9 September the second A-bomb was dropped on Nagasaki. The cumulative effect of these events, coupled with the invasion of

Okinawa, prodded the Japanese Government into surrender, despite the wishes of the hard-line minority.

The American triumph at Okinawa has to a certain extent been overshadowed by the continuing debate over the necessity and morality of dropping the A-bomb—indeed it has been argued that there was no need for the bomb to be dropped at all, that Japan could have been bombed and starved into surrender. Such arguments represent the triumph of hindsight over analysis. The military were not privy to the 'Manhatten Project' during the planning for 'Iceberg' or 'Olympic'. Moreover, any bombing campaign against Japan required bases nearer to the Home Islands than Iwo Jima, Saipan or Tinian. The capture of Okinawa was an inevitable stepping-stone in America's Pacific strategy.

The significance of the Okinawa Campaign is that it was a graphic demonstration to the Japanese that the Americans could, and would, take and hold an island 350 miles from the Japanese 'mainland' against a stubborn defence and massed suicide attacks. However, by confirming the views of those who believed that an invasion of Kyushu would be costly, 'Iceberg' undoubtedly gave the politicians a justification for the use of the A-bomb.

The capture of Okinawa was the last amphibious operation launched by the Americans in the Pacific. It was a triumph of American planning, organization and logistics. It was also an epic of courage and desperate resistance.

Appendices

APPENDIX 1
Numerical List of Task Forces and Task Groups engaged in Operation 'Iceberg'

Task Force	Task Group	Description
50		**Covering Forces**
	50.5	Search and Reconnaissance Group
	50.7	ASW Group
	50.8	Service Squadron Six
	50.9	Service Squadron Ten
51		**Joint Expeditionary Force**
	51.1	Western Islands Attack Group
	51.2	Demonstration Group
	51.3	Expeditionary Force Floating Reserve
	51.4	Area Reserve
	51.5	Transport Screen
	51.6	Service and Salvage Group
	51.10	Commander Air Support Control Unit
	51.15	SOPA Kerama Retto
	51.17	Hydrographic Survey Unit
	51.19	E Islands Support and Attack Group
	51.20	Seaplane Base Group
52		**Amphibious Support Force**
	52.1	Support Carrier Group
	52.2	Mine Flotilla
	52.3	High Speed Minesweeper Group
	52.4	Minesweeper Group
	52.5	Ditto
	52.6	Motor Minesweeper Group
	52.8	Net and Buoy Group
	52.10	Air Support Control Unit
	52.11	Underwater Demolition
	52.12	Underwater Demoltion Group 'Able'
	52.13	Underwater Demolition Group 'Baker'
	52.25	Advance Support Craft

53		**Northern Attack Force**
	53.1	Transport Group
	53.2	Transport Group
	53.3	Northern Tractor Flotilla
	53.4	Northern Control Group
	53.5	Northern Beach Party Group
	53.7	Northern Defence Group
	53.8	Northern Garrison Group
	53.10	Northern Air Support Control Unit
	53.11	Northern Support Craft
	53.12	Northern Small Craft Group
54		**Gunfire and Covering Force**
	54.1	Gunfire Support Group
	54.5	Battle Line
	54.6	Right Flank Forces
	54.7	Left Flank Forces
55		**Southern Attack Force**
	55.1	Transport Group
	55.2	Transport Group
	55.3	Southern Tractor Flotilla
	55.4	Southern Control Group
	55.5	Southern Beach Party Group
	55.6	Southern Attack Force Screen
	55.7	Southern Defence Group
	55.8	Southern Garrison Group
	55.9	Landing Craft Tank and Pontoon Barge Group
	55.10	Southern Air Support Control Unit
	55.11	Southern Support Craft
	55.12	Port Director Group
56		**Expeditionary Troops**
	56.1	Army Troops
	56.2	Northern Landing Force
	56.3	Southern Landing Force
	56.4	Western Islands Landing Force
	56.5	Demonstration Landing Group
	56.6	Expeditionary Troops Floating Reserve
	56.7	Area Reserve
57		**British Pacific Fleet**
58		**Fast Carrier Force**
	58.1	Fast Carrier Group
	58.2	Ditto
	58.3	Ditto
	58.4	Ditto
	58.7	Fast Battleship Bombardment Group (19 April only)
	58.8	Destroyer Scouting Group

59   **Striking Force**
        59.7   Fast Battleship bombardment Group
                   (24 March only)

APPENDIX 2
Fifth Fleet ships sunk or damaged in support of the operation against Okinawa, 24 March–21 June 1945

A: Summary by type

Type	Damaged	Sunk
Battleship	16	–
Carrier	13	–
Light carrier	4	–
Escort carrier	9	–
Heavy cruiser	7	–
Light cruiser	8	–
Destroyer	91	13
Destroyer-escort	30	–
Minelayer	1	–
Light minelayer	16	–
High-speed minesweeper	12	1
Minesweeper	14	2
Seaplane tender	2	1
High-speed (destroyer) transport	15	3
Cargo ship	15	3
Oiler	4	–
Transport	11	–
Ammunition ship	1	–
Evacuation transport	1	–
Survey ship	1	–
Repair ship	2	–
Floating dock	1	–
Tug	2	–
Merchant ship	1	–
Submarine-chaser	5	–
Motor gunboat	3	1
MMS	7	1
LCI	20	1
LCS	15	2
LCT	1	1
LSM	10	6
LST	30	1
Patrol vessel	1	–
Hospital ship	2	–
Totals	**371**	**36**

B: Summary by cause

Cause	Damaged	Sunk
Suicide air attack	164	27
Air attack	63	1
Shore battery	10	1
Mine	1	4
Suicide boat	7	1
Own AA fire	12	–
Operational	79	2
Typhoon	35	–
Totals	**371**	**36**

C: Alphabetical list of ships sunk or damaged

Name	Type	Date	Cause	Extent
Aaron Ward	Light minelayer	3 May	Suicide a/c	Major
Achernar	Cargo ship	2 Apr	Suicide a/c	Major
Adams	Light minelayer	26 Mar	Suicide a/c	Major
Adams	Light minelayer	1 Apr	Suicide a/c	Major
Agenor	Repair ship	5 Apr	Collision	Major
Alabama	Battleship	5 Jun	Typhoon	Minor
Allegan	Cargo vessel	3 Jun	Suicide a/c	Minor
Alphine	Assault transport	1 Apr	Suicide a/c	Major
Ammen	Destroyer	21 Apr	Air attack	Minor
Anthony	Destroyer	27 May	Suicide a/c	Minor
Anthony	Destroyer	7 Jun	Suicide a/c	Minor
ARD-28	Floating dock	6 Jun	Air attack	Minor
Arikara	Tug	11 Apr	Grounding	Minor
Atlanta	Light cruiser	5 Jun	Typhoon	Minor
Attu	Escort carrier	5 Jun	Typhoon	Minor
Audrain	Assault transport	6 Apr	AA fire	Minor
Bache	Destroyer	3 May	Suicide a/c	Minor
Bache	Destroyer	13 May	Suicide a/c	Major
Baltimore	Heavy cruiser	5 Jun	Typhoon	Major
Barnett	Assault transport	6 Apr	AA fire	Minor
Barry	High-speed destroyer-transport	25 May	Suicide a/c	Major[1]
Bataan	Light carrier	14 May	AA fire (5in)	Minor
Bates	High-speed destroyer-transport	25 May	Suicide a/c	[2]
Beale	Destroyer	7 Jun	Collision	Minor
Belleau Wood	Light carrier	5 Jun	Typhoon	Minor
Benham	Destroyer	17 May	Air attack	Major
Bennett	Destroyer	3 Apr	[3]	Minor
Bennett	Destroyer	7 Apr	Suicide a/c	Major
Bennington	Carrier	5 Jun	Typhoon	Major
Bennion	Destroyer	28 Apr	Suicide a/c	Minor
Berrien	Assault transport	10/11 Apr	Collision	Minor

178

Biloxi	Light cruiser	27 Mar	Air attack	Minor
Birmingham	Light cruiser	4 May	Suicide a/c	Major
Black	Destroyer	11 Apr	Air attack	Minor
Blue	Destroyer	5 Jun	Typhoon	Minor
Borie	Destroyer	2 Apr	Collision	Major
Bougainville	Escort carrier	5 Jun	Typhoon	Minor
Bowers	Destroyer-escort	16 Apr	Suicide a/c	Major
Bozeman Victory	Cargo ship	28 Apr	Suicide boat	Minor
Braine	Destroyer	27 May	Suicide a/c	Major
Bright	Destroyer-escort	13 May	Suicide a/c	Major
Brown	Destroyer	28 Apr	Air attack	Minor
Brown Victory	Cargo ship	28 May	Air attack	Minor
Brush	Destroyer	12 Apr	Air attack	Minor
Brush	Destroyer	5 Jun	Typhoon	Minor
Bryant	Destroyer	16 Apr	Suicide a/c	Major
Bull	High-speed destroyer-transport	20 Apr	Operational	Minor
Bunker Hill	Carrier	11 May	Suicide a/c	Major
Bush	Destroyer	6 Apr	Suicide a/c	**Sunk**
Butler	High-speed minesweeper	28 Apr	Suicide a/c	Minor
Butler	High-speed minesweeper	20 May	Suicide a/c	Minor
Butler	High-speed minesweeper	25 May	Suicide a/c	Major
Canada Victory	Cargo ship	27 Apr	Suicide a/c	**Sunk**
Carina	Cargo ship	4 May	Suicide boat	Major
Cassin Young	Destroyer	12 May	Suicide a/c	Major
Chase	High-speed destroyer-transport	20 May	Suicide a/c	Major
Chilton	Assault transport	2 Apr	Suicide a/c	Major
C. J. Badger	Destroyer	9 Apr	Suicide boat	Major
Clarksdale Victory	Cargo ship	27 Apr	Shore fire	Minor
Colhoun	Destroyer	6 Apr	Suicide a/c	**Sunk**
Colorado	Battleship	20 Apr	Accident[4]	Minor
Comfort	Hospital ship	7 Apr	Air attack	Minor
Comfort	Hospital ship	28 Apr	Suicide a/c	Major
Conklin	Destroyer-escort	12 Apr	Air attack	Minor
Conklin	Destroyer-escort	5 Jun	Typhoon	Minor
Connell	Destroyer	25 May	Suicide a/c	Minor
Coos Bay	Seaplane tender	31 Mar	Collision	Major
Corregidor	Escort carrier	20 Apr	Storm	Major
Cowanesque	Oiler	4 Apr	Storm	Minor
Cowell	Destroyer	25 May	Suicide a/c	Minor
Daly	Destroyer	28 Apr	Suicide a/c	Minor
Dashiell	Destroyer	5 Jun	Typhoon	Minor
Defense	Minesweeper	6 Apr	Suicide a/c	Minor
De Haven	Destroyer	5 Jun	Typhoon	Minor
Detroit	Light cruiser	5 Jun	Typhoon	Minor

Devastator	Minesweeper	6 Apr	Suicide a/c	Minor
Device	Minesweeper	20 Jun	Collision	Minor
D. H. Fox	Destroyer	17 May	Suicide a/c	Major
Dickerson	High-speed destroyer-transport	2 Apr	Suicide a/c	**Sunk**[5]
D. M. Cummings	Destroyer-escort	12 Apr	Suicide a/c	Minor
Donaldson	Destroyer-escort	5 Jun	Typhoon	Minor
Dorsey	High-speed minesweeper	27 Mar	Suicide a/c	Major
Dour	Minesweeper	20 Jun	Collision	Minor
Drexler	Destroyer	28 May	Suicide a/c	**Sunk**
Duluth	Light cruiser	5 Jun	Typhoon	Major
Emmons	High-speed minesweeper	6 Apr	Suicide a/c	**Sunk**
Endymion	Repair ship	20 Jun	Torpedo	Major
England	Destroyer-escort	27 Apr	Air attack	Minor
England	Destroyer-escort	9 May	Suicide a/c	Major
Enterprise	Carrier	11 Apr	Suicide a/c	Major
Enterprise	Carrier	14 May	Suicide a/c	Major
Essex	Carrier	11 Apr	Air attack	Minor
Evans	Destroyer	11 May	Suicide a/c	Major
Fieberling	Destroyer-escort	6 Apr	Suicide a/c	Minor
Foreman	Destroyer-escort	27 Mar	Suicide a/c	Minor
Foreman	Destroyer-escort	3 Apr	Air attack	Major
Formidable	Carrier (HMS)	4 May	Suicide a/c	Minor
Formidable	Carrier (HMS)	9 May	Suicide a/c	Minor
Forrest	High-speed minesweeper	27 May	Suicide a/c	Minor
Fox	Destroyer	17 May	Suicide a/c	Minor
Franklin	Carrier	19 Mar	Suicide a/c	Major
Franks	Destroyer	2 Apr	Collision	Major
Gayety	Minesweeper	4 May	Suicide a/c	Minor
Gayety	Minesweeper	27 May	Air attack	Minor
Gendreau	Destroyer-escort	10 Jun	Shore fire	Major
Gilligan	Destroyer-escort	27 May	Air attack	Minor
Gilmer	High-speed destroyer-transport	26 Mar	Suicide a/c	Minor
Gladiator	Minesweeper	12Apr	Suicide a/c	Minor
Goodhue	Assault transport	2 Apr	Suicide a/c	Minor
Gregory	Destroyer	8 Apr	Air attack	Major
Guest	Destroyer	25 May	Suicide a/c	Minor
Gwin	Light minelayer	4 May	Suicide a/c	Minor
Hadley	Destroyer	11 May	Suicide a/c	Major
Haggard	Destroyer	29 Apr	Suicide a/c	Major
Hale	Destroyer	11 Apr	Suicide a/c	Minor
Hale	Destroyer	27 Apr	Collision	Minor
Halligan	Destroyer	26 Mar	Mine	**Sunk**
Hambleton	High-speed minesweeper	5 Apr	Suicide a/c	Minor
Hancock	Carrier	7 Apr	Suicide a/c	Major

Hank	Destroyer	11 Apr	Suicide a/c	Minor
Harding	High-speed	16 Apr	Suicide a/c	Major
	minesweeper	16 Apr	Suicide a/c	Major
Harrison	Destroyer	6 Apr	AA fire	Minor
Haynsworth	Destroyer	6 Apr	Suicide a/c	Major
Hazelwood	Destroyer	29 Apr	Suicide a/c	Major
Hencrico	Assault transport	2 Apr	Suicide a/c	Major
H. F. Bauer	Light minelayer	5 Apr	Air attack	Minor
H. F. Bauer	Light minelayer	29 Apr	Air attack	Minor
H. F. Bauer	Light minelayer	11 May	Air attack	Minor
H. F. Bauer	Light minelayer	6 Jun	Suicide a/c	Minor
Hickox	Destroyer	26 Apr	Air attack	Minor
Hilbert	Destroyer-escort	5 Jun	Typhoon	Minor
Hinsdale	Assault transport	1 Apr	Suicide a/c	Major
H. L. Edwards	Destroyer	24 May	AA fire	Major
Hobbs Victory	Cargo ship	6 Apr	Suicide a/c	**Sunk**
Hobson	High-speed	16 Apr	Suicide a/c	Major
	minesweeper			
Hopkins	High-speed	4 May	Suicide a/c	Minor
	minesweeper			
Hopping	High-speed	9 Apr	Shore fire	Major
	destroyer-transport			
Hornet	Carrier	5 Jun	Typhoon	Major
Howorth	Destroyer	6 Apr	Suicide a/c	Major
Hudson	Destroyer	22 Apr	Air attack	Major
Hutchins	Destroyer	6 Apr	Suicide a/c	Minor
Hutchins	Destroyer	27 Apr	Suicide boat	Major
H. W. Hadley	Destroyer	11 May	Suicide a/c	Major
Hyman	Destroyer	6 Apr	Suicide a/c	Major
Idaho	Battleship	12 Apr	Suicide a/c	Major
Indefatigable	Carrier (HMS)	1 Apr	Suicide a/c	Minor
Indianapolis	Heavy cruiser	31 Mar	Suicide a/c	Major
Indiana	Battleship	5 Jun	Typhoon	Minor
Indomitable	Carrier (HMS)	20 May	Collision	Minor
Ingraham	Destroyer	4 May	Suicide a/c	Major
Intrepid	Carrier	16 Apr	Suicide a/c	Major
Isherwood	Destroyer	22 Apr	Suicide a/c	Major
J. C. Butler	Destroyer-escort	20 May	Suicide a/c	Major
Jeffers	High-speed	12 Apr	Suicide a/c	Major
	minesweeper			
J. Rodgers	Destroyer	5 Jun	Typhoon	Minor
J. Snelling	Cargo ship	28 May	Suicide a/c	Major
J. W. Ditter	Light minelayer	30 Apr	Air attack	Minor
J. W. Ditter	Light minelayer	6 Jun	Suicide a/c	Major
Kidd	Destroyer	11 Apr	Suicide a/c	Major
Kimberly	Destroyer	26 Mar	Suicide a/c	Major
Kline	High-speed	20 Apr	Collision	Minor
	destroyer-transport			
Knudson	High-speed	26 Mar	Suicide a/c	Minor
	destroyer-transport			

Lackwanna	Oiler	5 Jun	Typhoon	Minor
Laffey	Destroyer	16 Apr	Suicide a/c	Major
LC(FF)988	LCI	7 Jun	Collision	Minor
LC(FF)995	LCI	6 Jun	Operational	Minor
LCI58	LCI	27 Apr	Air attack	Minor
LCI(G)81	LCI	15 Apr	Grounding	Major
LCI82	LCI	4 Apr	Suicide boat	**Sunk**
LCI(L)90	LCI	3 Jun	Suicide a/c	Minor
LCI354	LCI	9 Apr	Operational	Minor
LCI407	LCI	16 Apr	Suicide a/c	Minor
LCI462	LCI	2 Apr	Grounding	Minor
LCI558	LCI	9 Apr	Air attack	Minor
LCI(G)568	LCI	2 Apr	Suicide a/c	Major
LCI580	LCI	2 Apr	Grounding	Minor
LCI580	LCI	8 Apr	Grounding	Minor
LCI580	LCI	28 Apr	Suicide a/c	Major
LCI(G)588	LCI	29 Mar	Suicide boat	Minor
LCI754	LCI	16 Apr	Grounding	Minor
LCI765	LCI	5 Apr	Grounding	Minor
LCI768	LCI	3 May	Grounding	Minor
LCI770	LCI	28 Apr	Air attack	Minor
LCI(M)807	LCI	1 Apr	Operational[6]	Major
LCI816	LCI	30 Apr	Grounding	Minor
LCS15	LCS	22 Apr	Suicide a/c	**Sunk**
LCS25	LCS	3 May	Suicide a/c	Major
LCS31	LCS	4 May	Suicide a/c	Minor
LCS33	LCS	12 Apr	Suicide a/c	**Sunk**
LCS36	LCS	9 Apr	Suicide a/c	Minor
LCS37	LCS	28 Apr	Suicide boat	Major
LCS38	LCS	11 Apr	Operational	Minor
LCS51	LCS	16 Apr	Suicide a/c	Minor
LCS52	LCS	26 May	Suicide a/c	Minor
LCS57	LCS	12 Apr	Suicide a/c	Major
LCS57	LCS	4 May	Suicide a/c	Minor
LCS88	LCS	11 Apr	Air attack	Major
LCS116	LCS	16 Apr	Suicide a/c	Major
LCS(L)119	LCS	28 May	Suicide a/c	Major
LCS(L)121	LCS	23 May	Air attack	Minor
LCS122	LCS	11 Jun	Operational	Major
LCS199	LCS	27 May	Air attack	Major
LCT876	LCT	9 Apr	Suicide a/c	**Sunk**[7]
LCT1054	LCT	7 Jun	Grounding	Minor
Leutze	Destroyer	6 Apr	Suicide a/c	Major
Lindsey	Light minelayer	12 Apr	Suicide a/c	Major
Little	Destroyer	3 May	Suicide a/c	**Sunk**
Logan Victory	Cargo ship	6 Apr	Suicide a/c	**Sunk**
Longshaw	Destroyer	9 Apr	Air attack	Minor
Longshaw	Destroyer	18 May	Shore fire	**Sunk**
Louisville	Heavy cruiser	5 Jun	Suicide a/c	Minor
Lowry	Destroyer	4 May	Suicide a/c	Minor

Loy	High-speed destroyer-transport	27 May	Suicide a/c	Major
LSM12	LSM	5 Apr	Grounded	[8]
LSM28	LSM	18 Apr	Air attack	Major
LSM59	LSM	21 Jun	Suicide a/c	**Sunk**
LSM82	LSM	13 Apr	Air attack	Minor
LSM135	LSM	25 May	Suicide a/c	**Sunk**
LSM137	LSM	14 May	Operational	Minor
LSM(R)188	LSM	29 Mar	Suicide a/c	Major
LSM189	LSM	12 Apr	Air attack	Minor
LSM190	LSM	4 May	Suicide a/c	**Sunk**
LSM192	LSM	1 Apr	Grounding	Major
LSM193	LSM	17 Apr	Grounding	Major
LSM194	LSM	4 May	Suicide a/c	**Sunk**
LSM195	LSM	3 May	Suicide a/c	**Sunk**
LSM270	LSM	7 Jun	Collision	Minor
LSM279	LSM	12 Apr	AA fire	Minor
LSM312	LSM	14 Apr	Operational	Major
LST70	LST	5 Apr	Broaching	Major
LST71	LST	5 Apr	Collision	Major
LST78	LST	11 Apr	Air attack	Major
LST166	LST	5 Apr	Collision	Major
LST288	LST	20 Jun	Operational	Minor
LST343	LST	5 Apr	Broaching	Major
LST447	LST	6 Apr	Suicide a/c	**Sunk**
LST449	LST	16 Apr	Shore fire	Minor
LST540	LST	5 Jun	Grounding	Minor
LST554	LST	5 Apr	Storm	Major
LST557	LST	10 Apr	Shore fire	Minor
LST568	LST	5 Apr	Operational	Minor
LST570	LST	5 Apr	Operational	Minor
LST599	LST	3 Apr	Suicide a/c	Major
LST608	LST	5 Apr	Storm	Minor
LST609	LST	5 Apr	Storm	Minor
LST612	LST	5 Apr	Storm	Minor
LST624	LST	5 Apr	Storm	Minor
LST625	LST	5 Apr	Storm	Minor
LST658	LST	6 Apr	Operational	Minor
LST675	LST	5 Apr	Storm	Minor
LST698	LST	5 Apr	Storm	Minor
LST723	LST	5 Apr	Storm	Minor
LST756	LST	5 Apr	Storm	Minor
LST762	LST	5 Apr	Storm	Minor
LST782	LST	5 Apr	Storm	Minor
LST808	LST	18 May	Air attack	Major
LST808	LST	20 May	Suicide a/c	Major[9]
LST884	LST	1 Apr	Suicide a/c	Major
LST890	LST	7 Apr	Collision	Minor
LST929	LST	19 Apr	Collision	Minor
Luce	Destroyer	4 May	Suicide a/c	**Sunk**

McDermut	Destroyer	16 April	AA fire	Major
McKee	Destroyer	5 Jun	Typhoon	Major
Macomb	High-speed minesweeper	3 May	Suicide a/c	Major
Maddox	Destroyer	5 Jun	Typhoon	Minor
Manila Bay	Escort carrier	16 Jun	Operational	Minor
Manlove	Destroyer-escort	10 Apr	Strafing	Minor
Manlove	Destroyer-escort	11 Apr	Suicide a/c	Minor
Maryland	Battleship	7 April	Bomb	Major
Mary Livermore	Cargo ship	28 May	Suicide a/c	Minor
Massachusetts	Battleship	5 Jun	Typhoon	Minor
Millicoma	Oiler	5 Jun	Typhoon	Minor
Minot Victory	Cargo ship	12 Apr	Air attack	Minor
Mississippi	Battleship	5 Jun	Suicide a/c	Minor
M. L. Abele	Destroyer	12 Apr	Suicide a/c	**Sunk**
Mobile	Light cruiser	18 Apr	Operational	Minor[10]
Morris	Destroyer	4 May	Suicide a/c	**Sunk**
Morrison	Destroyer	4 May	Suicide a/c	**Sunk**
Mullaney	Destroyer	6 Apr	Suicide a/c	Major
Murray	Destroyer	27 Mar	Air torpedo	Major
Natoma Bay	Escort carrier	7 Jun	Suicide a/c	Minor
Nevada	Battleship	27 Mar	Suicide a/c	Major
Nevada	Battleship	5 Apr	Shore fire	Minor
Newcomb	Destroyer	6 Apr	Suicide a/c	Major
New Mexico	Battleship	12 Apr	Suicide a/c and AA fire	Major
New Mexico	Battleship	12 May	Suicide a/c	Major
New York	Battleship	14 Apr	Suicide a/c	Minor
Norman Scott	Destroyer	12 Apr	Air attack	Minor
North Carolina	Battleship	6 Apr	AA fire	Minor
Oakland	Light cruiser	12 Apr	Air attack	Minor
O'Brien	Destroyer	27 Mar	Suicide a/c	Major
Oberrender	Destroyer-escort	9 May	Suicide a/c	Major
O'Flaherty	Destroyer-escort	15 Jun	Operational	Minor
O'Neill	Destroyer-escort	25 May	Suicide a/c	Major
Pakana	Ocean tug	27 May	Strafing	Minor
Pathfinder	Survey ship	6 May	Suicide a/c	Minor
PC462	Submarine-chaser	7 Apr	Operational	Minor
PC851	Submarine-chaser	16 Apr	Operational	Minor
PC1603	Submarine-chaser	26 May	Suicide a/c	Major[11]
PCS1396	Submarine-chaser	27 May	Suicide a/c	Minor
PGM11	Motor gunboat	14 Apr	Grounding	Minor
PGM17	Motor gunboat	4 May	Grounding	Major
PGM18	Motor gunboat	8 Apr	Mine	**Sunk**
PGM24	Motor gunboat	14 Jun	Operational	Minor
Pinkney	Evacuation transport	28 Apr	Suicide a/c	Major
Pittsburgh	Heavy cruiser	5 Jun	Typhoon	Major
Porterfield	Destroyer	27 Mar	Suicide a/c	Minor
Porterfield	Destroyer	10 Apr	AA fire	Minor

Pringle	Destroyer	16 Apr	Suicide a/c	**Sunk**
Pritchett	Destroyer	3 April	Bomb	Major
Purdy	Destroyer	12 Apr	Suicide	Major
Quilliam	Destroyer (HMS)	20 May	Collision	Major
Quincy	Heavy cruiser	5 Jun	Typhoon	Minor
Rall	Destroyer-escort	12 Apr	Suicide a/c	Major
Ralph Talbot	Destroyer-escort	27 Apr	Suicide a/c	Major
Randolph	Carrier	7 Jun	Operational	Minor
Rathburne	High-speed destroyer-transport	27 Apr	Suicide a/c	Major
Recruit	Minesweeper	6 Apr	Suicide a/c	Minor
Rednor	High-speed destroyer-transport	27 May	Suicide a/c	Major
Register	High-speed destroyer-transport	20 May	Suicide a/c	Major
Remey	Destroyer	12 Apr	Suicide a/c	Minor
Requisite	Minesweeper	6 Jun	Operational	Minor
R. H. Smith	Light minelayer	26 Mar	Air attack	Minor
Riddle	Destroyer-escort	12 Apr	Suicide a/c	Major
Rodman	High-speed minesweeper	6 Apr	Suicide a/c	Major
Roper	High-speed destroyer-transport	31 Mar	Collision	Minor
Roper	High-speed destroyer-transport	25 May	Suicide a/c	Major
Rooks	Destroyer	6 Apr	Air attack	Minor
St George	Seaplane tender	6 May	Suicide a/c	Minor
Salamaua	Escort carrier	5 Jun	Typhoon	Major
Sandoval	Assault transport	28 May	Suicide a/c	Minor
Sangamon	Escort carrier	4 May	Suicide a/c	Major
San Jacinto	Light carrier	6 Apr	Air attack	Minor
San Jacinto	Light carrier	5 Jun	Typhoon	Minor
San Juan	Light cruiser	5 Jun	Typhoon	Minor
SC667	Submarine-chaser	12 Apr	Grounding	Major
Shroeder	Destroyer	5 Jun	Typhoon	Minor
Sea Flasher	Merchant ship	3 Jun	AA fire	Minor
Shasta	Ammunition ship	5 Jun	Typhoon	Minor
S. H. Young	Cargo ship	30 Apr	Air attack	Minor
Shannon	Light minelayer	29 Apr	Suicide a/c	Minor
Shea	Light minelayer	22 Apr	Air attack	Minor
Shea	Light minelayer	4 May	Air attack	Major
Shubrick	Destroyer	29 May	Suicide a/c	Major
Sigsbee	Destroyer	14 Apr	Suicide a/c	Major
Sims	High-speed destroyer-transport	18 May	Suicide a/c	Minor
Skirmish	Minesweeper	26 Mar	Suicide a/c	Minor
Skirmish	Minesweeper	2 Apr	Air attack	Minor
Skylark	Minesweeper	28 Mar	Mine	**Sunk**
South Dakota	Battleship	6 May	Operational	Minor
Spear	Minesweeper	18 Apr	Suicide a/c	Minor

Spear	Minesweeper	6 Jun	Operational	Minor
Spectacle	Minesweeper	25 May	Suicide a/c	Major
Sproston	Destroyer	4 Apr	Air attack	Minor
S. S. Miles	Destroyer-escort	11 Apr	Suicide a/c	Minor
Stanly	Destroyer	12 Apr	Suicide a/c	Minor
Starr	Attack transport	9 Apr	Suicide boat	Minor
Sterret	Destroyer	9 Apr	Suicide a/c	Major
Stockham	Destroyer	5 Jun	Typhoon	Minor
Stormes	Destroyer	25 May	Suicide a/c	Major
Stringham	High-speed destroyer-transport	24 Apr	Operational	Major
Swallow	Minesweeper	22 Apr	Suicide a/c	**Sunk**
Swanson	Destroyer	5 Jun	Typhoon	Minor
Swearer	Destroyer-escort	?20 May	Air attack	Major
Taluga	Oiler	16 Apr	Suicide a/c	Major
Tatnall	High-speed destroyer-transport	20 May	Bomb	Minor
Taussig	Destroyer	6 Apr	Bomb	Minor
Taussig	Destroyer	5 Jun	Typhoon	Minor
Telfair	Assault transport	2 Apr	Suicide a/c	Minor
Tennessee	Battleship	12 Apr	Air attack	Major
Terror	Minelayer	30 Apr	Suicide a/c	Major
Thatcher	Destroyer	20 May	Suicide a/c	Major
Thornton	Seaplane tender	6 Apr	Collision	**Sunk**
Tjisadane	Attack transport	11 May	Suicide a/c	Minor
Tolman	Light minelayer	18 Apr	Grounding	Major
Trathen	Destroyer	14 Apr	Shore fire	Major
Twiggs	Destroyer	28 Apr	Suicide a/c	Major
Twiggs	Destroyer	16 Jun	Air attack	*Sunk*
Tyrell	Attack transport	2 Apr	Suicide a/c	Minor
Ulster	Destroyer (HMS)	1 Apr	Suicide a/c	Major
Vammen	Destroyer-escort	1 Apr	Booby trap	Minor
Victorious	Carrier (HMS)	9 May	Suicide a/c	Major
Wadsworth	Destroyer	22 Apr	Suicide a/c	Minor
Wadsworth	Destroyer	28 Apr	Suicide a/c	Minor
Wake Island	Escort carrier	3 Apr	Suicide	Major
W. Allison	Cargo Ship	25 May	Torpedo	Major
W. C. Cole	Destroyer-escort	25 May	Suicide a/c	Major
W. C. Wann	Destroyer-escort	12 Apr	Suicide a/c	Minor
W. D. Porter	Destroyer	10 Jun	Suicide a/c	**Sunk**
Wesson	Destroyer-escort	7 Apr	Suicide a/c	Major
West Virginia	Battleship	1 Apr	Suicide a/c	Minor
Whitehurst	Destroyer-escort	12 Apr	Suicide a/c	Major
Wichita	Heavy cruiser	27 Apr	Shore fire	Minor
Wichita	Heavy cruiser	12 May	AA fire	Minor
Wilson	Destroyer	16 Apr	Suicide a/c	Minor
Windham Bay	Escort carrier	5 Jun	Typhoon	Major
Witter	Destroyer-escort	6 Apr	Suicide a/c	Major
Wyandot	Assault transport	29 Mar	Air attack	Minor
YMS92	Motor minesweeper	8 Apr	Mine	Major

YMS96	Motor minesweeper	10 Apr	Collision	Major
YMS103	Motor minesweeper	8 Apr	Mine	**Sunk**
YMS311	Motor minesweeper	6 Apr	Suicide a/c	Minor
YMS321	Motor minesweeper	6 Apr	Air attack	Minor
YMS331	Motor minesweeper	4 May	AA fire	Minor
YMS427	Motor minesweeper	7 Apr	Shore fire	Minor
YMS427	Motor minesweeper	9 Apr	Air attack	Minor
YP41	Patrol craft	4 Jun	Operational	Minor
Zellars	Destroyer	10 Apr	Suicide a/c	Major

NOTES

1. Subsequently used as a decoy ship and sunk on 21 June by suicide aircraft.

2. Sunk during salvage operations.

3. *Bennett* sustained minor damage from a bomb or torpedo which failed to explode.

4. Powder explosion

5. Beyond repair and scuttled on 4 April.

6. *LCI(M)807* was damaged as a result of the accidental explosion of a mortar round on board, causing a sympathetic detonation of the rest of the ready-use ammunition.

7. Destroyed aboard *LST599*.

8. Constructive total loss.

9. Beached after the attack on 18 May and condemned after the attack on 20 May.

10. Cordite explosion in turret.

11. Subsequently decommissioned.

Select Bibliography

Admiralty, Naval Staff History, Battle Summary No. 47: 'Okinawa: Operation Iceberg, March–June 1945' (London, 1950)
———, Naval Staff History of the Second World War: 'War with Japan. Vol. VI: The Advance on Japan' (London, 1959)
D'Albas, Captain Andrieu, *Death of a Navy*, Devin-Adair (New York, 1957)
Appleman, Roy, et al, *The Last Battle*, Historical Department of the US Army (Washington, 1948)
Barker, A. J., *Suicide Weapon*, Pan/Ballantine (1971)
Belote, James H., and Belote, Wm M., *Typhoon of Steel: The Battle for Okinawa*, Harper and Row (1970)
Brooke, Geoffrey, *Alarm Starboard: A Remarkable True Story of the War at Sea*, PSL (1982)
Butow, Robert J. C., *Decision to Surrender*, Stanford University Press (1954)
Davidson, O. R. J., et al, *The Deadeyes: The Story of the 96th Infantry Division*, Infantry Journal Press (1947)
Dyer, George C., *The Amphibians Came to Conquer: The Story of Admiral Richmond 'Kelly' Turner*, US Government Printing Office (1972)
Gow, Ian, *Okinawa 1945: Gateway to Japan*, Grub Street Press (1986)
Hopkins, Captain H., *Nice To Have You Aboard*, Allen & Unwin (1964)
Ito, Masanori, *The End of the Japanese Navy*, W. W. Norton & Co (1956)
Johnstone R. W., *Follow Me: The Story of the 2nd Marine Division in World War 2*, Random House (1948)
Keegan, John, and Wheatcroft, Andrew, *Who's Who in Military History, from 1453 to the Present Day*, Routledge (London, 1987)
McMillan, G. J., *The Old Breed: A History of the 1st Marine Division in WW2*, Infantry Journal Press (1949)
Morison, Samuel Eliot, *The Two Ocean War: A Short History of the United States Navy in the Second World War*, Little, Brown (1963)
———, *History of United States Naval Operations in World War II. Vol. XIV: Victory in the Pacific 1945*, Little, Brown (1968)
Moskin, J. Robert, *The US Marine Corps Story*, Little, Brown (1992)
Nichols, C. C., and Shaw, H. I., *Okinawa: Victory in the Pacific*, Historical Branch, US Marine Corps (1955)
Pineau R., *History of the Second World War. Vol. 6: Okinawa*, Purnell & Sons (London)
Potter, E. B., *Nimitz*, USNI (1976)
Skulski, Janusz, *Anatomy of the Ship: The Battleship Yamato*, Conway Maritime Press (1988)
Spurr, R., *A Glorious Way to Die*, Sidgwick & Jackson (1981)
Stockman James R., *The Sixth Marine Division on Okinawa*, Historical Branch, US Marine Corps
Winton, John, *The Forgotten Fleet*, Coward McGann (1970)

Index